ALSO BY JAMES A. WARREN

Giap: The General Who Defeated America in Vietnam

American Spartans: The U.S. Marines:
A Combat History from Iwo Jima to Iraq

The Lions of Iwo Jima: The Story of Combat Team 28 and
the Bloodiest Battle in Marine Corps History,
coauthor with Major General Fred Haynes (USMC-RET)

Roger Williams's friendship with chief sachems Miantonomi and Canonicus ensured the assistance of the Narragansetts in establishing a settlement at the head of Narragansett Bay. Williams may very well have spent more time conversing with Indians than any other Englishman in seventeenth-century New England.

God, War, *and* Providence

The Epic Struggle of Roger Williams and the Narragansett Indians against the Puritans of New England

JAMES A. WARREN

SCRIBNER
New York London Toronto Sydney New Delhi

Scribner
An Imprint of Simon & Schuster, Inc.
1230 Avenue of the Americas
New York, NY 10020

First Scribner hardcover edition June 2018

Interior design by Kyle Kabel

Manufactured in the United States of America

1 3 5 7 9 10 8 6 4 2

ISBN 978-1-5011-8041-5
ISBN 978-1-5011-8043-9 (ebook)

In memory of two inspiring history teachers:

F. Edward Potter Jr., MOSES BROWN SCHOOL

and

William G. McLoughlin, BROWN UNIVERSITY

Contents

Note to the Reader

Anyone writing about politics and warfare in seventeenth-century New England faces several formidable obstacles in consulting primary sources. The documentary record, especially in the case of the colony of Rhode Island, is woefully incomplete. A disheartening number of treaties and agreements between the Puritan colonies and various Indian peoples that are described in English documents seem so egregiously lopsided given the balance of power at the time of their execution as to raise the question of whether the Indians comprehended the ramifications of the terms to which they were agreeing.

In the years after King Philip's War (1675–76), which resulted in the complete destruction of Indian political power in the region, self-serving legends proliferated among the victors concerning the Puritans' policies toward their Indian neighbors. These were carefully nurtured by Puritan descendants, among whom one finds many of the historians who dominated our understanding of the colonial era for centuries. Only in the second half of the twentieth century did the legends and distortions begin to raise the white flag to hard-won truths brought to the surface by the labors of more fair-minded and objective historians, ethnohistorians, and anthropologists, as well as Native Americans themselves. It's an ongoing process.

But the most formidable problem concerns the paucity of documents containing Indian voices that speak to the motivations, intentions, and experiences of the natives as they attempted to adjust to the vast changes in their world wrought by the arrival of Europeans. Yet since about 1970, scores of scholars, including a small cadre of scholars of Native American descent, have greatly expanded our knowledge of the Indian perspectives on the colonial encounter.

In the research phase of this project, I have consulted much of this fine work. But there are still yawning gaps in what we know about how the Indians felt and what they thought about their new neighbors, and surely there will always be. In telling the story of Narragansett resistance to Puritan expansion, in interpreting individual Indians' motivations, objectives, and intentions, I have had no choice but to engage in a good deal of speculation and educated conjecture based on fragmentary evidence. Accordingly, readers will find in the text of *God, War, and Providence* a hefty number of qualifiers, such as "probably," "it seems likely that," and "perhaps Miantonomi was attempting to," among others. It seemed only fair to let the reader know when and where my interpretations rest on limited evidence.

At his best, Roger Williams could be a profound and moving writer. He had a gift for employing striking figures of speech and evocative metaphors. But many of his compositions, especially his letters, were written in great haste. They are marred by rambling, run-on sentences, incomplete trains of thought, and haphazard punctuation. What is more, they are packed with obscure biblical references. Early editions of most of Williams's works are chock-full of printer's errors and annoying gaps and inconsistencies in the copy as well.

Both the superbly edited *Correspondence of Roger Williams* (Brown University Press/University of New England Press, 1988) and *The Complete Writings of Roger Williams* (Russell & Russell, 1963) retain many of the editorial quirks and errors found in the original manuscripts and printings, as of course they should. Such details are of great interest to scholars. Since *God, War, and Providence* was written primarily for a general audience, I felt an obligation to make Williams's writings—as well as those of his contemporaries—as approachable as possible and have edited them accordingly. Yet I hasten to add that every word in this book attributed to Roger Williams, or any other seventeenth-century historical figure, is theirs, not mine. But in this book, their words are unencumbered by archaic spelling, irregular punctuation, or (in Williams's case, particularly) obscure biblical references, and excessive italicization.

I have in quite a number of cases inserted definitions of obscure terms or an apparently missing word in the quotations in brackets. Readers interested in the exact wording and spelling of the original quotation can consult the original source, found in the endnotes.

God, War, *and* Providence

Introduction

A Winter Invasion in Narragansett Country

Samuel E. Brown's vivid nineteenth-century woodcut depicting the Great Swamp Fight—the dramatic culmination of the Narragansett's forty-year resistance campaign against the Puritans. One can still walk through the Great Swamp today, but even local historians and archaeologists aren't sure exactly where the Narragansetts' fort stood.

NARRAGANSETT COUNTRY, THE COLONY OF RHODE ISLAND AND PROVIDENCE PLANTATIONS, DECEMBER 19, 1675

A thick blanket of snow and biting wind greeted the first risers among General Josiah Winslow's Puritan army of a thousand men in the blue-black dawn. They had slept fitfully, shivering under blankets in the open fields around the burned-out remains of settler Jireh Bull's garrison house—a large dwelling fortified to withstand a sustained Indian assault—on the western shore of the Pettaquamscutt River. Bull's dwelling had been the scene of yet one more devastating Indian raid in the great Indian uprising that had begun six months earlier. Chilled to the bone, the English troops were gravely apprehensive about the mission that lay ahead.

They were about to launch a preemptive strike against the Narragansett Indians, thus opening an explosive new chapter in the greatest crisis in New England since the arrival of Europeans on its shores. Mounting out from camp, the army marched westward, in a ragged and broken column, for well over six hours in the howling wind, deeper and deeper into Indian country. At last, around 1:00 p.m., they arrived on the outskirts of a great and desolate cedar swamp. Suddenly they gazed out on an amazing sight. In the midst of the snow-covered, frozen swamp stood one of the largest Indian fortified villages ever encountered by white men in New England. Extending about four to five acres on an island in the middle of the swamp and enclosed by a palisade wall twelve feet high, it contained about five hundred wigwams and several thousand Indians. What appeared as the main entrance to the fort could only be accessed by traversing a single long tree trunk, which crossed a moat of frozen water between a berm of earth and felled trees and the opening in the palisade wall. The opening was well covered by several flankers and a blockhouse and was quickly deemed unassailable. Immediately Winslow ordered several companies of troops to disperse around the fort's perimeter in search of another way in.

Within a few minutes, some English soldiers spied another entrance, just large enough to permit the passing of two or three men at a time. It, too, was well covered by Indian musket fire from a blockhouse, but there was no time to waste. The soldiers had to penetrate the fort in strength before the Narragansetts had time to organize defensive positions within.

The troops of several companies rushed the opening and were greeted by a hail of musket fire and arrows for their trouble. Two company commanders were killed almost immediately in the initial assault, but fifteen or twenty men punched through the entrance. A resolute group of Narragansett warriors quickly converged on the breach, counterattacked, and forced the English out of the fort.

After regrouping, a larger, more determined force of English troops overpowered the first line of Narragansett defenders inside the fortress. Rapidly their comrades exploited the breach. Amid the din of musket fire and cries of the wounded, the adversaries engaged in close and frenzied combat, much of it hand to hand. Inside the fort, women and children hid in terror in their wigwams, which were packed with bags and tubs of corn and other provisions for the winter. Narragansett warriors and Puritan troops went at each other furiously with every weapon at their disposal: muskets, war clubs, tomahawks, sabers, knives, rocks, and fists. A great and furious battle had begun. It had been a long time coming, and nothing less than the future of all New England was at stake.

Known to history as the Great Swamp Fight, the attack catapulted the Narragansett Indian confederation into the greatest catastrophe in the history of New England: King Philip's War. At its height, many colonists feared the Indians might well force the entire English population to withdraw to a few of the largest coastal settlements. More than four thousand Indians, perhaps a third of them Narragansett, and a thousand English settlers would die in this brutal conflict. At the time there were some twenty thousand Indians and fifty thousand English settlers in New England, which makes King Philip's War one of the costliest military conflicts in all of American history in proportion to the size of the population. Many burned-out English towns weren't rebuilt for more than a decade, and the economy was in ruins. But the war's most significant outcome was the complete eradication of Indian political power and cultural autonomy throughout the region.

The causes of the war were rooted in the steadily deepening antagonism between an expanding, aggressive Puritan culture and an increasingly vulnerable, politically fractured Indian population.[1] From the very beginning of English settlement, the Puritans assumed that once the Indians came to understand that the "gifts" of civility and Christianity would free them from what missionary John Eliot called an "unfixed, confused and ungoverned life, uncivilized and unsubdued to labor and order," they would gladly submit to English political authority.[2]

This was a grave misapprehension. Many of the New England Indian tribes had lost as much as 90 percent of their population in a devastating epidemic (1616–19) and were thus warmly receptive to the Puritans' initial overtures of friendship and alliance. In exchange for land, corn, furs, and wide-ranging expertise about the natural world, the Indians received European tools, cloth, jewelry, and firearms, to say nothing of the prestige that came with their association with the newcomers. The major Indian tribes of southern New England were constantly jostling among themselves for control over territory and the allegiance of smaller Indian bands and groups. Alliances with the English often brought the promise of military assistance against rivals.

The early years of coexistence on the New England frontier (1620–50) were not without tension or conflict, but for the most part, relations between the natives and the English were marked by mutual accommodation, peace, and growing prosperity for Indian and Puritan alike. But the seeds of major conflict between Indian and Puritan worlds were deeply embedded in their encounters from the beginning.

As the size and imprint of the English population on the landscape expanded in the 1650s and 1660s, power relations between the two groups altered rapidly. When Indian sachems—their word for political leaders—clung tenaciously to their own religious beliefs and political autonomy, Puritan leaders read such resistance as stemming from impulses far more sinister than mere pride or ignorance. God smiled on the Holy Commonwealths of New England, and woe to those who stood in the way of their growth and prosperity. The Indians definitely stood in the way, and Native American resistance to Puritan political and cultural domination was widely interpreted by ministers and magistrates alike as confirmation of the devil's hold on the Indians' souls.

King Philip's War also marked the conclusion of a fascinating and unique bicultural experiment in Rhode Island—a decidedly non-Puritan colony that sought to remain neutral in the war, as did most of sachems of the Narragansett confederation, whose territory took in virtually all of contemporary Rhode Island. The Narragansetts were the most populous and stubbornly independent Indian confederation in all of New England.

Rhode Island had been founded in 1636 by the radical Puritan dissenter and Indian trader Roger Williams. Born in London in 1603 and trained in the ministry at Pembroke College, Cambridge, Williams was banished from Massachusetts in 1635 for his trenchant criticisms of Puritan religious intolerance and its exploitive Indian policies. In the spring of 1636 he established the tiny settlement of Providence at the head of Narragansett Bay as a refuge "for persons distressed of conscience." Williams, one of the first Englishmen to master the local Indians' language and take a sympathetic view of their culture and values, had obtained the land for his settlement from his close friends, the leading Narragansett sachems Canonicus and Miantonomi. By the mid-1640s, clustered in four settlements on the coast of Narragansett Bay, some five hundred English men, women, and children lived and worked peaceably among about ten thousand Indians.

The Narragansett confederation at the time of Rhode Island's founding was at the center of a vital and profitable trading network with the Dutch, the Mohawks, and a large group of Indian tributaries—subordinate bands and tribes who made regular tribute payments to Canonicus and Miantonomi in exchange for protection and trade—extending out from Narragansett Bay to New Amsterdam (Manhattan Island), Long Island, and the Connecticut River basin. In the wake of the Puritans' destruction of the Pequot tribe in 1637, and their subsequent conquest of all of eastern Connecticut, the colony of Rhode Island and the lands of the Narragansett Indians became crucial objectives of the Puritans' expansionist designs.

With the help of Williams and a handful of other like-minded allies in Rhode Island and London, the Narragansett Indians waged a tenacious and resourceful campaign of resistance against Puritan domination that lasted almost forty years. In the long struggle to maintain Narragansett autonomy, Williams, who was by turns a preacher, statesman, trader, farmer, and prolific writer of tracts on religion and politics, was the confederation's most effective and trusted advocate, mediating in countless disputes and war scares between the tribe and the Puritan colonies. A man of extraordinary courage and unshakable conviction, Williams vigorously condemned the Puritan oligarchy's effort to convert the Indians to Christianity as a thinly veiled program aimed at the destruction of Indian autonomy for its own material gain.

For their part, the Puritan authorities viewed Williams's Rhode Island as a cesspool of religious and political radicalism, and the stubborn Narragansetts as both a serious security risk and an obstacle to Puritan expansion. "Ultimately," writes historian Glenn LaFantasie, "the Puritan behemoths came to see the Narragansetts and the Rhode Island settlers as a single enemy, a united front to be subdued and conquered."[3]

God, War, and Providence tells the remarkable and little-known story of the alliance between Williams's Rhode Island and the Narragansetts, and their joint struggle against Puritan encroachment. This book is best conceived as a story of two closely intertwined narratives at the beginning of American history that on occasion merge into one, only to diverge in ways that are mutually illuminating. The first concerns the collision of Puritan and Narragansett Indian cultures from the time of the arrival of the Pilgrims to the conclusion of King Philip's War. The second story centers on the work of Roger Williams as the founder and leading architect of Rhode Island, and as the Narragansetts' closest English ally and advocate.

That Rhode Island survived the Puritan onslaught against all odds is due in no small measure to the Narragansetts' stubborn defense of their autonomy, as well as to the tenacious efforts of Williams and his followers—or so I have come to believe in researching and writing this book.

Williams's claims that the English had no right to settle on Indian lands without their consent, and that the Indians possessed a culture that deserved respect rather than condemnation, proved to be serious impediments to the fulfillment of the Puritans' plan to dominate the lands around Narragansett Bay. In establishing a colony in Rhode Island that respected Indian customs and rituals to a far greater extent than other English settlements, in challenging orthodox Puritan assumptions about the inseparability of Christianity and civility, and of church and state, Roger Williams was presenting a strikingly original, alternative version of what America should look like. In this respect, he was a man whose ideas were many years ahead of his time.

Chapter 1

1635: Indians and Puritans, Separate and Together

The early seal of the Massachusetts Bay Colony. The Indian importunes the settlers to "come over and help us." Civilizing and Christianizing the Indians was one of the major rationales for the Bay Colony, but many of the funds designated for Indian instruction were diverted to other projects.

By 1635, two colonies of English Puritans, Plymouth Plantation and Massachusetts Bay Colony, were firmly established along the coast of southern New England. A third colony, made up of perhaps a hundred recent émigrés from Massachusetts and a handful of Plymouth Colony traders, had begun to take shape on the banks of the Connecticut River near the modern city of Hartford, where the Dutch had earlier established a bustling trading post.

The Pilgrims of Plymouth had first arrived in November 1620 aboard the *Mayflower*. After an extremely hard first winter, during which almost half of the initial one hundred settlers had perished, the plantation—a common seventeenth-century synonym for *colony*—had grown slowly but steadily to self-sufficiency, thanks in large measure to the able assistance of local native inhabitants, especially Squanto, an English-speaking Indian from the deserted Patuxet village upon which Plymouth was settled, and Massasoit, chief sachem of the Wampanoag confederation. By 1635, Plymouth's population stood at six hundred.

Squanto had been captured by English explorers around 1614 and taken to Spain to be sold as a slave. He somehow escaped to England and learned the language before being brought back to New England by the merchant Thomas Dermer. All his fellow Patuxets had either died in the epidemic of 1616–19 or fled in its wake. In 1621, Governor William Bradford signed an alliance with Massasoit, granting the tribe exclusive trading rights with the colony, and providing for mutual defense in the not unlikely event of attack from one of the many other Indian tribes in the region.

Massachusetts Bay colonists first settled in the town of Salem, sixty miles north of Plymouth, in 1628, but by the early 1630s, Boston, with its excellent natural harbor, had become the center of colony government and the most populous English town in New England. The contemporary English chronicler William Wood described Boston as "a peninsula hemmed in on the south side with the Bay of Roxbury, on the north side with the Charles River," and "not troubled with the great annoyances of wolves, rattlesnakes, and mosquitoes."[1] Seven years after its founding, Massachusetts Bay Colony was home to six thousand English people, a good number in Boston itself, the rest dispersed in a handful of small towns ringing Boston proper.

Before the end of the decade, another five thousand English people would brave the Atlantic to settle in New England. Most settled in Massachusetts, which by 1640 had firmly established itself as the dominant and most dynamic of four New England

Puritan colonies: Plymouth, Massachusetts, Connecticut, and tiny New Haven, along the Quinnipiac River, destined to fold into Connecticut in 1662.

Like Plymouth, Massachusetts Bay had been settled on lands cleared and formerly inhabited by Indians—in this case, Massachusetts Indians under the sachem Cutshamakin, and the Pawtuckets under Sagamores John and James. By 1635, the Wampanoags numbered no more than five hundred; the Pawtucket and Massachusetts less than half that number. The great epidemic of 1616–19 had reduced the population of both tribes by as much as 90 percent, and then an outbreak of smallpox in 1633 further reduced their numbers. All these tribes welcomed the newcomers as trading partners, neighbors, and allies who could aid them in turning back raiding parties of the fierce Micmac tribe from northern New England.

The first English settlements of southern New England were surrounded by many other independent Indian bands and several confederations of bands—a grand total, it seems, of between fifteen thousand to twenty thousand Indians. The natives spoke slightly different dialects of the same eastern Algonquian language and possessed similar cultures and patterns of subsistence and settlement.

To the west of the traditional lands of the Massachusetts and extending into contemporary northwest Rhode Island were the Nipmucks. Farther west, in the northern Connecticut River valley, dwelled about a thousand Pocumtucks. South of the Pocumtucks, in the Connecticut River valley, lived the Podunks, Sequins, Wangunks, and several other small but strategically significant bands, referred to collectively as River Indians by the English.

East of the River Indians, centered on the Thames and Mystic River valleys respectively, were some three thousand Mohegans and the Pequots. To the east of the Pequots lay the Narragansett confederation. Its territory extended over the entire mainland of contemporary Rhode Island except for its northwest corner; the

East Bay, inhabited by Wampanoags; and the larger islands in Narragansett Bay. Their confederation was the largest and most prosperous Indian polity in the region, numbering between seventy-five hundred and ten thousand people.

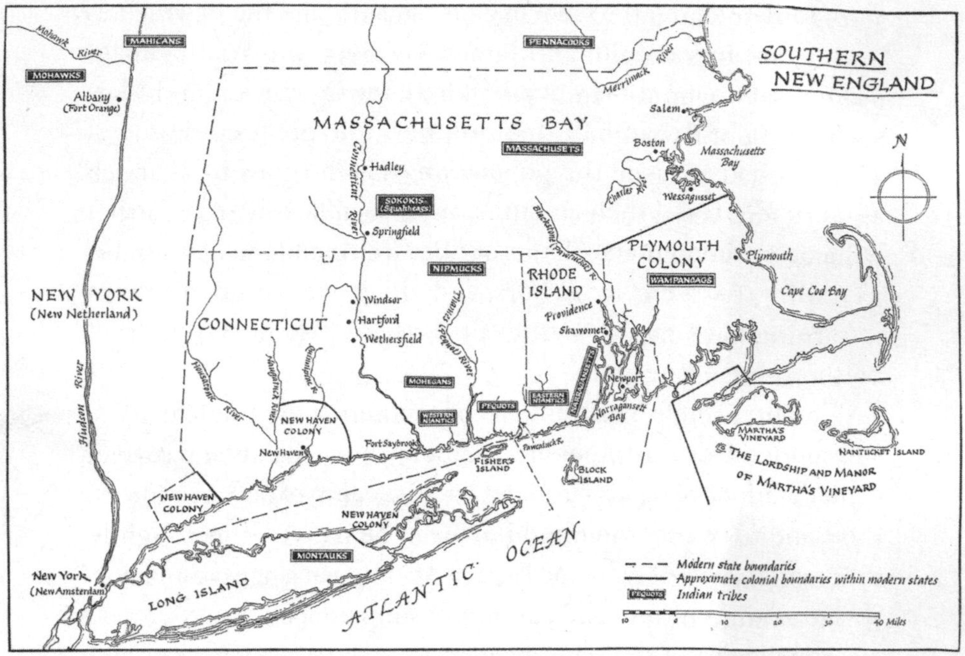

Southern New England, showing locations of major tribes and colonial boundaries, circa 1660.

THE LUSH NARRAGANSETT WORLD

Evidence of habitation near the Bay goes back about thirty-seven hundred years, and the remains of a Narragansett village dating from AD 1100 to 1300 have been uncovered by archaeologists recently. Narragansett Bay and its environs were extraordinarily rich in natural resources at the time of the first English settlements in New England. The Indians who dwelled there were masters of all the skills needed to exploit them. Contemporary English observers describe the Narragansetts as peaceable, industrious, and well led by an older sachem of few words and considerable wisdom called Canonicus, and his nephew Miantonomi, who by 1635 had already established a reputation in the region as a discerning and intelligent diplomat.

The first European to encounter the Narragansetts and record his observations was the great Italian navigator-explorer Giovanni da Verrazano, who sailed the eastern seaboard of America on behalf of the king of France in a futile search for a Northwest Passage. Even in 1524, the Narragansett predilection for industry and trade was evident. Verrazano's account of his encounter with the tribe is remarkably vivid in detail and bears repeating at length:

> We . . . proceeded to another place, fifteen leagues distant from [Block Island], where we found an excellent harbor [Newport]. Before entering it, we saw about twenty small boats full of people, who came about our ship, uttering many cries of astonishment. . . . Stopping, they looked at the structure of our ship, our persons and dress, afterwards they all raised a loud shout, signifying that they were pleased. . . . Among them were two kings more beautiful in form and stature than can possibly be described; one was about forty years old, the other about twenty-four, and they were dressed in the following manner: The oldest had a deer's skin around his body, artificially wrought in damask figures, his head was without covering, his hair was tied back in various knots; around his neck he wore a large chain ornamented with many stones of different colors. The young man was similar in appearance.
>
> This is the finest looking tribe, and the handsomest in their costumes, we have found in our voyage. They exceed us in size, and they are of a very fair complexion; some of them incline more to a white and others to a tawny color; their faces are sharp; their hair long and black, upon the adorning of which

> they bestow great pains; their eyes are black and sharp, their expression mild and pleasant. . . .
>
> They are very generous, giving away whatever they have. . . . We often went five or six leagues into the interior, and found country as pleasant as is possible to conceive, adapted to cultivation of every kind, whether of corn, wine, or oil; there are open plains twenty-five or thirty leagues in extent, entire free from trees or other hindrances. . . . The animals, which are in great numbers . . . are taken in snares, and by bows, the latter being their chief implement.[2]

The word *Narragansett* as used in this book has two distinct but closely related meanings. It refers in its narrower sense to a core group of some four thousand Indians dispersed in as many as twenty villages throughout the southern half of the Rhode Island mainland, and in a broader sense to a larger political entity known to the English of the seventeenth century as a great sachemdom—a loose confederation of Indian bands and tribes. The Narragansett confederation took in the Narragansetts themselves and a number of tributary tribes, including the Cowesett and Shawomet to the north, some Nipmuck bands to the northwest, and the Eastern Niantic to the south, in the areas we now know as Westerly and Charlestown, Rhode Island. Ties of kinship between the Narragansetts and the Eastern Niantics were especially strong.

All these tribes had close social and commercial ties to the Narragansetts, but each had its own sachem—often called a minor, or local, sachem by the English. He, or, in a handful of cases, she, was responsible for governing the internal affairs of the group. The independence of the local sachems in the Narragansett confederation had begun to diminish somewhat in the 1620s, as trade with the Dutch and the English became an increasingly important source of wealth for the Indians. By the mid-1630s, an emerging Indian-English-Dutch market economy, centered largely on the exchange of furs and foodstuffs for European goods, led to the concentration of political and commercial authority in the hands of Canonicus and Miantonomi.

Algonquian sachems, Narragansett and otherwise, almost always owed their positions to family descent. It fell to the great sachem to make all the critical decisions for his subjects, albeit with the advice of the minor sachems, a council of elders, and one or more powwows—men who presided over various rituals and tended to both the spiritual and bodily health of the people. Indians looked to their great sachem to dispense justice, mediate disputes between bands, allocate farming and hunting lands, conduct diplomacy with outsiders, and organize group activities, especially the seasonal migrations between the coast and the inland forests, and warfare. In exchange for protection and leadership, Miantonomi and Canonicus received allegiance and payments from their tributaries, as well as from their own local bands in the villages of southern Rhode Island.

Allegiance to the great sachem, however, was contingent on his ability to keep the local sachems and their subjects reasonably content through gift-giving and consensus building, and responsive leadership. Disaffected minor chiefs could alter the balance of power between the major Indian tribes by shifting their allegiance from one great sachem to another.

Political and social ties among the Algonquians were protean—which caused no small amount of confusion and frustration for Europeans. When individual Indians in Narragansett territory committed criminal acts or violated Indian-Puritan agreements, the English authorities would customarily go over the heads of the local sachems and seek satisfaction from Canonicus and Miantonomi directly. Much to the frustration of the English authorities, their ability to do so was often circumscribed by the power minor sachems enjoyed over members of their own bands, as well as by the ease with which unattached males, and even on occasion entire nuclear families, could migrate from one band to another.

The Narragansetts, like all southern New England Indians, were farmers and fishermen as well as hunters and gatherers. Each spring men and women worked together to clear new fields close to the coastline, cutting down trees, and breaking up the soil with clamshells and stone hoes. Women planted, nurtured, and harvested the staple crops of squash, beans, and corn, and they gathered fruit, nuts, and plants for both sustenance and medicinal purposes.

Puritans stereotyped Indian men as lazy, yet it's clear that men took on the hard labor of clearing the fields when new farming plots were needed. Narragansett men were also skilled trappers and hunters of deer, rabbits, beaver, and otter. Deer was by far the most important source of meat for the tribe. In the winter, hunting parties of as many as several hundred men roamed the forest, driving deer in the direction of a large V-shaped, funneled trap leading to a corral, where they could be easily dispatched with bow and arrow. Before the hunt, carefully controlled fires were set to clear away underbrush. While the cleared ground made hunting quite a bit easier, it did no permanent harm to the maple, oak, cedar, and pine trees. In fact, by decreasing the competition for nutrients in the soil, it enhanced the growth of the larger trees.

Pigeons, waterfowl, and turkeys formed a regular part of the Narragansett Indian diet and were found in numbers that astonished the English. Men fished with weirs, nets, and harpoons, both in Narragansett Bay proper and in the many fresh- and saltwater ponds and rivers in their territory. Shellfish, quahogs, and mussels were collected along the shoreline, usually by women, throughout the year.

Seaworthy dugout canoes carved out of the trunks of large hardwood trees were used for open-water fishing and travel between the mainland of Narragansett country and the islands in the Bay. These craft could transport as many as thirty Indians across miles of open ocean, even in blustery seas. The canoes were among the most striking examples of an Indian technology that proved far superior to its English counterpart in the New World environment. Roger Williams reported that the Narragansetts even knew how to rig a sail made of English cloth on a small pole in their canoes to gain speed.

Despite the hunting prowess of Narragansett men, corn was the staple of the tribe's diet. It was consumed in stews with beans, squash, fish, and meat. Cakes were also made from cornmeal, which was stored for winter consumption in great quantities in baskets buried in the ground.

Among the many groups of Algonquian Indians, the Narragansett distinguished themselves not only as traders, but as manufacturers. Narragansett baskets, woven by women, were highly prized throughout the region. Women prepared furs for both personal clothing and for trade. Men fashioned widely regarded pipes for tobacco they grew for their own consumption, as well as axes, chisels, hoes, and arrows made of flint and, later, European metals.

The coastline of Narragansett country was overrun with quahog and whelk, the raw material used for drilling and minting shell beads called wampum. Wampum had great symbolic and ceremonial value to all Algonquians long before Europeans arrived on the scene. It was given as tribute, to confirm agreements between native peoples, and worn as jewelry by individuals to designate authority and prestige. Shortly after the first English settlements in New England took root, wampum became the chief medium of exchange in the emerging European-Indian trade network. Vast stores of the stuff were traded by Narragansetts to the Indians in the hinterlands to the west and north in exchange for furs; the furs were exchanged with both the Dutch and the English for iron and steel knives, hoes and axes, brass pots, decorative beads and trinkets, cloth, firearms, and liquor. Almost all the metal objects used by Indians in New England in the seventeenth century "were of European origin," writes scholar Patrick M. Malone, "and they were made of various metals, including cast iron, wrought iron, steel, brass, copper and lead, among others."[3]

By entering into the market economy associated with the fur trade, the Narragansetts gained substantial purchasing power, which allowed them to obtain European versions of tools they had previously obtained only through their own labor-intensive manufacturing. Thus, the emerging market economy fostered growing dependency on the English and the Dutch, as well as a gradual decline in traditional subsistence patterns and skills, complicating relationships between Europeans and Indians, and between Indian tribes, in many unforeseen ways.

THE BAY AND ITS ENVIRONS

Geologists call Narragansett Bay an estuary, meaning a partially enclosed body of salty water into which freshwater rivers and streams drain, with a mouth on the open sea. The Bay is blessed with scores of coves, natural harbors, and shallow, smaller estuaries, with tidal pools and marshlands, and is gently rimmed by rocky coastlines and hardwood forests. Several navigable rivers drain into its waters from the hinterlands. In the seventeenth century a well-traveled network of trails amid the forests of New England permitted rapid movement on foot between various Indian bands and villages. The main artery of this trail network ran from the Pequot country in the southwest, straight through Narragansett country along the western coast of the Bay, and then all the way up to Massachusetts territory, near Boston, generally following the course of what is today Route 1, along the Old Post Road.

The Bay in the seventeenth century was easily accessible by overland and ocean travel, and well protected from the open ocean. Between its eastern and western shores lies an archipelago of some thirty islands. The largest of these—Aquidneck, Conanicut, and Prudence Islands—were usually inhabited by

Narragansett bands in the spring and summer months. Dutch Island, between the mainland and Conanicut Island, served as a trading post before the arrival of permanent English settlers in the 1630s.

Unlike the English settlers in New England, observes historian William Cronon, the Indians "held their demands on the ecosystem to a minimum by moving their settlements from habitat to habitat. . . . By using species when they were most plentiful, Indians made sure no single species became overused. It was a way of life to match the patchwork of the landscape. . . . Just as a fox's summer diet of fruit and insects shifts to rodents and birds during the winter, so too did the New England Indians seek to obtain their food wherever it was seasonally most concentrated."[4] Narragansett Indian territory contained a diversity of lush ecosystems. Each of these—forest, river, lake and pond, the deep salt waters of the Bay itself—provided a wealth of flora and fauna at different times of the year. Cod, striped bass, shellfish, and deer were especially plentiful. The Narragansetts used what they needed, no more, harvesting only when resources were plentiful. So their footprint on their environment was light.

The Narragansetts, like other Algonquians, lived within prescribed boundaries, but they moved their villages with the seasons to best exploit nature's bounty. In the fall and winter months, for the most part, they inhabited inland villages, amid the forests, though some hunting parties established temporary living quarters far afield from the main villages and lived in those camps for several weeks at a time. In the spring, the Narragansetts broke down their dwellings, packed their gear and goods, including mats made of earth, thatch, and bark used to cover sapling-framed wigwams, and trekked back to the coast, where they laid out new villages and cleared fresh fields or replanted old ones.

Winter villages were often located in shallow valleys for protection from the weather, where firewood was plentiful. Winter dwellings were considerably larger than summer ones, which were typically only sixteen to eighteen feet in diameter and housed a single family. Many winter homes were not wigwams, but longhouses up to a hundred feet long, with three or four fireplaces and roof vents placed at intervals. They could house as many as fifty people.

The Narragansetts had a rich spiritual life, but no formal, organized religion. Spirits permeated everyday activities and events, lending them meaning and purpose. The presence of spirits and gods explained good fortune as well as bad, and natural phenomena such as the stars, the wind, the sea, birds, and other animals were all invested with spiritual power. A nightmare signaled the gods' unhappiness; good fortune, their pleasure.

The Narragansetts had a panoply of spirit-gods but only one creator—Cautantowwit. According to Roger Williams, "Cautantowwit made one man and woman of a stone, which disliking, he broke them into pieces, and made another man and woman of a tree, which were the fountains of all mankind."[5] People who led good and useful lives returned to Cautantowwit's home in the southwest after death; the unworthy were destined to wander forlornly in the cosmos. Narragansett dead were usually buried in the fetal position, with the head facing toward Cautantowwit's home.

According to Williams, the Narragansett had a legend concerning the origin of corn and bean agriculture. A crow brought a single grain of corn in one ear and a single bean in another "from Cautantowwit, the great southwest god, to whose house all souls go, and from whom came their corn and beans."[6]

Whenever the Indians came across something they found remarkable or admirable, they were inclined to speak in spiritual terms to explain it. As Williams wrote, "There is a general custom amongst them, at the apprehension of any excellence in men, women, birds, beasts, fish, etc. to cry out *Manittoo*, a God, and therefore when they talk amongst themselves of the English ships, and great buildings, of the plowing of the fields, and especially of books and letters, they will end thus: *maniitowock*, they are gods."[7]

All the Algonquian of southern New England displayed remarkable loyalty and generosity toward family members and fellow band members. "These Indians," writes the early English chronicler William Wood,

> are of affable, courteous, and well-disposed natures, ready to communicate the best of their wealth to the mutual good of one another; and the less abundance they have to manifest their entire friendship, so much the more perspicuous is their love in that they are willing to part with their mite in poverty as treasure in plenty. . . . Such is their love to one another that they cannot endure to see their countrymen wronged, but will stand stiffly in their defense.[8]

NARRAGANSETT-PURITAN DIPLOMACY AND POLITICS: THE EARLY YEARS

Situated between the Massachusetts Indians to the north, the Wampanoags to the east, and the Pequots and Mohegans to the west, the Narragansetts occupied a strategic location in regional power politics and commerce. From the very first contact between the Pilgrims of Plymouth and the tribe, there was a strong undercurrent of wariness over the other's intentions, and in retrospect, it seems Miantonomi and Canonicus perceived earlier than most other sachems in the region the potential dangers posed by the newcomers, with their strange notions of land ownership, their firearms, and their books, which were objects of great awe, for they seemed to contain an immense fountain of both spiritual and temporal knowledge.

Unlike the vulnerable Wampanoags or the Massachusetts Indians, whose numbers had been drastically reduced by plague, the Narragansetts were not (initially, at least) disposed to see a formal alliance with the English as inherently beneficial. Because of the vitality of their confederation, their active trade with the Dutch, and their strategic locale, Miantonomi and Canonicus could afford to wait and see about establishing formal relationships with the nascent English colonies.

The sachems, however, were none too pleased about the Wampanoag-Plymouth alliance, for the Narragansetts had long squabbled over territory at the head of Narragansett Bay with the Wampanoags, and the advantages of the exclusive trading arrangement Massasoit had arranged with the English were many. Not only did that agreement appear to all but close the door on direct Narragansett-Plymouth trade; it strengthened the Wampanoags' political influence and prestige in the region considerably, as Indian bands in the vicinity of Plymouth, as well as those on Cape Cod, Martha's Vineyard, and Nantucket, now looked to conduct trade with the Pilgrims through Wampanoag intermediaries.

Not long after learning of the agreement, Canonicus sent a war party to support a raid on Massasoit's home village of Sowams, near Warren, Rhode Island, undertaken by a disgruntled Wampanoag minor sachem named Corbitant. Corbitant's force captured two of Massasoit's chief liaisons with the Pilgrims. One of these men, Hobbamock, escaped his captors, fleeing to Plymouth for help. Governor Bradford quickly responded, sending Captain Myles Standish, the fiery Pilgrim military commander, to the rescue along with fourteen troops. After a desultory engagement, Corbitant and the Narragansetts withdrew, releasing the other Wampanoag captive. Plymouth and Massasoit had gotten the better of the Narragansetts—this time, anyway.

Canonicus soon thereafter signaled both his displeasure and resolve by sending a bundle of arrows in a snakeskin to Governor William Bradford of Plymouth. Canonicus stood ready to protect his own people and the Narragansett alliance system against Puritan-

Wampanoag encroachment. Bradford recognized the gesture for what it was, promptly filled the snakeskin with powder and shot, and sent it back to Canonicus, who refused to accept it. Nothing was to come of this incident, but it seems an apt symbol for the vexed nature of Puritan-Narragansett relations in the years to follow. "Through their mutual act of rejection," writes anthropologist Paul Robinson, "each party signified its refusal to submit to the other."[9]

Southern New England in the early 1630s was in constant flux as the larger Indian tribes jostled to gain both control over smaller bands as well as favorable trade and defense alliances with European traders and colonies. Initially, at least, the Narragansetts seemed to get along much better with the colonists of Massachusetts Bay than they did with those of Plymouth. Due to its greater size and commercial dynamism, good relations with Massachusetts could more than offset whatever advantages accrued to the Wampanoag as a result of their arrangement with Governor Bradford. Miantonomi made the first of many visits to Boston in the summer of 1631. Arriving with his ally, the Massachusetts sachem Cutshamakin, as an intermediary, Miantonomi brought an animal skin for Governor John Winthrop, who requited the gift "with a fair pewter pot, which [Miantonomi] took very thankfully, and stayed all night."[10]

From many sources, we know that the Narragansetts had developed a wide-ranging trading network with fur-hunting peoples to the west, including the Nipmucks, the Pocumtucks, and, even farther to the west, the fierce and powerful Mohawks. William Wood tells us that in the early 1630s the Narragansetts regularly brought beaver, otter, and muskrat pelts to Massachusetts Bay, "returning back loaded with English commodities, of which they made a double profit by selling them to more remote Indians who are ignorant at what cheap rates they obtain them."[11]

The Massachusetts Bay trader John Oldham had established close trading ties with the Narragansett sachems by early 1634.

Oldham was even permitted by the sachems to set up a trading post on Prudence Island in Narragansett Bay. Oldham was killed by Indians two years later, and the island was subsequently purchased jointly by Roger Williams and John Winthrop from the Narragansetts and used for the raising of cattle and swine.

THE PURITANS, GOD-FEARING AND AMBITIOUS

The first Puritans had come to America from England after a long stay in Holland. However, most Pilgrims came to the New World directly from England to escape both religious persecution at the hands of an English king and a church they saw as afflicted with corruption, and the social dislocation caused by that nation's emerging market economy, with its calamitous price fluctuations and periodic depressions.

The Church of England was run by a hierarchy of bishops and priests more concerned with the worldly trappings of their offices than with what the Puritans understood to be the central business of life: preparation for redemption and salvation through Christ. Worship in the Church of England was decidedly short on good preaching and piety, both of which formed the bedrock of Puritan faith. The Church of England's services were organized around the *Book of Common Prayer*, a work containing the words of men, not God. Many of the rituals and forms of worship it prescribed bore the marks of medieval Catholicism, a religious tradition Puritans found at odds with the pure and simple church originally established by Jesus and His apostles.

To the Puritans, true worship involved direct engagement with the Bible, the revealed word of God. The Bible provided all the guidance human beings required to live on earth in a God-fearing and upright way. It was the key to all history, past and present. It gave life meaning and purpose. The Puritans journeyed across the North Atlantic to join with others already engaged in constructing a pious community based on biblical imperatives, dedicated, in the words of Governor John Winthrop's classic sermon, "A Model of Christian Charity," "to serve the Lord and work out our Salvation under the power and purity of His holy ordinances."[12] In short, Massachusetts was to become a model Christian commonwealth of close-knit towns, farms, and churches.

The Puritans were intensely preoccupied with salvation. It was probably the most important word in their vocabulary, the end for which they organized their individual and collective lives. What distinguished Puritans from other Englishmen, the historian Edmund Morgan observes, was "a deeper sense among Puritans of the great obstacle that lay between man and salvation." That obstacle was man's innate depravity, the stain on his soul that made him self-serving, lascivious, lazy, and greedy. "The Puritans insisted that man must keep the obstacle in full view and recognize that no saint or angel, no church or priest, could carry him over it."[13] Salvation could not be achieved through a person's own effort, but only through the grace of Christ, which came but to a few people, and even they could never be entirely sure about the matter.

Nonetheless, Puritans generally believed that one could approach saving grace through a series of prescribed steps that moved from acceptance of one's depravity, to contrition and humiliation, which, in turn, opened the door for the power of the Holy Spirit to transform the person through "saving grace" from sinner to "visible sainthood," and thus, full membership in God's church. Although God did not necessarily reward upright behavior with salvation, He surely smiled on those who shunned frivolous pursuits in favor of a life of industry, frugality, and charity.

Thus, the Puritans famously sacralized work, extending the religious concept of a minister's "calling" to the everyday labor of ordinary people. Edward Winslow, one of the leaders of the Plymouth Colony, got to the heart of the matter when he wrote that in the Puritan vision of New England, "religion and profit jump together."[14] Diligence, humility, integrity, self-discipline, and piety—these were the indispensable assets of the godly in the great struggle against the sway of the Antichrist.

Puritan values helped the colonists prosper in an unfamiliar and demanding land, and they "developed a culture that was both the most entrepreneurial and the most vociferously pious in Anglo-America," historian Alan Taylor astutely observes. "Puritans worked with a special zeal to honor their God and seek rewards that offered reassurance that God approved of their efforts." New England's well-ordered towns, farms, workshops, churches, and schools "constituted the Puritans' effort to glorify God."[15] The intense desire to close the gap between man and salvation was the engine propelling Puritan thought about this world, the next, and the relation between the two. It shaped the demanding Puritan moral code; it drove myriad debates about seemingly obscure theological points, causing Puritan churches to multiply by dividing. And it infused the powerful reform impulses that put Puritanism on a collision course with royal authority and traditional English institutions, culminating in the English Civil War of the 1640s.

Although King James I viewed Puritanism with great skepticism, he reluctantly tolerated its growing presence among clergy in Anglican parishes throughout the country. Not so his son and successor, Charles I, whose strong Catholic sympathies led to the dismissal of Puritan clergy, and then to outright persecution of Puritan laypeople. Under Archbishop William Laud, a great enthusiast for Catholic ritual and ceremony in worship, Puritan tracts were censured, and their authors sometimes pilloried and imprisoned.

In 1629, Charles dissolved Parliament and stepped up the persecution of Puritan congregations, opening the floodgates of the Great Migration to New England. Most of these émigrés joined their countrymen at home in believing that England was, and would remain, the world's indispensable nation, but Puritans alone believed themselves "destined to lead the world back to God's true religion and end the tyranny of the Antichrist."[16] Despite the depth of Puritan convictions, and they were profoundly deep, a strong current of anxiety ran through the Puritan mind, borne of uncertainty as to how to fulfill the mission. Was it necessary to form an entirely new church in the New World, or was it enough to work to reform that English church from within—even if the nature of the reforms needed to be worked out across three thousand miles of ocean?

Puritans differed on this key issue. The leaders of Plymouth had opted to separate from the Church of England and create their own church in the wilderness of the New World. The leaders of Massachusetts Bay took a different tack. They would stay within the Church of England, seeking to reform it from within by way of example, but do so far enough away from England to minimize external interference.

Most Puritans who came to America hailed from small, close-knit villages in England of about seventy families or so. When they crossed the Atlantic, they attempted to replicate these communities in the New World. The colony government allocated townships to groups of households who had just arrived from England, or to groups from crowded, older towns in New England. Houses were built close together, often centered around a village square, where the meetinghouse was used for both church services and town meetings. Fields lay near the town center and were distributed according to socioeconomic status and family size.

In Massachusetts, governmental power was in the hands of the General Court—what Minister John Cotton rightly called a "mixed aristocracy"—consisting in the early days of a governor, deputy governor, and eighteen assistants. The assistants were chosen by all freemen in the colony who were church members—perhaps 70 percent of adult males. Assistants alone chose the governor and the deputy governor. A bit later, the makeup of the General

Court was expanded to include representatives from each town, called deputies.

The General Court had both legislative and judicial functions, and while technically all church members were potential magistrates, invariably men of some wealth and educational achievement were chosen to lead, not only in Massachusetts, but in all the Puritan colonies. "In fact," writes historian Francis Bremer, "the broad franchise was instituted more for the purpose of binding the people to their government than to encourage the expression of popular views. God . . . had chosen the few to lead the many."[17]

While church and state in the Puritan colonies were separate institutions, they were in practice intimately related and mutually reinforcing in preserving both social order and religious conformity. Every town established its own independent church. Principles of town and colony government were firmly rooted in Scripture. The General Court was a civil institution, but one of its most important functions was to ensure religious uniformity. It fell to the court, not the church, to banish unrepentant religious dissidents and punish Sabbath breakers, for they threatened to bring God's wrath down on the entire community.

Ministers were prohibited from holding civil offices, but they exercised a great deal of political power. They could excommunicate freemen from the church, thereby stripping them of the vote, and magistrates invariably sought spiritual guidance from ministers and church elders when faced with any important political or military decision. More often than not, the advice provided was a crucial factor in decision making.

Having firmly established themselves on the coast of New England by the mid-1630s, the Puritans were remarkably quick to repress those among them who failed to adhere to the demanding religious and social code promulgated by a small group of like-minded magistrates and clergy. Liberty—liberty in the modern sense of the word, meaning to do what one chose, as one saw fit—was to the Puritan elite's way of thinking a dangerous thing. People left to their own devices would inevitably fall prey to sin and depravity. True liberty, wrote Winthrop, meant "liberty to that only which is good," and "to quietly and cheerfully submit unto that authority which is set over you."[18]

"The few" who were thought capable of holding positions of political leadership were by and large an austere and determined lot, men who took their positions seriously and did not suffer fools—or slackers—gladly. John Endicott, the first governor of Massachusetts Bay, was a strict disciplinarian and former soldier, quick to take offense if his judgment was brought into question. Thomas Dudley, the deputy governor for many of the early years in Massachusetts, had been steward of the Earl of Lincoln and prided himself on extricating his employer from debt by raising the rents of the tenant farmers, despite a looming depression and a steep decline in the price of crops. Dudley, cold and literal-minded, was frequently annoyed by Winthrop's willingness to compromise or to show leniency in judging minor infractions of the law.

The dominant political figures in the early history of Plymouth and Massachusetts, William Bradford and John Winthrop respectively, were exceptional men, gifted with uncommon intelligence and discernment. As long-serving governors who wielded extraordinary power even within the small circle of those deigned fit to govern, both men proved themselves outstanding administrators, judges, and politicians. Each man presided over a formidable array of disputes and challenges, ranging from the proper distribution of governmental power, to the regulation of prices and wages, to the colonies' often vexed relations with Indian peoples.

Born in 1590 in the Yorkshire village of Austerfield to a family of well-off farmers, Bradford knew tragedy early in life. He lost both parents before he was twelve. Raised by two uncles, he became a devout Puritan separatist before turning fifteen. Though he never attended university, Bradford was an autodidact who read widely and voraciously. He earned a reputation early on among the Pilgrims as a man of both thought and action, and he was an unusually keen judge of character.

After Plymouth's first governor, John Carver, died in the great sickness of 1620–21, Bradford was elected governor, then reelected each year for a decade. Time and again during the first years of the struggling colony, Bradford displayed personal courage, an abiding commitment to fairness and justice, and, perhaps most important, the ability to make quick, defensible decisions in crises. When a poorly prepared colony of English (i.e., non-Puritan) settlers at nearby Wessagusset (later renamed Weymouth) mistreated and stole from the Massachusetts Indians, Bradford learned from Massasoit that the tribe was plotting a surprise attack on both Wessagusset and Plymouth.

Considerably outnumbered by the hostile Indians, Bradford immediately recognized the crucial importance of responding quickly, and with decisive force—not only to preempt the impending attack, but to signal to all the Indians in the area Plymouth's resolve to defend itself vigorously in the face of conspiracy, despite its tiny numbers. Bradford ordered Myles Standish to plan and execute a surprise attack against the Massachusetts ringleaders. In March 1623, Standish did so, killing seven or eight Indians and scattering a score of others into a swamp. Soon thereafter the Massachusetts sachems sued for peace with Plymouth, and peace was to prevail between the Massachusetts and Plymouth for the rest of the seventeenth century.

It was Bradford, too, who extricated the colony from near financial ruin by negotiating with the key investors in England when the colony failed to turn a profit in the early years. He proved as adept at resolving internal squabbles and disputes as he was at guiding the colony's peaceful relations with the Wampanoags.

A man of considerable literary talents, in his book *Of Plymouth Plantation*, Bradford charts the evolution of the colony from 1620 to 1646 with clarity and penetrating insight into its failures as well as its successes. Bradford writes that he attempted to tell the story of the colony "in a plain style, with simple regard unto the simple truth in all things," as far as his "slender judgment" allowed.[19] But as events proved year in and year out, there was nothing "slender" about Bradford's judgment, or his character.

John Winthrop was one of the wealthiest and best-educated men to cross the Atlantic in the Great Migration. A third-generation son of landed gentry in Suffolk, he attended Cambridge, was admitted to Gray's Inn in London to study law in 1613, and returned to Suffolk in 1617, where he served as justice of the peace and lord of Groton, the family manor. Intensely religious, Winthrop struggled long and hard with how best he might serve God. After a considerable internal struggle, he came to believe that a person who sought "sure peace and joy in Christianity, must not aim at a condition retired from the world and free from temptations, but to know that the life which is most exercised with trials and temptations is the sweetest. . . . For such trials as fall within compass of our callings, it is better to arm and understand them than to avoid and shun them."[20]

Winthrop certainly lived his life in New England with this belief firmly fixed in his mind. By the time he was elected governor by members of the Massachusetts Bay Company in 1629, "his long struggle with his passions," writes biographer Edmund Morgan, "had left him master of himself in a way few men ever achieve. The fire was still there, and blown up by other men's wrath, it would occasionally burst out, but generally it lay well below the surface, imparting a warmth and power which everyone around him sensed. He never grasped for authority . . . [as] he was the kind of man upon whom authority was inevitably thrust."[21]

As both governor and assistant on the General Court, John Winthrop showed great tact and flexibility in mediating disputes both within the colony and among all the Puritan colonies, once they formed the Confederation of New England in 1643. But his supreme confidence in his ability to judge which kinds of institutions and ideas were congenial to God's wishes predisposed him to encourage intolerance among the magistrates for religious as well as political dissent.

As for the Indians, those tribes that readily submitted to Puritan jurisdiction and agreed to abide by English regulations he generally treated with courtesy and respect. But Indians who clung tenaciously to their own traditions and refused to defer to Puritan authority—as the Narragansetts so frequently did—were a different matter. As we shall see, there are compelling reasons to believe that Winthrop's seemingly judicious, well-crafted accounts of disputes between Puritans and Indians are peppered with distortions and curious omissions, especially in incidents where Indians put forward compelling defenses of their own sovereignty and autonomy. Unfortunately, every student of Puritan-Indian relations trying to find his bearings must rely heavily on Winthrop's writings, for in a great many cases his account of a given dispute or event is the only one we have.

The first scholar to bring this uncomfortable issue widely into the light was Francis Jennings, in his provocative book *The Invasion of America: Indians, Colonialism, and the Cant of Conquest*, published in 1975. Professor Jennings has some crucially important things to say about Winthrop's *Journal*, widely recognized as the quasi-official history of the early years of Massachusetts Bay Colony:

> An unbeliever could say that it presented history with a slant. An investigator may add that it is curiously selective and that the documents [concerning Indian relations] interpreted by Winthrop have a high mortality rate. Especially as regards Indian affairs, his interpretations have to be accepted in lieu of the prime sources [i.e., the actual texts of agreements] because of the latter's disappearance. In the tons of paper squirreled away by Winthrop and his descendants, the only text of an

> Indian treaty surviving his lifetime [is the 1645 treaty with the Narragansetts]. . . . The process of natural selection by which [the other treaties] became unfit to survive must be a matter of speculation, but one can say with confidence that the interpretations provided in Winthrop's [*Journal*] are unlikely to be accurate representations of the vanished texts. All this sounds like innuendo so let it be said forthrightly: Winthrop probably rewrote the substance of Indian treaties to meet the Puritans' political and ideological needs, and then he or a devoted descendant destroyed the originals.[22]

No one can prove that Jennings is correct, but for two reasons his thesis bears keeping in mind in understanding the struggle between the Narragansetts and the Puritans. First, many contemporary historians and other scholars who have sought to recover the Indians' side of the story through the use of archaeological and anthropological evidence believe Jennings's assessment is largely correct. And second, Jennings's thesis goes far in explaining quite a number of otherwise inexplicable actions and decisions.

DEEPENING ANTAGONISM

By 1635, the Puritans and the Indians in southern New England had for the most part established friendly, mutually beneficial relationships. Indian assistance had proved indispensable in ensuring the survival and growth of the two colonies. Contrary to widespread expectations, writes William Wood, the Indians proved "very hospitable, insomuch that when the English have traveled forty, fifty, or threescore miles into the country, they have entertained them in their houses . . . providing the best victuals they could, expressing their welcome in as good terms as could be expected. . . . The doubtful traveler hath often been much beholding to them for their guidance through the unbeaten wilderness."[23]

Despite the spirit of amity, latent forces and ideas were at work that threatened to transform the Indian-Puritan relationship from one of cooperation and friendship to one marred by misunderstanding, conflict, and for the Indians, an enduring sense of betrayal. The Puritan commitment to treat the Indian justly and equitably was unquestionably sincere during the critical early years of settlement. But that commitment diminished markedly over time. Conventional Puritan conceptions of Indian culture and character meant that, in the long run, the Indians would find justice and fair treatment at the hands of the newcomers to be elusive.

In journeying to the New World, recalled William Bradford, the Pilgrims expected to face "the continual danger of the savage people; who are cruel, barbarous, and most treacherous." The English believed they could expect little mercy from natives who "delight to torment men in the most bloody manner that may be; flaying some alive with the shells of fishes, cutting off the members and joints of others by piecemeal and broiling on the coals, eat the collops of their flesh in their sight whilst they live, with other cruelties too horrible to be related."[24]

The Puritan mind was Calvinistic, and Calvin saw the world as a struggle between the light of Christ and His people against infidels and pagans who, wittingly or unwittingly, served the devil, the Antichrist. The American Indians were such people, in this view. They were "barbarians"—wild, illiterate savages given to indolence, lying, and treachery.

The Puritans went to great pains to avoid the corruption and lassitude they imagined to come with extended contact with the Indian way of life, particularly their spiritual life, in which shamans (usually called powwows) presided over mysterious ceremonies, invoking the powers of a bewildering array of spirits and gods that inhabited animals and other natural phenomena. According to anthropologist William Simmons, the Puritans "believed that the Indian inhabitants worshiped devils, that Indian religious practitioners were witches, and that the Indians themselves were bewitched. . . . Unlike Indian beliefs about the supernatural qualities of Englishmen, which seemed to have been temporary and situational, Puritan commitment to the devil-and-witchcraft theory of Indian culture intensified rather than diminished with experience."[25]

The Puritans had also developed a cluster of ideas about their legal right to establish and expand their Holy Commonwealths within lands under the jurisdiction of one Indian sachem or another. Any patent issued by the English government granting its possessor political and legal jurisdiction was assumed to trump the rights of all Indian sachems within the boundaries prescribed by the document.

The Puritans looked to both biblical sources and the legal doctrine of *vacuum domicilium* to justify the occupation of Indian lands they claimed to find unoccupied and unimproved by the earnest labors of men. The doctrine was simple: lands not cultivated or "improved" in the English fashion were free for the taking. Puritan Robert Cushman noted that the Indians' "land is spacious and void, and there are few and [they] do but run over the grass as do also the foxes and wild beasts. They are not industrious, neither have [they] art, science, skill or faculty to use either the land or the commodities of it, but all spoils, rots, and is marred for want of manuring, gathering, ordering, etc."[26]

John Winthrop, in explaining *vacuum domicilium*, extended Cushman's thought, with unsettling repercussions for Indian sachems who understood themselves to hold jurisdiction over well-demarcated territories used for hunting and gathering as well as settlement: "As for the Natives of New England, they enclose no land, neither have they any settled habitation, nor any tame cattle to improve the land by, and so have no other than a natural right to those countries, so as if we leave them sufficient for their use, we may lawfully take the rest."[27] And so they did, though typically not before offering token compensation to Indians who "pretended" to have title to land they wanted for themselves to "avoid the least scruple of intrusion."[28] Ominously for the Indians, the Puritans appointed *themselves* the judges of how much land the Indians required. And in matters of dispute between Indians and Puritans, the final arbiters were always English courts and magistrates.

Among the most daunting and important tasks of building the Holy Commonwealths was to bring Christ and His blessings to the Indians. In the Puritan mind, Christ's blessings were inextricably tied to the adoption of the institutions, ideas, and patterns of life associated with English civilization. Thus, conversion required that the Indian not only jettison his religion, but his political allegiance and his entire mode of subsistence, and take up the manners and mores of the English.

What if the powerful Indians who occupied lands beyond Plymouth and the first towns of Massachusetts Bay, lands where the Holy Commonwealths envisaged expansion, proved hostile? What if the Indians refused to see the light and relinquish their heathen ways and their strange world of spirits and devils for the blessings of Christ and civilization?

The answer to that question was simple: it could not be allowed to happen. If reason, preaching, or diplomacy could not bring the Indians around, then military conquest was the only answer. Thus, even as the English sought "fair" trade arrangements, even as they purchased lands from both individual Indian occupants and sachems (who exercised dominion over well-defined territories) and entered into legally binding agreements with native peoples, they began to devise a variety of strategies to subdue the most powerful Indian tribes whose territories lay outside the boundaries of Plymouth and Massachusetts Bay. The primary target areas for expansion as of 1635 were eastern Connecticut and the lands around Narragansett Bay.

In Connecticut, the Puritans would succeed within a mere three years through a combination of alliances with local Indians and force of arms. Around Narragansett Bay, the Puritan quest for domination in political jurisdiction and occupancy would fail, but not for want of trying. The story of resistance to Puritan expansion around Narragansett Bay begins with the arrival in the New World of a Puritan minister of uncommon courage and imagination—a man who would in time become the founder of the first English settlement there: Roger Williams.

Chapter 2

A Godly Minister, Banished

Roger Williams's compass and sundial—two indispensable tools for navigating the New England wilderness. English settlements in early New England were islands in the midst of a vast and treacherous wilderness.

BOSTON, MASSACHUSETTS BAY COLONY,
FEBRUARY 9, 1631

Living under grinding duress in the bitter cold of their first New England winter, the settlers of Massachusetts Bay joyfully celebrated the arrival of the *Lyon*, a sailing ship out of Bristol, with its precious cargo of provisions, cattle, farming and building implements, lemon juice to prevent scurvy, and some twenty newcomers to the Holy Commonwealth. She had just set down anchor off the Boston coast. It was her third Atlantic crossing. The

Lyon had been part of the initial flotilla of the Great Migration in 1630 that carried John Winthrop and almost a thousand other settlers to the shores of Massachusetts. Scores of settlers had died since she last departed New England waters. In addition to delivering newcomers and goods, the *Lyon* brought a commodity in short supply: hope.

Of the twenty new arrivals aboard the *Lyon*, Governor Winthrop chose to describe only one man in his *Journal*: a "Godly minister" named Roger Williams.[1] Born in London around 1603, Williams early on showed signs of exceptional intellectual promise and religious piety. He came of age in what he himself described as "wonderful, searching, disputing and dissenting times."[2] England in the seventeenth century was passionately engaged in reflection and debate on political and ecclesiastical authority—of the proper relation between them, of their sources, and of their implications. Williams was destined to make important contributions to those debates in a long and stormy career as a theologian, a political theorist, a founder of a radical experiment in secular government, and an intermediary in many disputes between the Puritans and the Indians.

Roger Williams was born to a merchant-tailor father and a woman of the lower gentry, but we know little else of his early life. In his early teens Williams caught the attention of a towering figure in English jurisprudence and political philosophy, a man whose thought still resonates throughout the Western world today: Sir Edward Coke. His influence on the political ideas of the men who would frame the Constitution of the United States was particularly strong. As Coke's stenographer and clerk, Williams was exposed to many of the debates swirling around the issues of justice and power, natural rights, English common law, and the uneasy relationship between the rights and privileges of Parliament, the representatives of the people, and those of the king.

Coke befriended and mentored Williams. He secured him a

coveted place as a student at the prestigious Charterhouse school in London, and then at Pembroke College, Cambridge, where Williams trained for the ministry. It was almost certainly at Cambridge that young Williams first immersed himself in the movement to purify the Church of England.

Governor Winthrop made note of Williams's arrival in the New World because he had already met the promising young minister in old England and formed a favorable impression. Virtually everyone who knew Williams came to like him before too long. William Bradford called him "a man godly and zealous, having many precious parts."[3] He was warm, approachable, and charismatic. He spoke his mind confidently, yet his spirit was imbued with deep humility, a sense of his smallness and weakness in the face of God. As a Cambridge-trained minister in good standing, Williams would be expected to play an important role in building the Bay Colony and keeping its people on a godly course.

Above all else, perhaps, Roger Williams had the courage of his convictions. The clergy and the elders of the Bay Colony felt this man was well qualified to preach the word of God to the faithful, and so to nourish their piety and guide their way in a dark and dangerous world. His reputation as a gifted minister preceded him. Soon after settling into a new home with his wife, Mary, Williams was offered the prestigious post of teacher in Boston's church. The current teacher, John Wilson, was about to leave for England on the *Lyon* to persuade his wife to join him in Massachusetts.

To the astonishment of the elders of the church as well as the colony's leading political figures, Williams turned the offer down flat. John Winthrop explained why: he "refused to join with the congregation at Boston, because they would not make a public declaration of their repentance for having communion with the churches of England, while they lived there."[4] In other words, the congregation wouldn't formally declare itself separate from the Church of England.

So began five years of theological and political wrangling between the Massachusetts Bay authorities and Williams, leading in the end to his expulsion from the community in which he had fervently hoped to make a new life for himself and his family. The elders in Boston were taken aback not only by Williams's abrupt refusal of their generous offer, but by the vehemence with which he staked out his positions on matters of religion, government, and Indian affairs. So Roger Williams would become one of the early "unwilling wanderers" from Puritan orthodoxy in New England.

The question of whether a New England church community had formally separated itself from the Church of England or had committed itself to reform that Church from within—that is, whether it was a separating or nonseparating church—was the first issue of contention between Williams and Massachusetts. The question was of no small import both theologically and politically. To advocate complete separation from the Church was to court the wrath of King Charles I for the most obvious of reasons: he was the head of the Church. The line between acceptable religious dissent and political subversion was thin in a kingdom where the ecclesiastical and civil states were so "interwoven together," as one English aristocrat put it, "and in truth so incorporated in each other, that like Hippocrates' twins they cannot but laugh and cry together."[5]

Not long after Williams had turned down the offer to be church teacher in Boston, he challenged for the first time the authority of Boston's civil magistrates to monitor the spiritual life and religious practices of its people, and to mete out punishment for religious infractions. It was wrong, Williams protested, for the magistrates to involve themselves in violations of the first four of the Ten Commandments, known as the Decalogue, because the directives to love God, to refrain from taking His name in vain, to keep the Sabbath, and to avoid blasphemy were strictly matters of religious conscience, and thus, in Williams's mind, beyond the reach of any civil authority.

This, too, was an explosive assertion, but it seems from the contemporary sources that its implications for the Bay Colony were at first not fully grasped or were simply taken as the misguided and corrigible thinking of a headstrong minister. In mid-1631, the elders of Boston, including Governor Winthrop, in no way anticipated the sustained assault on their mode of worship or the relationship between church and state that Roger Williams was soon to mount. Quite the reverse: Winthrop and the leading men of the colony were confident that patient and methodical discourse between Williams and more experienced ministers in the colony would lead the young clergyman to see the error of his ways and disavow his outlier positions. Conformity on religious matters was deemed essential if the Holy Commonwealth was to thrive.

Soon after turning down the position in the Boston church, Williams and his young wife made their way to Salem, just north of Boston, where Puritan settlement in Massachusetts had first begun. There the church, under the guidance of the Reverend Samuel Skelton, had pronounced separatist leanings. Williams was well liked in Salem. He was apparently offered a position as an assistant to Skelton and would be given occasion to preach and meet with congregants to discuss matters of the spirit outside formal worship.

The Massachusetts General Court hadn't directly challenged Williams's move to Salem, but when word came down that he might be given a church position there, the Court warned the Salem congregation in writing that it would be wise to consult with them before granting him the position. The implication was clear. It was the first of many attempts by the authorities to silence Williams's voice. Salem was within the jurisdiction of the General Court as a town in Massachusetts Bay. Although the churches in the colony were meant to be completely independent in matters of organization and worship, it seems that Salem caved in under political pressure from the General Court and withdrew its initial offer of assistant to Williams.

Rather than challenging head-on the interference of Boston in the affairs of the Salem church, Williams and his wife pulled up stakes yet again, heading, they hoped, for a warmer reception among the Pilgrims of Plymouth, some forty miles south of Salem. The church there *was* of the separating variety, and in Plymouth Roger Williams stayed until the fall of 1633, outside the jurisdiction of the Massachusetts General Court and outside of trouble—at least for a while.

At Plymouth he joined the church and served briefly as the assistant to its minister. His sermons there, wrote Governor Bradford, were "well approved."[6] Unfortunately, none of the texts of those sermons have survived. Nor do we have many surviving comments from the hundreds of people, English and Indian alike, with whom Williams conversed about religious questions as he went about his day-to-day life. But circumstantial evidence suggests such conversations were frequent, and that he was a persuasive and thought-provoking speaker.

Yet at Plymouth, as in Massachusetts, Williams's unwillingness to compromise on matters of faith led him to part ways with the congregation. The church there proved insufficiently vigilant in enforcing separatist principles for him to remain a congregant. When he learned that some of its members who had worshipped in English churches in the old country had not been rebuked by their Plymouth minister for doing so, Williams objected strenuously. Many of the local inhabitants surely thought that their pious brother was making too much of a trivial matter, but when it came to Christ and religion, nothing was trivial to Roger Williams.

According to the minister-chronicler John Cotton, soon to emerge as Williams's most important intellectual adversary, it was at Plymouth that Williams first challenged the legitimacy of King

James I's royal patent giving the Massachusetts Bay Company the right to settle on the lands described in that document in his name. Williams did not see how the king could claim the right to grant English settlers land that had belonged for thousands of years to the current inhabitants—the Indians. After Williams returned to Salem in 1633, his refusal to refrain from challenging the legitimacy of the patent would get him into a great deal of trouble.

Although Williams and the Plymouth church formally parted company, Roger, his wife, and their daughter Mary—the first of six children born to the family—remained among the Pilgrims as part of the civic community for some time. During his two years in Plymouth, Williams embarked in earnest on a mission that would change everything for him, in addition to having a crucial bearing on Indian-Puritan relations for the next half century. He withdrew for extended periods from the tempestuous world of Puritan political and theological debate and headed south by small boat, loaded up with trade goods, to the shores of Narragansett Bay, where the Indian population was more heavily concentrated than anywhere else in New England.

He was intensely curious about the natives and wanted to learn all he could about their way of life. Besides, he also needed to make a living, and while trading with the Indians deep in their own country held some risks, it also promised considerable commercial reward. In Narragansett country Roger Williams went among the Indians to trade English axes, hoes, hatchets, cloth, kettles, knives, and trinkets for furs and wampum, as well as cornmeal and ground nuts to supplement the English settlers' still-tenuous food supply. He went to teach as well as to learn. He possessed, as he recalled more than forty years later, "a constant, zealous desire to dive into the Natives' language. . . . God was pleased to give me a painful, patient spirit to lodge with them in their filthy smoky holes (even while I lived at Plymouth and Salem), to gain their tongue."[7]

Traveling mostly by water, he mastered the details of the coastline and came to know the location of most of the Indian villages, as well as the numerous rivers, ponds, and swamps around the Bay. Trading deep in Indian country was physically demanding but rewarding spiritually and commercially, and the young minister—Williams was still in his late twenties—grew stronger and more confident as he built up an impressive network of friends and customers among the Narragansetts and Wampanoags.

Williams soon befriended Massasoit, chief sachem of the Wampanoags. But he formed especially close ties to Canonicus and Miantonomi, two men who would loom large in his life as friends and allies in the long struggle against the Puritan oligarchy's quest to dominate Narragansett Bay. During his trips to Narragansett country, Williams first began to make notes for a book about the language and culture of the local Indians, *A Key into the Language of America.* As many scholars have pointed out, Roger Williams shared some of the traditional Puritan views of the Indian, but the differences between his ideas and those of his fellow Puritans would prove far more important in the broad sweep of colonial history than the similarities.

Certainly he joined fellow Puritans in believing the Indian labored in spiritual darkness—they were, he thought, a "lost" people, and their behavior was at times "barbarous." He, too, expressed fears that Indian religious ceremonies and rituals might conjure up the devil, so he avoided direct participation in those ceremonies, even as he observed them.

Yet these sentiments hardly precluded him from learning all he could about the Indians' spiritual and temporal world, and exposing the Indians to what he knew of the Christian faith—but not imposing Christian beliefs or English culture upon them against their will. Christ had called upon him to love and treat his new neighbors with dignity and respect. Roger Williams had the humility to believe that neither he nor any other man or women—nor any earthly church—had a monopoly on religious truth. The truth for Williams, it might be said, could never be fully known by people, for they were too self-centered, too spiritually weak and prideful. But the truth must nevertheless be perpetually sought. If Williams brought any spiritual message to the Indians, it was this: seek the truth, and in time, you will be rewarded with God's favor.

Plainly, Roger Williams did not judge Indian culture and character with anything like the bias and cultural chauvinism of the Puritan elite. Much of what we know of Algonquian spirituality and culture at the time of the first English settlements comes from Williams's astute insights, gained through his discourses with the Narragansetts and Wampanoags. His understanding of the Indians, particularly the Narragansetts, was illuminated by a willingness to engage and observe the natives on their own terms, on their own ground. Dealing with them as he did, day by day and one-on-one, he came to value their friendship and the skills that ensured their survival in a wilderness that could be as brutal as it was unforgiving.

Williams found much in the way the Indians lived admirable. Indeed, their interpersonal ethics often seemed to him superior to those of Christian Europeans. As he would later write in *A Key*, "I could never discern that excess of scandalous sins amongst them, which Europe aboundeth with. Drunkenness and gluttony, generally they know not what sins they be; and although they have not so much to restrain them (both in respect of knowledge of God and laws of men) as the English have, yet a man shall never hear of such crimes amongst them of robberies, murders, adulteries, etc. as amongst the English."[8]

He praised the Indian's curiosity about spiritual matters. He found common ground with them in their tolerance of beliefs that differed from their own. Although Williams appears to have first entered the villages of the Narragansetts with a desire to convert them to Christianity, in time—and not much time, it seems—he came to see the conversion process along the New England frontier as one of a long list of orthodox Puritanism's anti-Christian projects. Carried on with the financial support of the state, it was inherently coercive, and thus antithetical to the teachings of Christ. It encouraged false conversions, undertaken simply for the sake of pleasing the missionaries and the Puritan governments that fostered their work. It was far better, Williams believed, to let God open up the Indians' souls to His message in His own time than to have it shoved down their throats by missionaries, even well-intentioned ones.

When all is said and done, Roger Williams came to find conventional Puritan (and English) views of the Indian to be wrongheaded, self-serving, and unchristian. "The unyielding rigor of his own religious convictions prompted him to treat the Indians with as much respect as shown by any English colonist of his generation," writes historian James T. Kloppenberg. "Since all people—Puritans as well as Wampanoag or Narragansett—are sinners, he urged the English to adopt an attitude of greater humility in their encounters with the native people of America."[9]

For their part, the Puritan authorities in Boston and Plymouth found Williams's views on the Indian as dangerous as they were blasphemous. John Winthrop wasn't the only Puritan who wondered if Williams had "gone Indian." Ironically, Puritan concerns over Williams's relationship with the Indians did not preclude them from turning to him time and time again to mediate disputes or negotiate agreements with the natives. Williams, the Puritan establishment held, was wrongheaded, prideful, theologically confused, and dangerous. He was a thorn in the side of the establishment. Yet he was an indispensable thorn when it came to treating with the Indians because he knew them better than any other Englishman in the region. And they trusted him.

WILLIAMS RETURNS TO SALEM, AND TO CONTROVERSY

Whatever the nature of Williams's theological disagreements with the authorities of Plymouth Plantation, we know that he pulled up stakes and returned to Salem in the fall of 1633. During his brief initial stay in that settlement in 1631, he had formed many close friendships and spiritual devotees. The congregation there was now looking for an assistant to their ailing minister, Samuel Skelton, who appreciated Williams's piety and was sympathetic to many of his ideas. Williams began to help Skelton with church affairs and apparently gained many supporters among recent settlers in Salem from East Anglia, though his position within the church was informal.

Not long after returning to Salem, Williams once again began to express his view that the royal patent was invalid. The minister–Indian trader had been thinking long and hard about land rights in America since his arrival in the New World. He had even written a treatise on the subject and shared it with both John Winthrop and William Bradford. No copy of this work has ever been found. We know of its existence largely from what's said about it in John Winthrop's *Journal*, as well as in a letter Winthrop sent to Salem magistrate John Endicott containing a detailed rebuttal of its argument.

According to Winthrop, Williams attacked English colonization as "a sin of unjust usurpation upon others' possessions."[10] The land belonged to the Indians, and any settler who sought a morally and legally legitimate claim to a landholding had to come to terms with its rightful owners. Williams stopped short of saying his king or his countrymen had stolen the land or forcibly evicted the natives, but that was the implication.

Like so many of Williams's criticisms of English and Puritan political and religious policies, this one was rooted in his radical theology and reinforced by his constantly expanding knowledge of Indian society and culture. King James, Williams said, had told "a solemn public lie" by claiming to be the first Christian king to discover New England.[11] Christ had given over neither His name nor His spiritual authority to any European kingdom or king to act in His name. There was, said Williams, no such thing as "Christendom." It was a word Williams found utterly repellent.

Williams believed churches of gathered believers in Christ anywhere on earth could be called Christian, but a nation, at least in the modern world, was strictly a civil, not a religious, entity—at least until Christ returned to earth and chose to anoint a given nation with His authority, and there was no sign whatsoever of *that* happening in the 1630s. The king of England, therefore, was committing blasphemy in claiming he acted as Christ's agent in "discovering" New England and granting settlement rights to His subjects through a patent.

Williams also rejected the English legal doctrine justifying the occupation of Indian lands, *vacuum domicilium*. He knew from firsthand experience that the Indian sachems were particular about the boundaries of their territories, and that certain lands were assigned for planting, hunting, and village settlement to various bands and often reassigned with the changing of the seasons. Williams therefore viewed *vacuum domicilium* as a specious doctrine that reflected ignorance of Indian ideas of property and settlement. So, too, he rejected outright the conventional Puritan view that thc Indians were wild, ungovernable savages. He found "their civil and earthly governments [to] be as lawful and true as any governments in the world."[12]

On December 27, 1633, the General Court formally condemned Williams's opinions on the royal patent and Indian land rights and attempted to refute them, principally on the grounds that they were offensive to the king. The Court demanded a retraction. Exactly what Williams said in response is not known, regrettably, but according to Winthrop, he "gave satisfaction of his intention and loyalty."[13] Apparently, Williams promised not to repeat his allegations in public in the future. He was duly persuaded that he was giving voice to opinions that could well threaten the civil order it was the duty of every citizen to protect. So he simply stopped expressing his views in public. For at that very moment, the king and Archbishop William Laud, the chief clergyman of the Church of England, were threatening to send a royal commission across the Atlantic to rein in the authorities in Boston for abusing their authority, and refusing to recognize the sovereignty of the king.

In 1634, the Salem congregation, broadly speaking, seems to have remained supportive of their charismatic and headstrong teacher. The General Court, however, kept a wary eye on Williams, whose supporters seemed to be growing in number as the year progressed. It seemed to some on the Court that the headstrong minister might succeed in drawing many members of the congregation toward the dangerous shoals of separatism.

Other questions must surely have been on the minds of the colony's magistrates sitting on the General Court: What other strange and misguided ideas did Williams harbor about the relation between religious and civil authority? What other rights and privileges did he think the Indians enjoyed? Had Williams truly recanted his position about the patent in his heart, or just in his words? If he hadn't truly abandoned his views, would he keep them to himself? They soon learned the answer to the latter two questions. He had not and would not.

In April 1634, Williams preached against administering oaths of fidelity to God by the government to unconverted Christians—that is, Christians who had yet to experience the crucial "rebirth" in Christ through the work of the Holy Spirit. Oaths should only be administered to regenerate Christians, said Williams, because an oath was a part of Christian worship. Here was yet another vexing and contentious issue, albeit one that seems far more bizarre and remote to twenty-first-century sensibilities than the land-ownership issue, but that nonetheless was of critical importance to orthodox Puritans.

In the fall, the Court learned Williams had again been speaking out privately against the royal patent, "antichristian" churches, and the exploitive Indian-land policies of the government of the Bay Colony. He even went so far as to draft a letter to the king, beseeching him to recognize "the evil of that part of the patent which respects the donation of land, etc."[14] Considering the hazards such a letter would invite, it seems astonishing that Williams was not censured and threatened with outright banishment in late 1634, but he was not. He did agree to refrain from sending the letter to the king, once it was borne in on him that the ramifications of doing so might well prove disastrous for the colony.

Exasperation over Williams's ideas and behavior continued to mount in Boston. Sometime during the summer of 1635, Salem defied the General Court's wishes, formally appointing Williams teacher in their church. In July, the Court again attempted to persuade Williams to back away from his dangerous opinions, citing his erroneous view that the state had no right to punish the first four sins enumerated in the Decalogue because those commandments concerned a person's relationship with God and had no bearing on civil affairs. When the Court consulted the other ministers in the colony—all of whom were in attendance at the meeting of the General Court—their opinion was that Williams should be removed from the office of teacher in the Salem church. The Court decided to refrain from either formal censure or from removing Williams. He was given time to reflect and recant.

Emboldened by support from the church membership in Salem, Williams stood firm. Minister John Cotton of Boston, a towering figure in orthodox Puritanism, entered the fray, attempting to persuade his fellow minister to admit the error of his ways, for the sake of his own soul as well as for the sake of peace between the Salem congregation and its sister churches. Cotton failed, just as he would fail again and again in a protracted series of letters and treatises in the coming years to convince Williams that his radical views on the separation of church and state were wrong.

Williams's intransigence, however, soon forced a dramatic showdown before the General Court. In October 1635, Williams was summoned to Boston yet again, to stand before the magistrates. This time the critical issue was his refusal to retract two provocative letters he had written. The first was to all the churches of the Bay Colony, protesting the magistrates' effort to repress his own views as well as those of the Salem congregation. A second, more explosive, communication called on the Salem congregation to separate itself formally from the other Massachusetts churches—churches that Williams described in the letter as "antichristian." In Williams's view, any church that did not support the right of its sister congregations to engage in independent, open discourse on matters of the spirit should not be called a Christian church at all.

The Court was by this time losing what little patience it had left. It took the extraordinary step of exerting sustained political pressure on the Salem congregation to recant, threatening to block the town's purchase of much-needed additional land on Marblehead Neck for settlement if it didn't distance itself from Williams and his outrageous opinions. Support among the beleaguered members of the congregation for their outspoken dissenter began to give way. John Winthrop reported that the church "disclaimed his [Williams's] errors, and wrote in humble submission to the magistrates, acknowledging their fault in joining with Mr. Williams in that letter to the churches against them."[15] The degree of reluctance and resentment felt among the people of Salem in doing this we can only surmise. It seems likely that practical realities overtook personal inclinations. Separatist views, and support for Roger Williams, though, lingered in Salem for some time.

The General Court had come to believe Williams was constitutionally incapable of keeping subversive views to himself, or of paying due respect to either religious or civil authority. It had finally heard quite enough. On October 9, 1635, it issued the following decree:

> Whereas Mr. Roger Williams, one of the elders of the church of Salem, hath broached and divulged diverse new and dangerous opinions, against the authority of magistrates, [has] also written letters of defamation, both of the magistrates and churches here, and that before any conviction and yet maintain the same without retraction, is therefore ordered that the said Mr. Williams shall depart out of this jurisdiction within six weeks now next ensuing, which if he neglect to perform, is shall be lawful for the Governor and two of the magistrates to send him to some place out of this jurisdiction, not to return any more without license from the Court.[16]

Through his seemingly inexhaustible energy and drive, Roger Williams had already demonstrated that he had an iron constitution. Yet, immediately after his banishment, at the age of about thirty-two, Williams became ill—a sickness, by his own account, "near unto death."[17] For a time, he could not speak. Apparently the strain of sustained controversy, with all its personal and political implications, had taken a devastating toll on his body and spirit.

Taking into account his illness, the Court granted him a short extension, but soon came to regret it. Williams regained his voice and kept talking up subversive ideas in private conversations with anyone who would listen. It soon became clear: Roger Williams had to go, and fast, for the spiritual purity—and perhaps even the political survival—of the colony was at stake. In mid-January, the General Court ordered John Endicott, a Salem magistrate and former soldier, to track down Williams and escort him to a ship about to embark for England.

Endicott arrived too late to accomplish his mission. Joined in all probability only by his trusted teenage servant, Thomas Angell, Williams slipped the noose and headed into the cold, windswept wilderness.

The brooks were frozen solid; the vast forests were blanketed by snow, deserted, except for small bands of Indian hunting parties. Williams was on the move again, on his way to a place seemingly beyond the reach of *all* English authority. He was heading back to see his friends Canonicus and Miantonomi. He was heading back to Narragansett country.

Chapter 3

"For Persons Distressed of Conscience": Providence

Alonzo Chappel's 1857 oil painting, *The Landing of Roger Williams in 1636.* Was the founder of Providence greeted by a party of Narragansetts on the western shore of the Seekonk River, as legend—and this painting—has it? We will never know for sure.

Decades after the event, when Roger Williams reflected on his experience during the fourteen-week journey from the comforts of hearth and home at Salem to the headwaters of Narragansett Bay—a distance of about seventy-five miles—he would describe it as a severe trial. Although he soon enough proved ready and willing to reestablish amicable relations with a number of important people in Massachusetts Bay, the shock of banishment never left him. In 1644, he wrote of the "miseries, poverties, necessities, wants, debts, hardships of sea and land" he had suffered "in a banished condition."[1] Williams maintained until the end of his life that he had been treated in a decidedly unchristian fashion. "His expulsion from Massachusetts Bay took on a symbolic importance," observes the editor of his correspondence, "for it signified in a dramatic way both the sufferings he had undergone as a witness of Christ and the evils of persecution that the Bay authorities had committed in the name of God."[2] He owed his survival not only to the goodwill of a handful of Indian guides along the way, but to the considerable body of knowledge about the wilderness he had gleaned from living and trading among the Indians.

Yet what we know of Williams's sensibility suggests he probably viewed his banishment as something of a blessing as well. The door to a fresh chapter in his life had opened. He was destined now to serve God and humanity in some as-yet-unknown way, and that awareness energized him, body and soul, and filled him with hopeful expectation. Roger Williams thrived on challenge and uncertainty, and there was something distinctively modern in his rejection of the conventional Puritan view of the world as static and predetermined. "I desire not to sleep in security and dream of a nest which no hand can reach," he wrote to John Winthrop in the summer of 1636, echoing Paul's first letter to the Corinthians. "I cannot but expect changes, and the change of the last enemy, death."[3]

Why did the outcast choose to go south to the Narragansetts? The decision emerged from dire circumstances, from personal history, and from the urging of his friend and mentor John Winthrop. As Williams recalled toward the end of his life, Winthrop "privately wrote to me to steer my course to the Narragansett Bay and Indians, encouraging me from the freeness of the place from any English claims or patents. I took his prudent motion as a hint and voice from God and (waiving all other thoughts and motion) I steered my course from Salem (though in winter snow which I feel yet) unto these parts . . . wherein . . . I have seen the face of God."[4]

He had not fled religious repression in the mother country five years earlier only to return home in defeat and disgrace. He did not wish to live among the Dutch in New Amsterdam, though he knew their language well and would have been welcomed there.

Yet surely Winthrop's suggestion only confirmed Williams's personal inclination. Probably well before his formal banishment, he had all but decided that if forced to leave Puritan New England, he would try to make a life among the friends he had made during his sojourns deep into Indian country near Narragansett Bay. "Many years before [settling in Providence] I came in person to the Narragansetts," Williams recalled, "and therefore when I came [to Providence to settle] I was welcome to Ousamaquin [another of Massasoit's names] and that old prince Canonicus, who was most shy of all English, to his last breath."[5] Williams could not have come to Narragansett much earlier than 1632, for he had only arrived in Boston in February 1631, so "many years" was a bit of a stretch, but one takes his point.

Williams had to come to some sort of understanding with both Ousamaquin and the Narragansett sachems regarding his settling on lands both tribes claimed. The specifics of those early arrangements are lost to us. But whatever they were, they proved congenial to both tribes. Neither the original sachems nor their successors ever took issue with the legitimacy of Williams's original settlement once it began to take root. The same could not be said for the Puritan leadership.

WINTER JOURNEY

The winter of 1635–36 was extremely cold, and Williams's trip to Narragansett country was often arduous and occasionally harrowing. But the journey was also surely punctuated by moments of elation and great hope. Bands of Indians offered him food and shelter, as well as camaraderie. And he had time to think, to plan, to reflect.

The sequence of events during the fourteen weeks between Williams's departure from Salem and his arrival at the head of Narragansett Bay has been the subject of a great deal of speculation. Most of the early secondary accounts have it that Williams took up residence for several weeks at Sowams that winter, the main Wampanoag village, located in the vicinity of Bristol, Rhode Island. He had already formed a strong bond with Massasoit. It only made sense that he would seek advice and shelter from the most important sachem of the Wampanoag people. From Sowams Williams probably corresponded via Wampanoag messengers with the dozen or so men from Salem and Boston who had shown interest in establishing a new settlement at the head of Narragansett Bay.

In late March 1636, Williams was joined by perhaps a half dozen of those followers and their families, including men who would have a strong hand in shaping Rhode Island politics in the years ahead—William Harris, Francis Wicks, and William Arnold, the forebear of the infamous Revolutionary War general, Benedict Arnold, among them. This small band of men and women began to build the rudiments of a crude settlement at the outer reaches of Plymouth territory, on the western shore of the Seekonk River. Informed politely but firmly by Plymouth governor Edward Winslow that they should cross to the eastern bank, outside the proper boundaries of Plymouth, Williams and his party packed up their meager possessions and embarked by canoe for their final destination.

A SETTLEMENT IS BUILT

Legend has it that Williams and his followers crossed the Seekonk River by canoe and were welcomed by a party of Indians on the spit of land in Providence known today as Fox Point, near the corner of modern Gano and Williams Streets, around April 20. After consultations with this band of Narragansetts—Miantonomi was almost certainly there to welcome his friend and new neighbor—Providence's first English settlers took to their canoes once again, rounded Fox Point, and came north, to the junction of the Woonasquatucket and Moshassuck Rivers, close to an Indian village called Moshassuck. Here, at the base of a two-hundred-foot-high hill, near a spring and a cove surrounded by meadows, the new town began to take shape. In 1661, Williams looked back on the first days of the new community:

> I had the frequent promise of Miantonomi (my kind friend) that it should not be land that I should want about those bounds mentioned, provided that I satisfied the Indians there inhabiting; I having made covenants of a peaceable neighborhood with all the sachems . . . and having in a sense of God's meaningful Providence unto me in my distress, [I] called the place Providence; I desired it might be for a shelter for persons distressed of conscience.[6]

Williams's home lot stood with the others along a path at the base of what later generations of Rhode Islanders would know as College Hill, home of Brown University and the Rhode Island School of Design, close to the intersection of Bowen and North Main Streets. Today, Roger Williams National Memorial, the only national park in the entire state of Rhode Island, sits astride the site of Williams's Providence home.

The view from the summit of that hill must have been awe

inspiring to this small party of weary travelers. They had arrived at last. A nineteenth-century historian, Henry C. Door, described it eloquently:

> The Great Salt River flowed far below broad and unconfined. On the east it was bordered by ancient forest trees, and on the west by deep marshes studded with islands overgrown with coarse grass, and nearly covered by every spring tide. At the head of the bay the channel widened into a cove, with a broad gravelly beach on the east and north, and a border of salt marshes on the west. . . . Still farther westward, low sand hills scantily covered with pines rose above the marsh. . . . On its western side, the hill upon which our explorers stood ascended abruptly from the very margin of the Salt River, but slowed with an easy descent to the Seekonk nearly a mile away on the east. Both its eastern and western hillsides were thickly wooded with oak and cedar.[7]

The records of the initial years of the Providence settlement have been lost for at least three centuries, so any account of how the community first organized itself has to be speculative. Relying on the sometimes contradictory recollections of Williams, William Harris, William Arnold, and several others, it appears that the first series of agreements binding the community together and establishing procedures for its governance were determined by simple majority rule of the male heads of households.

In a summer 1636 letter to John Winthrop, just three months after the first crude shelters began to take shape on Towne Street, Roger Williams put forward a draft of the new colony's first compact for the governor's comments. Winthrop's advice has not survived, but the official compact signed by all the heads of households in Providence is virtually identical to the draft in Williams's letter to Winthrop. That document has no date affixed, but Rhode Island historians generally agree that the number of head-of-household signatories, thirteen, places its signing no later than 1638. Its radically egalitarian slant, absence of deference to traditional authority, and tacit assumption of complete religious liberty—remarkably, there was no mention of God in the document at all—hint strongly that the compact did not go down well in Boston or Plymouth. It read in part:

> We whose names are hereunder, desirous to inhabit in the town of Providence, do promise to subject ourselves in active or passive obedience to all such orders or agreements as shall be made for public good of the body, in an orderly way, by the major assent of the present inhabitants, masters of families, incorporated together into a town fellowship, and such others whom they shall admit unto them, only in civil things.[8]

Canonicus and Miantonomi deeded the land exclusively to Williams, who, in turn, distributed it among the first families in more or less equal portions and established the town's common farming grounds atop the hill. Each head of household was required to pay Williams a tax of thirty shillings toward a town fund, and to reimburse him thirty English pounds for labors and expenses associated with his obtaining the deed. Not all fulfilled this obligation, apparently, and most of the settlers, being of modest means, paid their debts in small, irregular installments.

Over the next five years, other religious dissenters, strong-minded individualists, and freethinkers would come to the lands in and around the Bay. Providence grew very slowly, but more than eighty exiles from Massachusetts settled on nearby Aquidneck Island in 1638 alone. Williams brokered the sale of Aquidneck from the Narragansett sachems for a group led by the wealthiest of Rhode Island's founding fathers, the merchant William Coddington, a former magistrate from Massachusetts Bay. Coddington and the rest of the original settlers on Aquidneck were followers of the extraordinary religious thinker Anne Hutchinson.

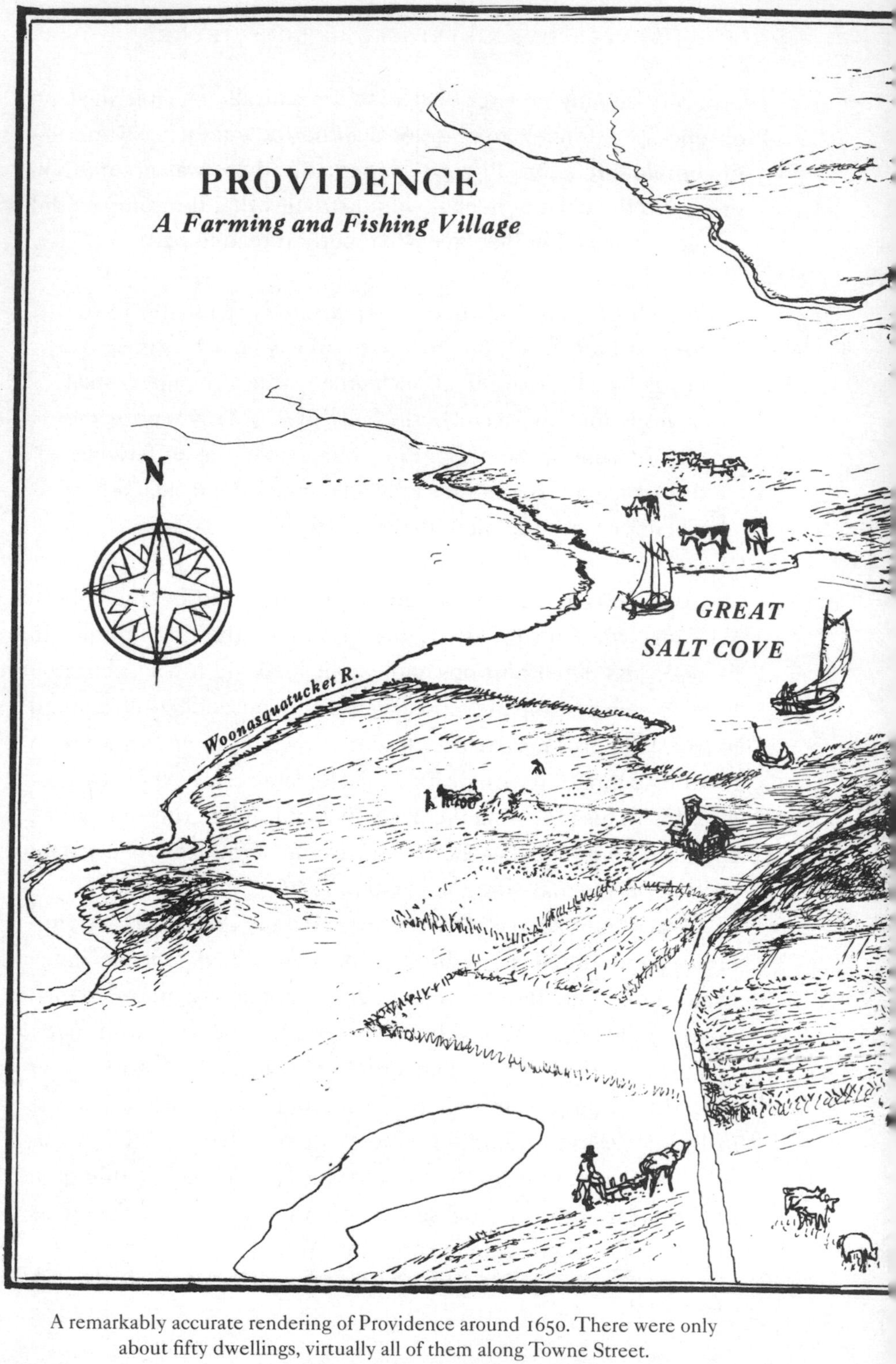

A remarkably accurate rendering of Providence around 1650. There were only about fifty dwellings, virtually all of them along Towne Street.

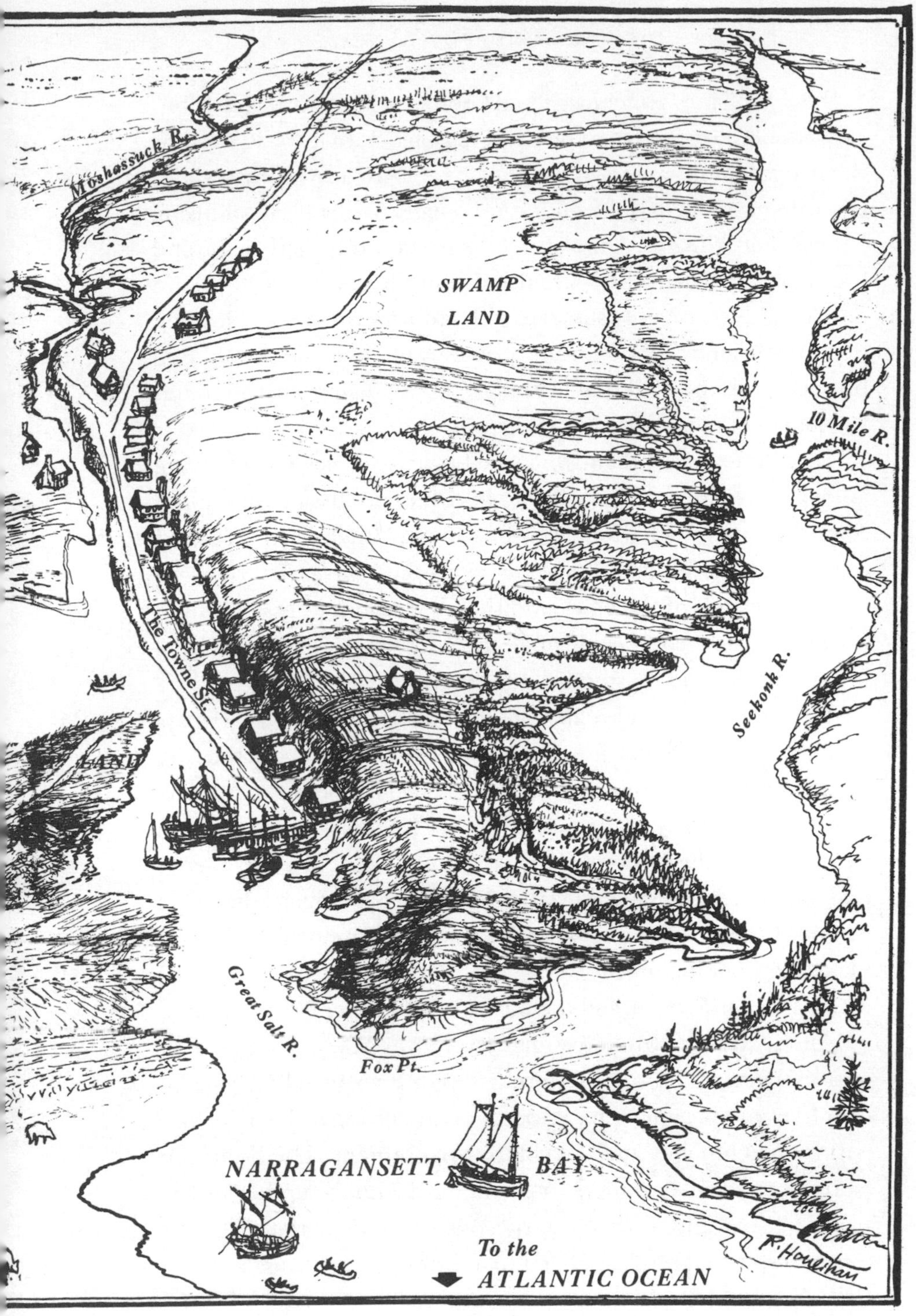
Moshassuck R.
SWAMP LAND
10 Mile R.
The Towne St.
Seekonk R.
LAND
Great Salt R.
Fox Pt.
NARRAGANSETT BAY
To the ATLANTIC OCEAN
R. Houlihan

Like Williams, Hutchinson had been banished from Massachusetts for both religious and political reasons. Born in 1591, she was the daughter of Francis Marbury, a devout Anglican minister, and the wife of a successful London merchant, William Hutchinson. Like Roger Williams, Anne Hutchinson was both charismatic and pious. She also had a first-rate mind, and the confidence to share her thoughts on weighty subjects with ordinary citizens and leading magistrates alike. John Winthrop, who would become the leading prosecutor in the civil trial leading to her banishment, called her "a woman of ready wit and bold spirit."[9]

A skilled nurse and midwife, she began to develop a following among the women of the colony by leading discussions about the Sunday sermon each Monday in her home. Hutchinson preached a spirit-centered religion. She believed the Holy Spirit dwelled within the souls of the elect, and that no amount of prayer, Bible reading, or good works could open the door to salvation. Only God, in His infinite and mysterious wisdom, could do that.

Her stress on the indwelling of the Holy Spirit seemed to bypass the Bible and the church in salvation and thus "empowered the laity at the expense of the ministry."[10] Before too long, she was viewed by Winthrop and many of the colony's other leaders as a woman who lacked the humility to know her place, and a threat to good order in both the church and state. That threat loomed ever larger as her ideas gained currency among some of the influential men of the colony, including Coddington, Sir Henry Vane, Williams's close friend and confidant John Easton, and the physician-preacher John Clarke.

An ascendant Hutchinsonian faction in Massachusetts Bay ousted Winthrop from the governorship in 1636, installing Vane in his place, and began to press assertively for changes of leadership within the churches and the colony government. The Winthrop faction's resistance to the appointment of Anne's brother-in-law John Wheelwright as pastor in the Boston church, and to Anne's role as a spiritual ringleader, led to a bitter power struggle.

Winthrop was reelected governor in 1637. Wheelwright was soon thereafter tried and convicted of sedition. When seventy-five people petitioned for a reversal of the decision, they were disarmed and threatened with banishment. In November 1637, Hutchinson herself was tried by the colony for "traducing" the ministers. By all accounts she put up an able and cogent defense, but when she claimed she had experienced a divine revelation that God would ruin the colony for persecuting her, she was publicly condemned for preaching the subversive doctrine of antinomianism—the idea that God spoke directly to his believers. She was subsequently banished from the colony. So were many of her followers.

In the spring of 1638, Hutchinson made her way to Portsmouth, at the northern end of Aquidneck Island, where she joined the new plantation started by William Coddington and about twenty other families. In 1639, after a schism at Portsmouth of cloudy origins, a significant number of the wealthier, more entrepreneurially minded families, led by Coddington, settled at the southern end of the island, near one of the finest natural harbors on the east coast of America. They called the new settlement Newport. It would prove to be the largest and most prosperous of Rhode Island's settlements up through the American Revolution, and one of the most religiously diverse towns in all of colonial America.

Anne Hutchinson never played an important role in Rhode Island politics, but she stands as a prominent symbol of that colony's place as a haven for "persons distressed of conscience" and had probably been invited to settle there by Williams personally. She would resettle in New Netherland after the passing of her husband, only to be killed in an Indian uprising against the Dutch, along with a number of her children, in 1643.

Rhode Island's fourth town was established in 1642, about twelve miles south of Providence on the edge of Narragansett Bay, in the territory of the Shawomet Indians. Originally called Shawomet, it was soon renamed Warwick in honor of the English earl who returned the settlement to the jurisdiction of Rhode Island after Massachusetts secured control over the place for a number of years (more on this story later).

Warwick's primary founder was Samuel Gorton, another radical Puritan. Among all of Rhode Island's religious radicals, he was perhaps the most eccentric, and certainly the most scornful of the Puritan oligarchy's penchant for hypocrisy and arrogance. This self-proclaimed "professor of the mysteries of Christ" was reviled by the established order.

The exact nature of his beliefs remains obscure even today, but most of what we know he held to be true was anathema to the Puritan establishment. He shared Williams's belief in absolute religious liberty and the separation of church and state. He did not believe ministers should be supported by taxes; they were appointed by God and preached at the behest of the Holy Spirit. Theology, being a human rather than godly construct, was largely rubbish. No one should be obligated to attend church services. The ideal form of worship was the voluntary gathering of the pious for prayer in the hopes that the Holy Spirit would speak through a particular man or woman. Like Williams, Gorton denied the unique holiness of the Puritan experiment in the eyes of God. The Puritans of New England were not a chosen people. God's covenant was with the entire human race.

Before settling in Warwick, Samuel Gorton had fled from Plymouth to evade prosecution for blasphemy and took up residence at Portsmouth. But he was forced to leave there, and later Providence, for refusing to recognize the legitimacy of the civil authority. Taken to court for some obscure offense at Portsmouth, he declared the judges "just asses" who had no proper legal authority.[11] He found any government that did not scrupulously respect English common law to be contemptible and illegitimate, and in his view few colonial governments did so.

Sometime between the settlement of Providence and of Portsmouth, Williams was given a choice piece of land in the heart of Narragansett country by Canonicus himself, right at the edge of an excellent natural harbor near the contemporary village of Wickford in North Kingstown. Here he established an important trading post that also served as a meeting place for English and Narragansett diplomatic conferences for decades to come. By 1639, trading had again become a crucial source of income for the founder of Providence, as his gratis services to the communities that had sprouted up around Narragansett Bay by the early 1640s, along with a large and growing family—Roger and Mary had six children in all—left him perpetually strapped for cash.

Williams's acceptance of a plot of land for a lucrative trading post in the heart of Narragansett country, and his purchase with John Winthrop of Chibachuweset (later named Prudence) Island in Narragansett Bay to raise cattle and goats, goes far to confirm that Williams saw trading, farming, and statecraft as going hand in hand. The trading post, at a location the Indians called Cocumscussoc, is today a museum site, though nothing remains of Williams's first dwelling there. It was easily accessible to canoes and pinnaces—small European sailing ships of one or two masts—of buyers and sellers alike. Cocumscussoc also stood astride the main north-south Indian trail between Boston and the Pequot country.

Until 1651, when he sold the post to Richard Smith, another local Indian trader, Roger Williams would spend considerable stretches of time there away from his family and home in Providence, reading, writing, and entertaining many Indian visitors, who came to trade and share news. Williams once remarked that he earned the considerable sum of about a hundred pounds sterling a year from his trading ventures.

A handful of forward-looking individuals from the four towns on Narragansett Bay saw from the earliest years the need to establish some sort of central governmental structure over the Narragansett towns, if for no other reason than to prevent them from being swallowed up by one or more of the orthodox Puritan colonies. Of these men, Roger Williams was by far the most important in the future development of the colony, in part because of his crucial role in establishing an egalitarian, strictly secular government in Providence, which the other towns would emulate.

Williams, too, was the first Rhode Islander to establish and exploit close ties with influential liberals in Parliament, and their assistance would prove indispensable in fending off the Puritan colonies' efforts to extend their jurisdiction over Rhode Island's towns and the Narragansett Indians. After he returned from England with a parliamentary charter for the colony of Rhode Island in 1644, Williams would serve as its first chief executive, working tirelessly to put his liberal political ideas into practice.

Williams's radical ideas on church and state and religious liberty did not begin to see print until he made his way back to London in 1643. But it seems quite likely from what survives of his extensive correspondence that many of his ideas, at least in their inchoate form, were well-known among leading Puritans in New England before he embarked for London in 1643. Those concepts, which ultimately formed the distinctive political foundation of the colony of Rhode Island, were that the church was an entirely separate entity from the state. It was a voluntary association of individuals, and one of the many civil corporations that the state was obligated to protect. The magistrates' authority was temporal, not spiritual, just as the authority of the church was spiritual, not temporal.

Williams disavowed the Puritans' cherished belief that their Holy Commonwealths were in a special covenant with God. There was no "chosen nation" in the seventeenth century, nor had there been one since Moses's Israel. Williams believed, as Edmund Morgan puts it, that "since the coming of Christ the only way God had contracted with men . . . was through the churches of Christ, which were scattered throughout the nations and were forbidden by their founder to propagate or defend His religion by force. . . . No body of men who now employed force in defense of religion, whether at home or abroad, could claim the name Christian."[12]

Nor had God provided human beings with a model form of government that could be divined in the Scriptures, whether Old or New Testament. Governments, Williams came to believe, derived their powers from one source, the will of the governed, and it followed that the type of government they established should reflect the particular manners, mores, and customs of the individuals who formed them. The world was full of different people who held radically different ideas about God and worship from either the Puritan orthodoxy or himself. Many of these people were not Christians at all, but the nature of their spiritual beliefs was no reason for excoriating them, or denying them a place in a secular community as either citizens or as officeholders—unless those beliefs incited civil disorder or unrest.

Finally, a secular government that defended liberty of conscience did a great deal more to encourage the pursuit of religious truth and social civility than the current government of Massachusetts, or any state that enforced one particular brand of worship. Freedom of conscience was necessary because no one could know for certain which form of religion was the one God had intended people to follow.

Little wonder, then, that the Puritan colonies were wary of Roger Williams's efforts to establish a secular colony just fifty miles south of Boston. A truly viable colony government in Rhode Island would not begin to emerge for almost a decade after the founding of Providence. In the late 1630s and early 1640s, the "union" of small towns on Narragansett Bay was informally maintained and barely a union at all, for each town was loath to surrender power to outsiders, even those who clearly had common interests a few miles down the road. Stubbornly local in orientation, disputatious in the extreme, the Narragansett settlements were united only in their rejection of strong central control and traditional Puritan forms of governance and worship.

Around Narragansett Bay, too, there was a decided resistance to conventional ideas and to displays of deferential behavior toward the educated elite. Quickly, colonial Rhode Island developed a reputation as a place "where the people think otherwise." John Winthrop was more cutting in an early appraisal: Rhode Island, he wrote in 1642, was "under no government, [and] increasingly offensive."[13] The people there, opined Winthrop and the minister Thomas Weld in a pamphlet, were "loose and degenerate in their practices."[14] Even the Dutch in New Amsterdam shared this dim view of the cantankerous settlers in Narragansett country. Said one government official there, "Rhode Island . . . is the receptacle for all sorts of riff-raff people and is nothing else but the sewer latrina of New England. . . . All the cranks of New England retire thither."[15]

Ironically, the ideal of religious freedom that Williams hoped would stimulate piety as well as social cohesion and civility did just the opposite for most of the seventeenth century. The settlers in the Narragansett Bay towns, writes historian Sydney James, created exclusive religious "fellowships that militantly left secular affairs alone. Religion, by the reckoning of most Christians . . . had gone haywire. Uneducated men and even women preached, pretending to utter words furnished by the Holy Ghost. Cranks and fanatics multiplied, producing weird and dangerous new doctrines, while far too many people used their freedom as liberty to shuffle aside all duty to the divinity."[16]

As the cranks multiplied, spreading out along the reaches of the Bay, what had begun as a rather minor irritant began to gnaw away at the devout but politically ambitious men in Boston, Plymouth, and Connecticut. Their frequent scoffing about the state of affairs around Narragansett Bay and the English who'd taken up residence there belied deeper concerns. They worried that heresies and blasphemies that passed for religious thought in Rhode Island would spread north and east and infect the devout. They worried even more that Williams and Coddington and the others would outflank them and secure a legal basis for a proper colony around Narragansett Bay before they were able to accomplish the task themselves.

The Puritans fretted, too, over the unorthodox manner in which Williams and a few other settlers were purchasing land in Rhode Island from the Indians. The General Court in Boston saw the documentation of land sales as critical for maintaining order in the region. Accordingly, all native land purchases had to be authorized and documented in government record books according to English standards. Much to the chagrin of Boston, Williams and the other dissenters in Narragansett Country were able

> to circumvent the Boston land system and establish claims through direct purchase from sachems, often in ceremonies that combined elements of Native and English legal systems. Based as they often were on friendship with Native leaders, a form of cultural capital most available to wandering separatists like Williams, these ceremonies offered an expedient means to . . . found settlement communities beyond the political reach of the Massachusetts Bay Colony.[17]

Williams's deed for Providence, like a number of others he helped to execute for Rhode Island settlements, was a hybrid document. These were framed in the traditional Algonquian manner as tribute arrangements, with due respect for the native practices of reciprocity and ritual exchange, and then "translated" into the language of English contract law. Williams was keenly aware of this hybridity. He understood it was essential to abide by Indian tribute customs and rituals in deal making to ensure peace around the Bay.

Unlike his contemporaries in Boston and Plymouth, Roger Williams did not assume English customs and mores, legal and otherwise, must always trump those of the Indians. Quite the reverse. He observed Indian custom to the letter. "He had no patent, no deed, no boundary lines, no financial or legal backing," writes biographer Ola Winslow. He had "no authorized claim of any sort, no capital except the small sum for which he had mortgaged his house in Salem, and a bundle of such toys and necessities as served for exchange with the Indians. His only basis for negotiating a bargain with [the Narragansetts] was the claim of mutual friendship with the sachems. . . . In their eyes as well as his own, this friendly relation was sufficient."[18]

As controversy swirled over who owned what in Providence and other lands around the Bay in the late 1650s, Williams reminded his neighbors, "It was not price nor money that could have purchased Rhode Island. Rhode Island was obtained by love."[19] And in a disposition at the end of his life, he reiterated his belief that Rhode Island's founding was more the product of a humane understanding on the part of friends who were binding themselves together as neighbors than a strictly legal or diplomatic transaction:

> And therefore I declare to posterity that were it not for the favor that God gave me with Canonicus, none of these parts, no, not Rhode Island had been purchased or obtained, for I never got anything out of Canonicus but by gift. . . . And I never denied him nor Miantonomi whatever they desired of me as to goods or gifts, or the use of my boats or pinnace and the travels of my person day and night, which though men know not, nor care to know, yet the all-seeing eye hath seen it and his all-powerful hand has helped me.[20]

Williams's knowledge of Indian tribute rituals and Indian conceptions of land would prove of incalculable value in preserving trust and amicable relations between the early Rhode Island settlers and the Narragansetts for almost forty years. The strength and independence of the Narragansetts throughout those years proved indispensable in preserving a space for Williams and other dissenters to work out novel ideas, new ways of thinking and living in frontier towns beyond the reach of the magistrates' grasping hands of Boston, Plymouth, and Hartford.

In turn, Canonicus and Miantonomi had in Williams a trusted teacher and guide to English ways and customs, and, even more important, an ally and advocate who could provide invaluable service to the Narragansetts as they tried to navigate the dangerous shoals of Indian-English power politics. And those shoals, as we shall see, were getting more treacherous all the time.

Chapter 4

Troubles on the Frontier: The Pequot War

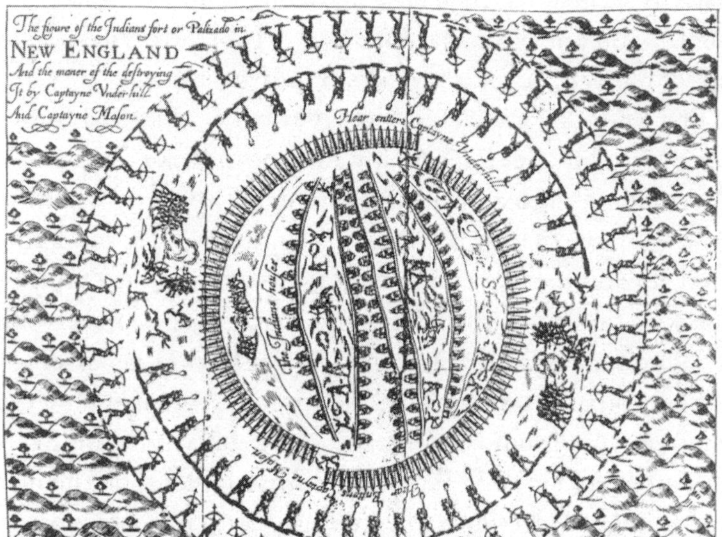

This extraordinarily detailed drawing of the attack on the Pequots' fort at Mystic first appeared in John Underhill's *Newes from America*, published in London in 1638. English troops are shown shooting unarmed Indians as Pequots struggle to escape beyond the English lines. The English way of war was far more destructive of human life than traditional Indian warfare, and it shocked and frightened the natives.

In the early 1630s, the Narragansetts found themselves engaged in on-again, off-again warfare with their perennial enemies to the west, the Pequots, for the loyalty and tribute of the small bands of Indians who lived on the Connecticut River, and for control over the land between the Pawcatuck and Thames Rivers. These Narragansett-Pequot clashes were part of a larger, regional conflict that drew in a small number of Dutchmen hunkered down at a trading post near modern Hartford, English traders from Plymouth Plantation, several hundred settlers from Massachusetts Bay intent on establishing a new colony on the Connecticut River, and the Pequots' disaffected kindred tribe, the Mohegans, led by Uncas. That wily sachem was then busily poaching bands from the Pequot sachem Tatobem's orbit, having failed to gain the Pequot sachemship for himself, despite several spirited attempts.

The Pequots' attacks on the river tribes that had formerly been their tributaries forced those Indians to seek protection from either the Narragansetts or the Mohegans, both of whom took to the warpath against the Pequots. In early 1634, the Pequots killed several members of a Narragansett party attempting to trade with the Dutch at their trading post. Eager to preserve their highly profitable trade relationship with the Narragansetts, the Dutch responded swiftly. They captured Tabotem and held him for ransom. A ransom was paid by the Pequots, but a bit too late: the Dutch handed over Tatobem's corpse rather than the man.

The Pequot reaction to the killing of Tatobem was measured, revealing the weakness of their strategic position in the volatile Connecticut River valley. A Pequot raiding party boarded a ship at the mouth of the Connecticut River and killed its captain. Unfortunately, the ship was not Dutch. Nor was the captain. The Pequots had killed Captain John Stone, a rogue English trader-pirate who had led a colorful criminal career in New England and the West Indies. He had stolen a sailing vessel in Plymouth and been booted out of Massachusetts for suspected adultery, among a host of other offenses.

Having killed an Englishman, even a rogue Englishman, the Pequots would be expected to answer for doing so before trade with the English could resume. Finding themselves in active conflict with the Narragansetts, the Dutch, and the Mohegans simultaneously, and now facing trouble with the English, the Pequots were in a real bind. As John Winthrop reported in his *Journal* at the time, the Pequots "could not trade safely anywhere."[1]

Now, let the reader beware. The many gaping holes in the evidence, and problems in sorting out the exact chronology of events, prevent us from uncovering the intentions of the Bay Colony and Connecticut regarding the Pequots in the impending war with anything like certainty. All of the historians writing in the years immediately after the Pequots' fate was sealed—and for three centuries after that—accepted pretty much uncritically the intentions the Puritans ascribed to themselves in their written recollections. Both participants and chroniclers present the two Puritan colonial governments, in Boston and in Hartford, as fair-minded arbitrators in a series of messy disputes among Indian peoples and European traders, and as defenders of peace and order. The Pequots are depicted as bellicose expansionists who had to be challenged to restore peace along a roiling frontier. After the Pequots repeatedly failed to make reasonable compensation to the English for a series of criminal acts, including the murder of Stone and conspiring with other Indians to slaughter English people on the Connecticut River, the Puritans were left with no choice but to attack the warmongers and destroy them as an independent tribe.

Since the mid-1970s, historians have carefully reexamined the fragmentary documentary record and the contemporary histories. Their work has hardly clarified definitively the tangle of motives and intentions of the participants, but they have succeeded in demolishing the conventional view of the war that persisted for hundreds of years.[2]

Recent accounts of the conflict differ on the exact sequence of events and many details, but they all reach the same broad conclusion: the Puritan "arbitrators" in Boston and on the Connecticut River were neither disinterested nor fair-minded in working out a solution to the crisis with the Pequots.[3] Wilcomb Washburn, a judicious scholar of Puritan-Indian relations if ever there was one, puts it this way: "While it is dangerous to reason from assumed motives of the participants, it is fair to assert that both the established colony of Massachusetts and the newer colony of Connecticut sought to profit from the destruction of this powerful tribe. The causes of the war given by the [contemporary] English seem strained and arbitrary."[4]

"Strained and arbitrary" is putting it mildly. Moreover, the Pequots without question made a sustained, good-faith effort to appease the English for any offenses they had committed, inadvertent or otherwise, in the interest of reestablishing amicable relations. The English responded to Pequot peace overtures with both words and actions clearly designed to provoke war rather than secure peace.

Why? The answer is plain enough: the English believed it was both their right and destiny to establish control over eastern Connecticut with a view to establishing a powerful new Puritan colony there. To that end, the English bullied the Pequots into submission with the help of their Indian rivals under the guise of restoring order and obtaining justice.

In November 1634, Pequot emissaries had arrived in Boston, seeking to reestablish trade relations with Massachusetts, sort out the issue of Captain Stone, and gain Massachusetts's assistance in brokering a peace agreement with the Narragansetts. In exchange, the Pequots indicated they would happily welcome English settlement within their territory. They would also pay tribute to the English for their services in restoring peace, for this was how all such arrangements were made between different Indian groups in the region long before the Puritans had arrived on the scene.

The draft treaty proposed by the English was decidedly lopsided. The ordinarily meticulous record keepers of the Bay Colony (or their descendants) somehow lost all the copies of the text, leading more than one contemporary investigator to question whether the document was more of a Puritan ultimatum than a viable draft agreement, and thus best not viewed by the prying eyes of posterity. Massachusetts Bay agreed to establish trade relations with the Pequots and sort out the Pequots' problem with the Narragansetts. In return, the Pequots would surrender the killers of John Stone and pay the hefty sum of four hundred fathoms of wampum and seventy beaver and otter skins as tribute.

The value of the tribute equaled 250 pounds sterling at the time, which was slightly less than half of the total property taxes levied by Massachusetts on its entire population in 1634![5] Little wonder the Pequot diplomats in Boston indicated they themselves couldn't agree to such terms. A payment of four hundred fathoms might be appropriate if Massachusetts was offering to defend the Pequots if they were attacked, but this guarantee was decidedly not part of the proposed deal. The Pequot emissaries agreed to present the offer to Sassacus, their new chief sachem, upon their return home, and in time he would respond.

No matter its exact value, the tribute demanded was sufficiently draconian to amount to extortion. The Puritan authorities were probably well aware the "tribute" could not be paid in full under the best of circumstances, and the requirement for turning over the killers of Captain John Stone was surely unreasonable. The Pequot emissaries had been completely straight with the Massachusetts authorities concerning their mistaking Stone for a Dutchman and recognized their responsibility to make amends for his death, even granting that Stone had provoked them into the act by capturing two Pequots at the mouth of the Connecticut River.[6]

John Winthrop himself said that the Pequot explanation for the death of Stone "was related with such confidence and gravity, as, having no means to contradict it, we inclined to believe it."[7] He indicated in his *Journal* that the magistrates were not inclined to press the matter, which makes perfectly good sense. After all, how much could the Puritan authorities expect by way of retribution for the *mistaken* killing of a rogue who had taken two Pequots prisoner? Surely, not a great deal.

The Pequots were well aware that turning over Stone's killers meant the perpetrators, too, would be killed. Since Stone had provoked the Indians to act, a sizable wampum payment was surely adequate compensation, and that was all Sassacus was willing to pay.

Soon after the Pequots arrived in Boston to parley, a Narragansett sachem whose name has been lost to history, joined by twenty men, came to Boston at the General Court's request. The Massachusetts delegation had little trouble persuading the Narragansetts to cease their attacks on the Pequots. The Narragansetts were keen to strengthen their alliance with Massachusetts Bay, not least because it was rapidly on the path to becoming the most powerful political force in the region. Massachusetts could offer the Narragansetts not only continued peace, friendship, and a written guarantee of free trade, but also—surreptitiously—a small percentage of the tribute Massachusetts expected to receive under its new arrangement with the Pequots.

It seemed a fair arrangement to the Narragansett sachems. According to Winthrop, a treaty was drawn up reflecting those terms and signed by Canonicus's mark, a bow, and by Miantonomi's, an arrow. (Again, all copies of the actual treaty have been lost.)

Relations between the Puritans and the Pequots, and between the Pequots and the Narragansetts, were by all accounts peaceable throughout 1635 and early 1636. By the end of 1635, several hundred Puritans had settled at the mouth of the Connecticut River at Fort Saybrook, as well as at a handful of locations upriver, notably at Windsor and Wethersfield, where they were warmly welcomed by the Pequots and their tributaries. The Puritans clearly wanted to expand their limited settlements near the river substantially, as the land in the valley was far more fertile than the land around Boston, and the fur trade in the valley was bustling. The Connecticut River valley was seen by the oligarchy as an ideal place for immediate expansion, not least because of what Winthrop described as the "fruitfulness and commodiousness of Connecticut, and the danger of having it possessed by others, Dutch or English."[8]

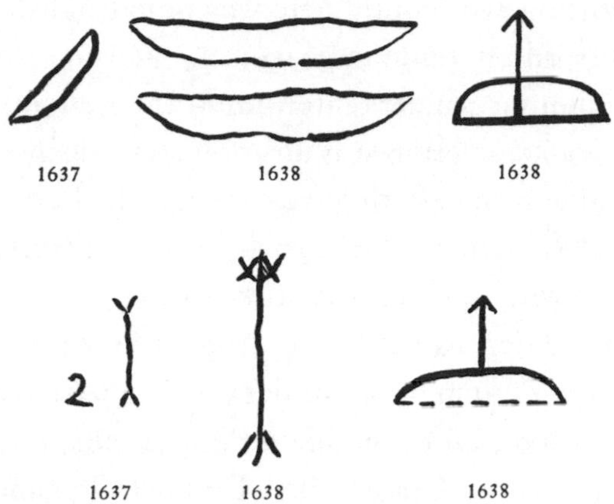

The marks of Canonicus (*top*) and Miantonomi (*bottom*). Most Indian sachems' marks depicted a common object that represented power or authority.

Before too long, Sassacus did make a substantial wampum payment to Massachusetts, along with some other gifts, as a sign of the Pequots' honorable and friendly intentions. But he made no attempt to turn over the suspected killers of Stone, probably in large measure because Winthrop had sent signals that doing so was no longer a requirement for the maintenance of good relations. Nor did Sassacus see any reason to pay the whopping tribute payment of four hundred fathoms. Since the Pequots had welcomed several hundred Puritans to settle on Pequot lands—and expected many more—four hundred fathoms was deemed unreasonable.

In July 1636, John Winthrop Jr. led a delegation to the Pequots at the behest of Massachusetts Bay. He presented the Pequot delegation with an ultimatum: either pay the full tribute payment and turn over Stone's murderers or face retribution. We have no record of what the Pequots said at the meeting, but clearly they would not negotiate at the point of a gun. They wouldn't make the four-hundred-fathom payment or turn over Stone's killers. They would, however, continue to welcome English settlers into their territory, and to trade in peace.

The Puritan magistrates interpreted the Pequots' seemingly reasonable negotiating stance as unacceptable defiance and recalcitrance. It had to be met with force to terrify the Pequots into submission. So, like so many "defensive" wars in history, the Pequot conflict began with a preemptive strike by the party that presented itself as on the defensive. In late August 1636, three pinnaces carrying ninety Puritan troops under Captain John Endicott were sent on an expedition to the main Pequot village at the mouth of the Thames River. Upon arrival, Endicott demanded that the Indians turn over Stone's killers and the entire tribute payment immediately—or face the consequences.

The expedition had been mounted, we should note, in light of a series of rumors of a Pequot conspiracy to attack all the English settlements on the Connecticut. Uncas, the Pequots' bête noire, was the source of most of these rumors, for he hoped to provoke the Puritans into attacking his rivals and had already begun to position his Mohegans to reap the benefits of the Pequots' downfall.

William Pynchon, the most knowledgeable Indian trader in the region, informed the magistrates that these rumors were patently false, but the Puritan leaders had their own reasons for taking a different view. In fact, there is "little if any evidence to support the image of the Pequots as savage killers threatening the lives of English settlers in the Connecticut wilderness," writes the most meticulous modern historian of the conflict. "That image was the product of Puritan mythmaking, not of real occurrences on the frontier."[9] Nonetheless, the government of Massachusetts Bay used these rumors as an important justification for the Endicott expedition.

The Pequot spokesman who parleyed with Endicott at the water's edge pleaded with all sincerity, "We crave pardon, we have not willfully wronged the English."[10] He then admitted that Sassacus himself had killed Stone, but it had been a mistake, and surely it was beyond reason to demand that the tribe turn over its own sachem to face death for committing an understandable error. Endicott had a well-earned reputation as among the most severe and uncompromising of Puritan leaders. He was having none of it.

After an hour or so of unproductive verbal exchange, the English launched a preemptive attack on the Indians, who promptly retreated into the woods, firing off a few arrows as they withdrew. All the Pequot projectiles fell short of the mark. The English forces then burned down the Pequots' cornfields and wigwams in the immediate vicinity, and (according to Narragansett sources, at least) killed thirteen Pequots before returning to their ships.

Sassacus interpreted Endicott's expedition to Pequot Harbor not as a reasonable request for further negotiations between two governments in dispute, but as a deliberate act of war. After a while, the Pequots responded accordingly. For several months they laid siege to Fort Saybrook, the Puritan trading post established by John Winthrop Jr. at the mouth of the Connecticut, killing or wounding several members of its small garrison when they roamed outside the fort proper in search of food.

Political wrangling between Massachusetts and Connecticut over strategy and division of the prospective spoils delayed the English response. Another issue complicated matters greatly. The Puritans' most reliable source of intelligence on Indian intentions reported that far from intimidating the Pequots, the Endicott expedition had enraged Sassacus, prompting him to approach the Western Niantics about forming an alliance to do battle against the white men. The Niantics had agreed to join the fight. The two Indian peoples were determined to "live and die together, and not yield [the suspected murderer of Captain Stone] up."[11]

The source of this intelligence was Roger Williams. The founder of Providence had the best Indian contacts of any Englishman in the Narragansett-Pequot orbit. Shortly after conveying what he had learned about the reaction to the Endicott raid to Boston, Williams filed more ominous news via letter. Pequot emissaries to the Narragansetts were attempting to convince their traditional enemies to join with them in a war against the English colonies because, as Williams reported to Winthrop, the Pequots claimed "the English were minded to destroy all Indians."[12] William Bradford had apparently been right. When he had first learned of Endicott's expedition, he remarked in great exasperation, "We have occasioned a war, etc., by provoking the Pequots."[13]

Bradford wanted no part in the impending struggle. His counterparts in Massachusetts Bay and Connecticut, however, took the not uncommon view among Puritans that the recalcitrant Pequots, in failing to respect Christian authority and submit to English demands, were the devil's agents, testing Puritan resolve to do God's work in the wilderness. If they were not dealt with harshly, the forces of darkness would grow stronger, all the Indians would rise up, and the Holy Commonwealths would be destroyed. There was, too, a more worldly motive: both colonies wanted the Pequot country clear of autonomous Indian tribes in order to expedite English settlement there.

The idea of a Pequot alliance with the Western Niantics did not put the oligarchy off the idea of a war of conquest. But a war against the Narragansetts *in addition* to the Pequots and Western Niantics was an entirely different matter. The Narragansetts alone could field two thousand warriors, or so it was widely believed. They were important trading partners with Massachusetts. Even granting superior Puritan military technology and God's sanctification of the venture, the prospect of a conflict with the Narragansetts in league with the Pequots was not a happy one for the magistrates.

In light of these realities, Williams the outcast was suddenly transformed into Williams the emissary. At the request of the governor in Boston, Williams was asked "to use my utmost and speediest endeavors to break and hinder the league labored for by Pequots. . . . The lord helped me immediately to put my life into my hands, and, scarce acquainting my wife, to ship myself, all alone, in a poor canoe, and to cut through a stormy wind, 30 miles in great seas, every minute in hazard of my life, to the [Narragansett] sachem's house."[14]

Roger Williams was perhaps above all a man of peace. Time and again in future years he would be called on to mediate disputes between Puritans and Indians. This time the stakes were personal. Williams was a close ally and personal friend of both Narragansett sachems. He not only feared for the lives of his Narragansett friends. He was well aware that in a war between Puritans and Narragansetts, Providence might well be destroyed. Almost certainly war would lead to the occupation of all of Narragansett country by a Puritan army, and that didn't auger well for Williams's fledgling experiment.

Accordingly, he used his considerable powers of persuasion to convince the Narragansett sachems to refrain from allying themselves with their rivals to the west. As Williams relates the deliberations, it took no small amount of work to bring Canonicus around, for he blamed the English for the smallpox plague that had fallen on the Narragansetts in 1633. Williams pacified the old sachem by pointing out that the sickness had afflicted the English as well and had come from God, not the English themselves. Canonicus agreed to invite Puritan emissaries to his village for further discussions.

In early October 1636, a delegation from Massachusetts Bay made its way to the Narragansetts' village in the vicinity of Wickford. Whether Williams was there we do not know. Given Canonicus's demonstrable willingness to trust Williams but not his countrymen, it seems likely that he was on the scene. One of the members of the Massachusetts Bay delegation, Edward Johnson, left a well-observed account of the meeting. Johnson and his fellow delegates were "entertained royally, and treated to a meal of boiled chestnuts and a sweet pudding made of beaten corn . . . with blackberries, somewhat like currents." The Indians "afterward gave them audience, in a state house, round, about fifty foot wide, made of long poles stuck in the ground, like your summer houses in England, and covered round about, and on the top with mats, save in a small place in the middle the roof, to give light, and let out smoke."[15]

Sitting on the ground with their knees touching their chins, Canonicus's council listened to the Englishmen speak "with much sober gravity. . . . It was a matter of much wonderment to the English, to see how solidly and wisely these savage people did consider the weighty undertaking of a war, especially old Canonicus, who was very discrete in his answers."[16] The delegation returned with a limited victory: a promise of neutrality. The Puritans had hoped for a more encouraging result.

Later that month, however, Williams and the Massachusetts sachem Cutshamakin were instrumental in persuading Miantonomi to travel to Boston for further discussions of the looming crisis. There the Narragansett sachem and his retinue parleyed with Governor Winthrop. According to Winthrop, Miantonomi spoke with great sincerity of his intentions. He remarked that his people "had always loved the English and desired firm peace with us: They would continue in war with the Pequots and their confederates until they were subdued, and desired that we should do so: They would deliver our enemies to us, or kill them."[17]

A day after this speech, a treaty was produced and signed, with a copy being sent to Williams to confirm the fine points. Winthrop summarizes the terms of the October 1636 treaty in his *Journal* as follows:

1. A firm peace between us and our friends of other plantations, (if they consent,) and their confederates (if they will observe the articles, etc.,) and our posterities.
2. Neither party to make peace with the Pequots without the other's consent.
3. Not to harbor, etc., the Pequots, etc.
4. To put to death or deliver over murderers, etc.
5. To return our fugitive servants, etc.
6. We give them notice when we go against the Pequots, and them to send us some guides.
7. Free trade between us.[18]

It is quite clear from documents concerning Narragansett-Puritan negotiations after the Pequot War that Winthrop also promised the Narragansetts some sort of hunting and fishing rights in conquered Pequot lands, as well as an unspecified number of Pequot noncombatants for adoption into the Narragansett confederation in the event of success. (Winthrop's failure to list those promises in his *Journal* is a prime example of the Massachusetts governor's distortion of the record to fit the Puritans' larger geopolitical designs.) The Narragansett sachems formalized the alliance by sending the Bay Colony a gift of forty fathoms of wampum and a Pequot head.

On the basis of this treaty's promise of mutual friendship and reciprocity, the Narragansetts played a prominent role in devising the plan of attack for the Puritan invasion of the Pequot country, in addition to providing warriors to assist in the assault. In hindsight, the Narragansett sachems would rue the day they put their marks to this parchment.

THE ATTACK ON THE PEQUOT FORT

Winter of 1636 passed without incident. Spring was another matter. On April 23, 1637, two hundred Pequots raided the upriver English settlement at Wethersfield, killing six men and three women, and capturing two small girls. The strike had been provoked by Endicott's assault, but that hardly diminished its shattering effect on the lives of the isolated English settlers in the Connecticut River valley. They were terrified of additional Indian attacks.

Just a month later, a formidable army composed of perhaps seven hundred men from Connecticut, Massachusetts Bay, and their Mohegan and Narragansett allies began their march on a fortified, palisaded village on the Mystic River containing about four hundred Pequots, mostly women and children. The Narragansetts and Mohegans provided substantial manpower, as well as accurate intelligence on the dispositions of the Pequots, and a clever scheme of maneuver that avoided detection by Pequot scouts until the last minute.

In the predawn hours of May 26, the Puritan army caught the Pequots by complete surprise in a two-pronged assault, with each of the fort's two openings attacked by a separate company. The Indians initially put up fierce resistance from within the fort. When the Pequot warriors refused to come out from the cover of their wigwams and fight in the open, Captain John Mason, commanding Connecticut's forces, ordered the Pequot village to be set alight. "We must burn them," the captain later recalled telling his troops, and so they did: within an hour, the entire fortified village was consumed by fire and smoke.

Some of the Pequots climbing the ten-foot-high palisades to escape were shot down by the English; others, terrified, rushed wildly into the flames and perished; a few boldly charged upon the enemy and fell by the sword or by musket fire. The Narragansetts, numbering perhaps two hundred, hadn't themselves entered the village; they were stationed around the perimeter of the fort, and it fell to them to kill or capture the terrified Pequots who escaped the inferno.

Captain John Underhill of Massachusetts leaves us with the most detailed and harrowing account of the action:

> Captain Mason entering a wigwam, brought out a firebrand, after he had wounded many in the house. Then he set fire on the west side [of the fort], where he entered; myself set fire on the south end with a train of powder. The fires of both meeting in the center of the fort, blazed most terribly, and burnt all in the space of half an hour. Many courageous fellows were unwilling to come out, and fought most desperately through the palisades, so they were scorched and burnt with the very flame, and were deprived of their arms—in regard the fire burnt their very bowstrings—and so perished valiantly. . . . Many were burnt in the fort, both men, women, and children. . . . It is reported by themselves, that there were about four hundred souls in this fort, and not above five of them escaped out of our hands. Great and doleful was the bloody sight to view the young soldiers that never had been in war, to see so many souls lie gasping on the ground, so thick, in some places, that you could hardly pass along. It may be demanded, why should you be so furious? (as some have said). Should not Christians have more mercy and compassion? But I would refer you to David's War. When a people is grown to such a height of blood, and sin against God and man, and all confederates in the action, there he hath no respect to persons, but harrows them, and saws them, and puts them to the sword, and the most terriblest death that may be. Sometimes the Scripture declareth women and children must perish with the parents. Sometimes the case alters; but we will not dispute it now. We had sufficient light from the word of God for our proceedings.[19]

Echoing the recurring Puritan theme that the war was at root a struggle between the forces of good and evil, John Mason described the fiery death of the Pequots as an act mandated by God to punish savages guilty of arrogance and treachery against the Chosen People: "God was above them, who laughed [at] his Enemies and the Enemies of his People to scorn making them as a fiery

Oven. . . . Thus did the Lord judge among the Heathen, filling the place with dead bodies."[20]

Sassacus could see the conflagration at Mystic from Weinshauks, the Pequots' other fortified village about two miles to the southwest. The Pequot sachem hastily assembled a force of several hundred men to mount a counterattack, but when he apprehended the strength of the enemy force and the extent of the horrors that had befallen the inhabitants of the Mystic fort, he lost heart, and the Pequot force returned to Weinshauks.

All in all, well over three hundred Pequots perished in a single morning. The English, exhausted, exultant, and low on food and ammunition, withdrew to Pequot Harbor, boarded their ships, and sailed away, while their Indian allies returned to their home territory on foot.

The devastating attack on the Mystic fort had broken the spirit of resistance among the Pequots. Sassacus could no longer hold the tribe together. Several hundred Indians of the tribe fled in the immediate aftermath of the English assault, seeking refuge among the Montauks and the Narragansetts to the east. Sassacus and two hundred warriors fled west, toward the Hudson River.

Mopping-up operations in Connecticut continued for several weeks. In mid-July, a force of English troops cornered Sassacus and his warriors in a swamp near New Haven. About eighty were killed, one hundred taken prisoner, and twenty, including Sassacus, escaped. Some of these captives were sold as slaves in the West Indies. Others would be distributed among the Mohegans and Narragansetts as reward for their military assistance—but not in a manner that the Narragansetts had been led to expect (more on this in the next chapter). In August, a Mohawk war party captured the Pequot sachem. Wanting to placate the new powerhouse in the region, they killed him and turned over his hands and scalp to English soldiers, effectively putting an end to the conflict.

Word of the attack on the fort at Mystic spread fast among

the Indian peoples of the region, and they recoiled in horror at the accounts. No war between Indians had ever inflicted such carnage. "It is naught [wrong], it is naught," protested the Narragansetts right after the attack, "because it is too furious, and slays too many men."[21] The Narragansetts were all the more disturbed by the fighting at Mystic because they had requested before the operation commenced that Pequot women and children be spared. Underhill and the English troops felt differently.

In the wake of the destruction of the Pequots, many Indians in the region rushed to secure friendship and protection from the victors before they, too, became the objects of violent English conquest. "Two of the Montauk sachems came to Mr. [Israel] Stoughton [a Puritan military officer from Connecticut] and tended themselves to be tributaries under our protection. And two of the Nipmuck sachems have been with me to seek our friendship," reported John Winthrop from Boston.[22]

After the Pequot War, the English were indisputably the dominant power in all of southern New England. How they would use that power was the paramount question on the minds of all the sachems in southern New England.

Ironically, the Narragansetts' treaty of friendship and alliance with Massachusetts in 1636, and their participation in the Pequot War, put both the Narragansett confederation and Roger Williams's Rhode Island squarely on their path of resistance to the Puritan Goliath's expansionist designs. For the Puritans were not inclined to abide by their obligations to the Narragansetts once Pequot power had been effectively shattered, and Williams's reward for his crucial assistance was a prolonged and concerted campaign by the oligarchy to place Providence and the other Rhode Island towns under its jurisdiction. The conflict between Rhode Island's inhabitants, Indian and English alike, and the Puritan oligarchy was about to begin in earnest.

Chapter 5

"Did Ever Friends Deal So with Friends?"

Unknown artist's portrayal of the execution of Miantonomi. This great sachem's death led to warfare between the Narragansetts and the Mohegans, who served Connecticut interests faithfully after the Pequot War. Miantonomi saw earlier than most Indian leaders the dangers posed by the growth of the Puritan settlements.

A few weeks after the Narragansett warriors returned home from the devastating attack on the Pequots—when all parties knew clearly that the war was over, except for the mopping up—Miantonomi and Canonicus must have gathered their sachems and counselors in a longhouse to discuss the ramifications of the Pequots' demise. As allies of the English, with only an inchoate grasp of the newcomers' geopolitical ambitions, the

Narragansetts had some reason to be cautiously optimistic about the future.

The English had promised substantial rewards for the tribe's participation in the conflict, including hunting and fishing rights in the former Pequot territories between the Pawcatuck and Thames Rivers. The sachems had been assured that a certain number of Pequot noncombatants would be turned over to them for adoption into the Narragansett confederation. That would be a welcome development, for it meant a stronger, more productive, and populous Narragansett nation.

There is little question, too, that at this early juncture in the story, Miantonomi and Canonicus expected their powerful English allies' support as they carried out the day-to-day business of statecraft. But even granting the Puritans' new status as the dominant military power in the area, the Narragansett sachems expected reciprocity and friendship to remain guiding principles in their relations with the colonists. Canonicus and Miantonomi took it as a given that as great sachems they would maintain control over their confederation's internal affairs and territory and continue to play a prominent role in regional diplomacy.

The sachems wanted to cultivate new alliances with Montauks on Long Island, and with several bands of River Indians who had been tributaries of the Pequots. The confederation's enhanced status as allies of the English in the recent war would likely make these Indians receptive to Narragansett overtures. And the Narragansett sachems would continue to strengthen the sinews of its alliances with the powerful Mohawks to the west, as well as with Massachusetts and the other Puritan governments. Canonicus and Miantonomi hoped to expand the size and the strength of the confederation by pursuing an activist diplomatic strategy of flexibility and adaptability.

But the Narragansett sachems were also realists. They had been shocked by the ferocity of the English attack, by the killing and burning of women and children, and they were surely both intimidated by and apprehensive of their allies' ultimate intentions. Would the English seek a relationship with the confederation of cooperation and compromise, or would they seek to extend their control over other Indian tribes now that the Pequots' political power had been utterly smashed? By the fall of 1637, this was a pressing question in Narragansett circles, and surely it occurred to a leader as astute and intelligent as Miantonomi that the English might well pursue an aggressive rather than cooperative strategy. If this proved to be the case, the Narragansetts would have to revise their political strategy considerably.

But as of late 1637, the Narragansett sachems chose to hope for the best, and to act on that hope. Miantonomi did not challenge the English when they began to act as arbiters in disputes among Indian peoples in the former Pequot territory, for such a development promised, at least in theory, to deter the chronic low-intensity warfare among Indian communities that pervaded the region. Besides, Miantonomi felt sure his people would need English assistance in containing Uncas's aggressive designs once Narragansett hunting and fishing parties began their forays into the Pequots' former domain.[1]

Alas, the sachems' hopeful expectations were soon dashed against the hard rocks of experience. Over the next several years, at virtually every turn, the Puritan oligarchy sought to frustrate Narragansett diplomatic objectives and deny the tribe access to Pequot territory and former Pequot tributaries. By 1643, a union of the four orthodox Puritan colonies—Massachusetts, Plymouth, Connecticut, and tiny New Haven (founded in 1638)—was finally established after years of internal wrangling. The chief purposes of the United Colonies of New England were to create a united English front to deal with the Indians and the Dutch, and to direct the expansion of the Holy Commonwealths, largely at the Indians' expense.

Not surprisingly, Rhode Island was excluded from the United Colonies. It was peopled almost exclusively by English dissenters hostile to orthodox Puritan ideas and institutions. Besides, by the time of the formation of the United Colonies, Massachusetts, Plymouth, and Connecticut were clearly intent on integrating either part or all of the outcast colony into their own jurisdiction.

FALLOUT FROM THE PEQUOT WAR

From the very beginning, the leaders of the new colony of Connecticut displayed an intense hostility and mistrust toward the Narragansetts. Their antagonism was due to the persistence of the Narragansetts' strong tributary ties and trading alliances with many Indian bands between the Pawcatuck and Connecticut Rivers, including several erstwhile tributaries of the Pequots that had shifted their allegiance to the Narragansetts just before the outbreak of the Pequot War.

The leaders of the River Colony—as Connecticut was often called—were determined to integrate those bands into their own trading network, and to expand their political jurisdiction over as wide an area as possible, including the eastern fringes of the Narragansett confederation, where Miantonomi's brother-in-law, a shrewd and politically savvy sachem named Ninigret, led the Eastern Niantics, as well as several former Pequot bands on the west side of the Pawcatuck. To accomplish this ambitious agenda, the River Colony's leaders looked for assistance from an Indian they soon came to regard as an indispensable ally: Uncas.

Direct experience with the Narragansetts in Pequot War operations had hardened Connecticut's negative views of Narragansett attitudes and intentions. In his first encounter with Ninigret, just before the Mystic attack, Captain John Mason found that the Niantic chief "carried himself very proudly" toward the English troops and refused the captain and his men entry into his village proper. Mason, sensing treachery might be in the offing, surrounded the fort to prevent Niantic messengers from escaping to contact the

Pequots. Ninigret, though, had no intention of contacting his rivals to the west. He'd agreed to provide warriors to the English for the impending fight, and he did so, but after the attack on the Mystic fort, Mason judged the Narragansetts (including the Niantics, for they were quasi-independent members of the confederation) to be tentative, unreliable warriors.

Another Connecticut officer, Captain Israel Stoughton, found the Narragansetts in the campaign to be eagerly "set upon their own ends, to get booty, and to augment their own Kingdom."[2] In June 1637, Captain Daniel Patrick, who had led a Massachusetts detachment in the Pequot campaign, told Roger Williams in a letter that his troops had a "great itch" to attack the Narragansetts, for he found them to be haughty and boastful. Indeed, Patrick confessed that he had developed the impression that Miantonomi's people sought "to be the only lords of the Indians."[3] Were the Narragansetts truly being cocky and obnoxious, or was it simply that their lack of deference rubbed these Puritan officers the wrong way? It may well have been a bit of both. Negative reports about the Narragansetts quickly made their way to Governor John Winthrop, who wrote to Williams about such "grievances and threatenings" in early August 1637. Winthrop's letter has never been found, but Williams's two replies, on August 20 and September 9, make it plain that the Puritans were troubled over reports alleging the desertion of several Narragansett scouts from the Puritan army after the Mystic attack; over the harboring of Pequots; and over the Narragansetts' seizure of goods and payments from erstwhile Pequot tributaries on Long Island that the colonial powers felt belonged to them.

Williams immediately acquainted Canonicus and Miantonomi with the contents of Winthrop's letter. The sachems responded earnestly, believing they could prove themselves "honest and faithful . . . yet they could relate many particulars, wherein the English had broken (since these wars) their promises." Miantonomi was particularly upset, it seems, about his failure to receive confirmation from Winthrop of the Narragansetts' right to hunt and fish in the former Pequot lands. Now that the English and their Indian allies had vanquished the Pequots, he could not understand why his friend the governor had yet to make such a confirmation.

There were other Narragansett grievances. After the big battle at Mystic, the English troops had denied Miantonomi access to a Pequot minor sachem and some eighty of his followers captured by Miantonomi's brother Pessacus during the attack. Had Governor Winthrop wished to see captives of war in *his* possession, Miantonomi assured Williams, he would have certainly obliged.[4] Here, and elsewhere, the absence of reciprocity rankled.

The sachems steadfastly denied that they had harbored a number of Pequot women that belonged to Massachusetts. Yes, a handful had come to their village, but they had since vanished from the Narragansetts to destinations unknown. Miantonomi agreed to send out men to find them and return them to Winthrop if they could be located.

Meanwhile, the Narragansett leaders were deeply disturbed over developments in the Pequot country. Much to their dismay, Uncas seemed to have the run of the place. The Mohegan sachem was encamped along the Pequot (Thames) River along with three hundred Indians, "most of them Pequots and their confederates," reported Williams to Winthrop in September 1637. Many of those Indians, Williams wrote, remained under Uncas's control only because he had ordered them "under pain of death not to come to Canonicus."[5]

Additionally, four minor Pequot sachems and eighty Indians were reportedly on Long Island. The Narragansett sachems were eager to receive permission from the English authorities to launch a raid to capture them, kill the sachems, and adopt the Pequots into their own confederation. But again, no such permission was in the offing from Boston.

Throughout the late 1630s, Williams often found himself on the defensive, having to allay English fears of Narragansett treachery he knew from daily contact with his neighbors to be misplaced: "Concerning Miantonomi I have not heard as yet of any unfaithfulness toward us."[6] Indeed, the founder of Providence could detect "some sparks of true Friendship. . . . [If it] could be deeply imprinted into him that the English never intended to despoil him of the [Pequot] country, I probably conjecture his friendship would appease in attending us with 500 men (in case) against any foreign enemies."[7]

With the Mohegans operating extensively among the villages in the former Pequot lands between the Pawcatuck and Thames Rivers, apparently with Connecticut's blessings, the frustrated Narragansetts looked elsewhere to enhance their fortunes. Ninigret crossed Long Island Sound with eighty warriors in June 1638 and attempted to coerce the Montauk sachem Wyandanch, a former Pequot tributary, to ally himself with the Narragansetts rather than the Mohegans and their Connecticut patrons.

Wyandanch at first declined, refusing to accept Ninigret's admonition that the English were deceivers who would, in the end, take Montauk wampum but leave them to fend for themselves against their enemies. Surely Ninigret's bitterness vis-à-vis the English was the result of their failure to follow through expeditiously on their promises made to his ally and brother-in-law Miantonomi before the Pequot War. Among all the Narragansett sachems to deal with the English in the period between the Pequot conflict and the outbreak of King Philip's War, Ninigret was perhaps the most suspicious of English intentions—and the most assertive when it came to defending Narragansett freedom of action.

When Wyandanch refused to reconsider, Ninigret took thirty fathoms of the Montauks' wampum by force and burned a number of wigwams in their main village. Humiliated and intimidated by Ninigret, Wyandanch then agreed to pay tribute to the Narragansett in exchange for protection and trade. Yet not long after Ninigret's war party departed, Wyandanch reported the incident to the Connecticut authorities.

Captain John Mason led a cavalry detachment to Ninigret's village near the coast of modern Charlestown, Rhode Island, to demand that the Narragansett sachem repay the wampum he had taken. Acting reluctantly on the advice of Williams, Ninigret did as Mason asked, and a punitive English-Mohegan invasion into Niantic country was nipped in the bud. This was the first encounter between English and Narragansett that threatened to erupt in violence as a result of the confederation's effort to strengthen its alliance system in the wake of the Pequot War. It would not be the last.

In the late summer of 1638, Connecticut, having failed to arrive at a formal agreement with the other orthodox colonies to regulate Indian affairs and divide up the spoils of the Pequot conquest, now determined to impose its own brand of order within its self-proclaimed sphere of influence. The magistrates of the River Colony summoned Miantonomi and Uncas to appear in the fledgling town of Hartford to negotiate a treaty. Uncas had no reason for alarm. The intention of Connecticut regarding the Mohegans was merely to formalize a cozy arrangement of mutual benefit already informally agreed upon: Uncas was to establish dominion over as many Indian bands as possible from the Pawcatuck to the Connecticut Rivers, pay a portion of the tribute he received from those Indians to Connecticut, and ensure their compliance with Hartford's directives. Connecticut also looked to Uncas to keep the diverse Indian bands within the colony's boundaries out of trouble with the ever-growing number of white settlers in the area.

Why, though, did the Narragansett sachems have to sign a treaty with the English at Connecticut when they already had a perfectly serviceable one with a Massachusetts government they understandably believed to speak for all Englishmen? Miantonomi would soon find out.

Williams stayed in Miantonomi's village for several days in mid-September, before the delegation of 150 Narragansetts traveled to Hartford on foot, helping the sachem prepare for the sojourn. Williams's letter to Winthrop reporting on this busy time makes evident these were days marked by turbulence and apprehension. Several Narragansett men filed into the village to complain to their sachem of being robbed and attacked by Pequots and Mohegans while traveling in Connecticut. One man reported that the Wunnashowatuckoogs, tributaries of the Narragansetts in eastern Connecticut, had just been raided by a large force of Mohegans and their allies. More than twenty of their cornfields had been burned. Members of the tribe had been robbed as well. A Mohegan had told a group of Narragansetts that the Mohegans planned to "lay and wait to stop Miantonomi's passage to Connecticut" and "threatened to boil him in a kettle."[8]

Halfway into the hundred-mile journey, two Englishmen suggested that Williams and the Narragansetts leave the lush forest trails and take to the water to avoid an ambush. Miantonomi would have none of it. They would press on along the forest trail, but the Narragansett prince ordered a group of warriors to march on the flanks to protect the main column, which included Williams, several sachems, and Miantonomi's wife and family.

Once Uncas and Miantonomi finally stood face-to-face before the Connecticut delegation at Hartford around September 20, they had an extended verbal jousting match, with each man accusing the other's people of illicitly harboring Pequots, and committing various crimes. But before too long, the two sachems were persuaded by their hosts to shake hands and dine on venison provided by Narragansett hunters.

We know little of the negotiations at Hartford. Williams and Miantonomi must have asked why the Narragansetts had to sign a treaty with Connecticut after having signed one with Massachusetts already. Surely they were told by the Connecticut representatives that the Narragansett treaty with Massachusetts Bay did not apply to the English in the Connecticut settlements. Connecticut was a sovereign colony; its magistrates made their own agreements with Indians regarding security matters.

We do have the text of the treaty, though according to at least one meticulous scholar, it appears there were almost certainly some secret clauses as well.[9] Under the terms of the Treaty of Hartford of September 1638, signed by Uncas, Miantonomi, and several representatives of Connecticut, the long-standing conflict between the two tribes was formally declared resolved. Future disputes were to be arbitrated by the authorities in Hartford, and if either Indian party failed to abide by Hartford's decision, then Connecticut would be obliged to send a military expedition to ensure that it did so.

Although Boston had promised the Narragansetts the right to hunt and fish in Pequot lands, now, according to the new treaty, both the Mohegans and Narragansetts forfeited any such rights; *Connecticut* was to determine who could do what in the former Pequot lands. The Pequot name was declared extinct. Eighty Pequot captives were awarded to each tribe. Ninigret was awarded twenty for the Niantics. The sachems were to pay an unspecified annual tribute payment for each Pequot received.

Yet in just a few weeks, anyone who cared to look could see that Mohegan men were hunting and fishing in the Pequot territories, and Uncas had incorporated several hundred Pequots into his domain, apparently with Connecticut's blessing. Roger Williams noted several sizable new villages under Uncas's control populated by Pequots sprouting up near the Thames River alone.[10] These developments signaled an ominous shift in the balance of power between Uncas and Miantonomi. Connecticut's support of Uncas, Plymouth governor William Bradford wrote, "did much

[to] increase his power and augment his greatness, which the Narragansetts could not endure to see."[11]

Little wonder frustration continued to mount among Narragansett councils. In spring 1639, a frustrated Miantonomi adopted a conciliatory approach with Governor Winthrop, sending him a gift of thirty fathoms of wampum and a beautifully crafted basket for Mrs. Winthrop, along with a letter penned by Williams, in which the Narragansett chief requested "the continuance of your ancient and constant friendship toward them and good opinion of their sincere affection to the English." Again, Miantonomi asked that his people be granted access to former Pequot lands for hunting and fishing. Williams reminded Winthrop that he had not yet "ratified the promise made [to the Narragansetts] . . . vis. the free use of the Pequot country for their hunting. . . . Since the last year at Connecticut with Mr. Haynes and the magistrates you have not yet pleased to come to action."[12]

As Miantonomi's patience wore thin waiting for Massachusetts to make good on its promise, Connecticut's hostility to the Narragansetts remained implacable. In late August 1639, Uncas informed the Connecticut magistrates that Ninigret had established a tributary community of Pequots on the eastern bank of the Pawcatuck River—by long tradition the western edge of Narragansett territory. The Hartford magistrates ordered the ubiquitous Captain Mason and a force of forty English cavalrymen to drive them off by burning their wigwams and confiscating their corn. So far as Hartford was concerned, this was Connecticut's territory by right of conquest. Uncas, along with a hundred warriors in twenty canoes, was glad to assist.

The Pequots fled into the woods upon seeing the Connecticut force approaching from downriver. As Uncas's men began to ransack the village, about sixty Niantics descended on them with clubs and tomahawks from a nearby hill. A brief melee followed, in which seven Niantics were captured by Mason's men. Yotaash, one of

Miantonomi's brothers, stepped forward and offered to exchange several Pequots who'd killed Englishmen in the recent war for the Niantics' return. Mason agreed. Uncas was asked to hold the Niantic prisoners until the exchange could be made.

Mason and Uncas decided to spend the night; they would complete the destruction of the village the next day before taking to their boats. In the morning, three hundred well-armed Narragansetts arrived on the banks of the Pawcatuck, itching to attack the Mohegans. When Mason made it plain the Narragansett force would have to engage his own troopers as well as Uncas's men if they wanted a fight, the Narragansetts reluctantly demurred—they had seen how the English fought firsthand at Mystic and wanted no part of it. "They would not fight with the Englishmen for they were spirits, but would fight with Uncas."[13]

There was no further fighting to speak of, but as the English-Mohegan force prepared to depart in their boats, Thomas Stanton, Mason's interpreter, shot a jeering Pequot through both thighs with a single musket round.[14]

It had been a humiliating experience for Ninigret, Yotaash, and the Narragansett confederation as a whole. A full year later, Roger Williams was on the way to Mohegan country to try to arrange for the return of the Niantics. Whether they were ever exchanged for Pequots, as Yotaash and Mason had agreed, is unknown. "The English," historians Julie A. Fisher and David J. Silverman astutely observe, "knew that their influence in Indian country—and, with it, access to Indian land—depended on chipping away at the tribute relationships that structured Indian politics. With the Pequots defeated and Uncas wise to his dependence on the English, the Narragansetts were now the colonists' main target."[15]

For several years after this incident, the English authorities in both Boston and Hartford persistently harassed the Narragansetts about harboring rogue Pequots and failing to keep up with tribute payments on the Pequots they had been allotted for their part in the Pequot War. Considering the festering resentment felt by the Rhode Island Indians, it's undoubtedly true that some Narragansett and Niantic bands did harbor Pequots that hadn't been allocated to them by the English authorities. After all, Uncas was gathering up as many Pequots as he could manage, with Connecticut's blessing. And Miantonomi surely felt that withholding tribute payments at times was entirely justified, given English sluggishness in fulfilling their obligations to the confederation. He may well have felt that withholding tribute would provide an incentive to the English authorities to follow through on their promises.

Meanwhile, the Connecticut authorities continued to encourage Uncas to build up a wider sphere of influence among the Indian bands in the central and eastern parts of the colony, and they relied on him to keep those tribes peaceable and in good order. In the fall of 1640, Uncas in return rewarded his supporters in Hartford. He deeded to the colonial government exclusively "all the land that doth belong, or ought of right to belong, to me by whatever name it be called, whether Mohegan, Yomtokc, Aquapanksuks, Porktannoks . . . or any other, which they may hereafter dispose of as their own."[16] Yet Uncas shrewdly reserved ample lands within that grant for himself, and no Englishman could settle on those lands "without consent or approbation of the said magistrates or governor of Connecticut."[17]

This clever arrangement bestowed a kind of reciprocal legitimacy on both parties, thereby enhancing the legal status of each: Uncas's rights to his lands were now a matter of colonial record; Connecticut now had an Indian deed to back up its rather shaky settlement and jurisdictional claims. The deed was a direct affront to Narragansett commercial and diplomatic interests, for the lands Uncas had deeded contained a number of villages and minor sachems with close ties to the Narragansett-Niantic confederation. It was a recipe for war.

NO JOY AND NEW WAR SCARES

By early 1640, it was all too clear: the Narragansetts' postwar strategy of asserting autonomy while seeking to secure Puritan support for their diplomatic and trade initiatives was not working. Roger Williams reported to John Winthrop in July of that year that Miantonomi felt betrayed by English partiality to the Mohegans. Probably around that time the Narragansett sachem realized he had two choices: he could go the same route as Uncas, becoming a kind of agent/subject under English jurisdiction, thereby gaining Boston's support in maintaining his own leadership over the Narragansett confederation, or he could begin to resist the efforts of the English colonies to nibble away at Narragansett autonomy by forming a countervailing coalition of Indian peoples, united in their resistance to English expansion. He chose the latter.

Miantonomi looked initially to his powerful trading partners, the Mohawks, the easternmost Iroquoian people, as key players in the coalition. The Mohawks, however, enjoyed a reputation among the English as ferocious warriors, and when a flurry of rumors that Miantonomi had approached them with gifts reached the governments of the four orthodox colonies, the news set off a war scare.[18] In June 1640, Plymouth's governor, William Bradford, filed this report to John Winthrop:

> I am informed by good intelligence, that the Narragansetts have made a great collection amongst their people; and sent a great present, both of white and black [wampum] beads to the Mohawks, to entreat their help against you, and your friends, if they see cause. And the Mohawks have received their present, and promised them aide, bidding them begin when they will, and they will be ready for them, and do encourage them, with the hope of success.[19]

In September, Massachusetts sent out a small party with an interpreter to Narragansett to parley with both Miantonomi and Ninigret. The two sachems denied they were conspiring with the Mohawks against the English and confirmed that they wished to remain on friendly terms. The Bay Colony took no further action. Apparently the magistrates were inclined toward taking the two sachems at their word—at least for now—recognizing that Bradford's "good intelligence" was probably inspired by Uncas's keen predilection for malicious rumormongering against his rivals to the east.

Rumors, though, persisted. Miantonomi traveled to Boston again in November 1940, where he had a tense exchange with the proud, ham-fisted governor, Thomas Dudley. It began when Miantonomi rejected the Pequot interpreter whom Dudley wanted to use in the negotiations because the Narragansett did not trust her. Dudley refused, at least initially, to provide another translator. He also refused to let Miantonomi dine at his table until he apologized for his breach of manners in turning down the governor's interpreter.

After a bit of time, it appears another translator was found, and the conference got under way. Miantonomi again confirmed his desire to remain in friendly alliance with the English. But Winthrop's terse account of the meeting suggests that the Narragansett sachem left Boston with a sense that he had been denied the respect due him as the leader of an important sovereign power: "It was conceived by some of the court that he kept back such things as he accounted secrets of state, and that he would carry home in his breast an injury, the strict terms he was urged to for not observing our custom in matter of manners, for he told us that when our men came to him, they were permitted to use their own [manners], and so he expected the same liberty with us. So he departed and nothing was agreed."[20]

Indians and English alike in southern New England remained alert to rumors of a Narragansett-led conspiracy in the months ahead. In September 1642, three letters came into Boston from prominent men in various parts of Connecticut, including one that drew on intelligence from Dutch sources. Taken together, the letters indicated that the Indians all over the country planned to combine "to cut off all the English" by sending diverse "small companies" to the homes of leading colonists under the guise of trading with them, breaking into their homes, seizing their weapons, and then undertaking a general uprising. The Narragansetts were the ringleaders.[21]

These letters give every appearance of drawing on an Indian's now-famous recapitulation of Miantonomi's appeal to the Montauks during the summer of 1642 to join an Indian uprising against the English, or "we [Indians] shall all be starved." Connecticut military officer Lion Gardener apparently reported the Indians' rendition of the speech (or perhaps his own rendition of the Indians') sometime late that summer to some well-placed source, and news of the report spread fast and wide throughout Connecticut.

The first *published* version of this famous call to arms doesn't appear in the historical record for almost twenty years, when Gardiner inserts it into his *Leift Lion Gardener his relation of the Pequot Warres*, published in 1660. According to this account, Miantonomi arrived at the Montauk village with a troop of men,

> and instead of receiving presents, which they used to do in their progress, he gave them gifts, calling them brethren and friends, for so are we all Indians as the English are, and say brother to one another; so must we be one as they are, otherwise we shall all be gone shortly, for you know our fathers had plenty of deer and skins, our plains were full of deer, as also our woods . . . and our coves full of fish and fowl. But these English have gotten our land, they with scythes cut down the grass and with axes fell the trees; their cows and horses eat the grass, and their hogs spoil our clam banks, and we shall all be starved; therefore it

> is best for you to do as we, for we are all Sachems from east to west, both Montauks and Mohawks joining with us, and we are resolved to fall upon them all, at one appointed day.[22]

Dozens of historians over the centuries have taken Gardener's account as accurate reportage, presenting the speech as unambiguous proof of Miantonomi's intention to lead a violent uprising against the English. This view is unfortunate, and more than a little naive, for the sachem's message is rendered with a sculptured eloquence that is atypical of the few recorded utterances of Algonquian sachems in the mid-seventeenth century that have survived.

A critical investigator might well conclude that the text of the speech in Gardener's manuscript was the result of a second- or thirdhand account by an Indian who had an ax to grind against the Narragansetts, which was then embellished for dramatic effect by an educated Englishman (Gardener) who *without question* had an ax to grind against them.

We will never know whether the speech was a complete fabrication, a dramatically embellished account of a real speech, or a reasonable approximation of what Miantonomi actually said. We do know that Gardener's version of Miantonomi's speech has been cited uncritically by Puritan apologists ever since as a justification for the draconian treatment that was visited upon the proud Narragansett sachem at the hands of the United Colonies.

The September 1642 letters warning of Narragansett conspiracy, though, are authentic. Predictably, the Connecticut authorities assumed the worst after reading them. They urged Massachusetts to join them in launching a preemptive strike against the Narragansetts, requesting that Massachusetts send one hundred troops to join a Connecticut force of equal number to mount an attack on the conspirators.

Cooler heads prevailed in Boston. The magistrates there took the precaution of disarming the local Indians, but not for long, and after weighing the evidence and making some discreet inquiries, Winthrop reported, "We thought it not sufficient ground for us to begin a war, for it was probable that it might be otherwise, and that all this [talk of conspiracy] might come of the enmity which had been between Miantonomi and Uncas, who continually sought to discredit each other with the English." Rumors to this effect had been raised "about every year" and "proved to be but reports raised up by the opposite factions among the Indians."[23] The chronic rumormongering that went on among the Indians was as widely known in Connecticut as it was in Massachusetts, but as we have seen, Connecticut's magistrates had a marked preference for equating unsubstantiated rumor with fact when it came to the Narragansetts' intentions.

Nonetheless, Miantonomi was again summoned to Boston to give satisfaction. He did just that. "In all his answers," writes Winthrop, "he was very deliberate and showed good understanding of the principles of justice and equity, and ingenuity withal. He demanded that his accusers might be brought forth, to the end, that if they could not make good what they had charged him with, they might suffer what he was worthy of . . . if he had been found guilty, viz., death." After two days of discussions, Miantonomi "did accommodate himself to us to our satisfaction."[24] Lacking Massachusetts's support, Connecticut refrained from launching an attack against the Narragansetts on its own initiative.

ENCROACHMENT—AND HUMILIATION—BY A DIFFERENT METHOD

If the Boston magistrates were satisfied with Miantonomi's assurances, they chose a strange way to show it. Four English settlers of Pawtuxet, which is located about ten miles south of the original Providence settlement and had been deeded to Roger Williams by

Miantonomi and Canonicus in 1636, had just petitioned Massachusetts, asking for its protection against the insolences and violent attacks of a small sect of ultraradical Puritan dissenters under the leadership of Samuel Gorton, the self-proclaimed "professor of the mysteries of Christ." Gorton and his small group of followers had recently taken up residence there.

Gorton was detested by the authorities in both Plymouth and the Bay Colony. He was called by members of the elect there a "miscreant," a "proud and pestilent seducer," and "a man whose spirit was stark drunk with blasphemies and insolences."[25] Massachusetts was more than happy to respond favorably to the request of the disgruntled partitioners at Pawtuxet, led by William Arnold and his son, Benedict. The Bay Colony blithely declared Pawtuxet under its jurisdiction and appointed several of the partitioners magistrates there. Pawtuxet was well outside the bounds of Massachusetts as described in its charter, and well within the bounds of the deed granted to Williams's Providence settlement by the Narragansett sachems. Those hard facts mattered not a bit to the Boston magistrates, for they sensed that in coming to the aid of the Arnold faction, they could help themselves.

Rarely were the orthodox Puritans candid when it came to explaining their motives for jurisdictional expansion, especially when such expansion raised tricky legal and ethical questions. The Pawtuxet annexation, which remained in effect until the late 1650s, when the area was finally returned to Rhode Island thanks to pressure from the authorities in London, was one of those times. Boston accepted jurisdiction, wrote Governor Winthrop, "partly to rescue these men from unjust violence, and partly to draw in the rest in those parts, either under ourselves or Plymouth, who now lived under no government, but grew very offensive, *and the place was likely to be of use to us, especially if we should have occasion of sending out against any Indians of Narragansett and likewise for an outlet into the Narragansett Bay*, and seeing it came without our seeking, and would be no charge to us, we thought it not wisdom to let it slip [italics added]."[26]

So began a cunning scheme by Massachusetts to gain a beachhead on the shores of Narragansett Bay. Within a few months, it would lead to a direct challenge to Miantonomi's sovereignty in the heart of his own country, and to the right of the early Rhode Island settlers to govern themselves in Pawtuxet.

In reality, the Pawtuxet partitioners were the antagonists in the conflict. It was the Gortonists who were the victims. Soon after their arrival, Gorton and his followers challenged the Arnold faction's complete dominance of the town's affairs, and the Arnolds found Gorton's religious practices entirely beyond their ken. For both these reasons, the Arnolds wanted Gorton and company out of the neighborhood.

With powerful Massachusetts breathing down his neck, Gorton and company in January 1643 purchased a large tract of land south of Pawtuxet from Miantonomi and began to settle there. It was called Shawomet, after the name of the small band of Indians who dwelled there, and it took in a significant part of the territory of the modern towns of Warwick, Coventry, and West Warwick.

Massachusetts was not well pleased. Brazenly, it moved to block the sale. Now it colluded with Pomham, sachem at Shawomet, and Socononoco, sachem at Pawtuxet, to void Miantonomi's sale of both of those tracts of land. Pomham had actually cosigned the Shawomet deed to Gorton along with Miantonomi. Sococonoco had earlier "resold" Pawtuxet to the Arnold faction, thereby undermining Miantonomi's original 1636 sale to Roger Williams.

With a promise of protection from Massachusetts in hand and probably with some additional monetary incentives or "gifts" from the expansionist oligarchs, these two minor sachems of the Narragansett confederation agreed to claim that Miantonomi had coerced them into making a sale to the rogue Gorton. They also asserted that the Gortonists were persecuting and mistreating them. Neither claim contained an iota of truth.

Yet again, Miantonomi was summoned to appear in Boston, this time to defend his right to sell Shawomet. The Massachusetts General Court followed its time-honored practice of stacking the deck with pliant Indian witnesses who confirmed exactly what the Bay Colony leaders wanted to be said for the record, but what was in fact manifestly false. Cutshamakin, the pliant ally of Massachusetts Bay, testified that Pomham and Soconoco were not tributaries of Miantonomi but independent sachems in their own right. Then Cutshamakin directly contradicted himself by admitting that both men had in fact paid tribute to Miantonomi because he was, indeed, their great sachem![27] Ignoring the latter assertion entirely, the "magistrates 'proved' to their own satisfaction that they had rightfully acquired what they coveted," observes historian Francis Jennings wryly, "and they sent him [Miantonomi] home with orders to keep hands off."[28]

Years later, Williams would write to the Massachusetts General Court reminding the magistrates what they knew very well in 1643 but had cynically ignored in order to achieve their desired ends: "I humbly offer that what was done [the selling of Shawomet to Gorton] was according to the law and tenor of the natives . . . in all New England and America, viz., that the inferior sachems and subjects shall plan and remove at the pleasure of the highest and supreme sachems, and I humbly conceive that it please the Most High and Only Wise to make use of such a bond of authority over them without which they could not long subsist in human society, in this wild condition in which they are."[29]

Wanting to make the case appear as cut-and-dried as possible for posterity, Winthrop chose not to record in his *Journal* even the gist of Miantonomi's testimony regarding the sale of Shawomet. The reason is plain enough: because that testimony was sure to throw serious legal and moral doubt on the action Massachusetts was about to take. Far better, then, simply to quip that the Narragansett sachem said nothing convincing in his defense. As historian Daniel K. Richter remarks in *Facing East from Indian Country: A Native History of Early America*, "The colonial histories told by English-speaking victors shout across the centuries, but stories told in Native voices are far more difficult to hear."[30]

For Miantonomi, it was yet another humiliating experience at the hands of the Massachusetts General Court. Massachusetts's acceptance of jurisdiction over Pawtuxet and Shawomet marked the colony's abandonment of its obligations toward the Narragansetts as established in the treaty of 1636. If Boston was willing to violate so central a tenet of Indian political life as the right of a principal sachem to dispense of lands occupied by his own minor chiefs, then Narragansett sovereignty meant nothing to the authorities in Boston. At Shawomet and Pawtuxet, the Boston magistrates had engaged in the cynical strategy of divide and rule by luring local sachems away from the Narragansett confederation into their own, self-declared jurisdiction.

Cut off from his tributaries now in his own backyard as well as in Connecticut, unable to obtain for his people their promised rewards for participation in the Pequot War, and under widespread suspicion of conspiracy, Miantonomi by spring 1643 was in a precarious position. His only English supporters were his neighbors in Providence and Aquidneck. They had little power to speak of in Indian-Puritan diplomacy, and no military power at all.

Miantonomi's most influential English friend, Roger Williams, understood the gravity of the situation. By the time Miantonomi returned home from Boston—around late May 1643—Williams was in New Amsterdam, making preparations to sail to London. He was going in part to publish several manuscripts he had been laboring over since coming to the New World, and more urgently to seek parliamentary help in warding off the predations of the orthodox Puritan colonies against the towns and Indians on Narragansett Bay.

It wasn't going to be an easy task. In May the four orthodox colonies had at last formed the United Colonies of New England, defined as a "league of friendship and amity for the offense and defense, mutual advice and succor upon all just occasions both for preserving and propagating the truth and liberties of the Gospel and for their own mutual safety and welfare."[31] Should "God bless their [the Confederated colonies'] endeavors" in an altercation with outsiders—Indians or Puritan dissenters in Rhode Island, for instance—"the spoils of whatever is gotten by conquest" were to be equitably divided among the signees.[32]

William Bradford of Plymouth went so far as to claim that the danger of Narragansett conspiracy was the primary impetus for the formation of the Confederation. Dealing with a looming crisis between the Narragansetts and the Mohegans would be the Confederation's first order of business at its initial meeting in September in Boston.

In the spring of 1643, one of Uncas's Pequots attempted to kill the Mohegan sachem. Uncas accused Miantonomi of hiring the assassin and brought the case before the United Colonies commissioners. The evidence that Miantonomi was behind the crime was hazy and circumstantial at best, but a bit of haze and a few curious circumstances were all the authorities required to believe Uncas's charge, though a formal verdict in the case would have to wait until the commissioners gathered in September.

However, a far more serious development than an alleged assassination attempt arose in midsummer. Open hostilities broke out between Uncas and one of Miantonomi's close allies—possibly a kinsman—on the Connecticut River who had resisted Uncas's rapid ascendancy in the area. Sequessen, sachem of the Suckiags, got the worst of the fighting, losing seven or eight of his men in a single attack, and then suffering the indignity of having his bands' wigwams burned by Mohegan warriors.

Mindful of the Treaty of Hartford and of the suspicions of his intentions among the English magistrates, Miantonomi asked both Connecticut and Massachusetts for permission to strike back at Uncas. Connecticut's John Haynes replied noncommittally: "The English had no hand [in the affair]."[33] Winthrop appeared to give the Narragansett sachem the green light: "If Uncas had done him or his friend wrong, and would not give satisfaction, we should leave him to his own course."[34]

Miantonomi rapidly marched a formidable army of about a thousand warriors to a place called the Sachem Plain today, just outside Norwich, Connecticut. There, Uncas's men, only half that number, somehow got the better of the Narragansetts early in the opening skirmish. Miantonomi, weighed down with English armor given him by one of the followers of his friend Samuel Gorton, was captured and brought to Uncas's village, Shantok, on the Thames River, as a prisoner. A ransom of 160 fathoms of wampum was paid to the Mohegans by the Narragansetts to spare their sachem's life. Uncas, ever mindful of his obligations under the Hartford Treaty and wanting to remain in the good graces of the English, delivered his captive to the English jail at Hartford, hung on to the ransom, and awaited English justice to take its course.

Miantonomi's fate was to be decided by eight commissioners—two from each colony. By all accounts, the deliberations were carried out expeditiously despite the rather large gaps in the evidence against the accused. John Winthrop, the chief commissioner, summarized the verdict in his *Journal*: the commissioners, "taking into serious consideration what was safest and best to be done, were all of the opinion that it would not be safe to set him [Miantonomi] at liberty, neither had we sufficient ground for us to put him to death. In this difficulty we called in five of the most judicious elders [out of a pool of eighty] . . . and propounding the case to them, they all agreed that he ought to be put to death."[35]

Queasy about the ramifications of following through on their decision with their own judicial apparatus, the commissioners asked Uncas to execute his archrival, but only after he had taken the condemned sachem into Mohegan territory. Many, though by no means all, early accounts have it that Miantonomi was executed by a hatchet blow to the head, somewhere between Hartford and Windsor. The executioner was Uncas's brother, Wawequa.

The official records of the United Colonies and Winthrop's *Journal*—the most important official and quasi-official sources—present Miantonomi's alleged conspiracy "to cut off all the English" as by far and away the most serious offense justifying the execution. Other reasons, though, clearly came into play. The alleged assassination attempt on Uncas is presented as fact, but in this case, as in others regarding offenses by inconvenient Indians in the mid-seventeenth century, the commissioners saw no need to present reasonable proof of the "fact" in the record.

Further, it was said that Miantonomi had violated the Hartford Treaty in attacking Uncas without first obtaining permission from the English. But Miantonomi *had* abided by the Treaty of Hartford in seeking permission for the attack, and it had been granted by none other than John Winthrop, while Connecticut's evasive response could reasonably be read as indicating it had no intention to interfere. Finally, there was the nagging problem of the accused's character: Winthrop reported that Miantonomi "was of turbulent and proud spirit, and would never be at rest."[36]

Many distinguished scholars of Puritan-Indian relations have been struck by the disingenuousness of the official explanations for putting Miantonomi to death, and it is not hard to see why. In judging the case and in documenting it, the Puritan authorities flagrantly misrepresented themselves as objective arbiters in a long-standing conflict between two Indian peoples. In fact, the Mohegans were for all intents and purposes an integral part of the Puritan political machine, not an autonomous political entity, as the Narragansetts clearly were.

As for the conspiracy, Miantonomi was unquestionably pursuing new alliances and renewing old ones with Indians throughout the region, including the Mohawks. But the pursuit of an alliance is a very different thing from conspiring to make war. The notion that Miantonomi would take up arms against the United Colonies doesn't jibe at all with what we know of the man's character, or with his shrewd assessment of English military power. Just a year before the verdict was rendered, Winthrop had described Miantonomi as a man who "was very deliberate and showed good understanding of the principles of justice and equity."[37] The most fair-minded Puritans, particularly Williams, who knew Miantonomi best, concurred with this assessment.

In surveying the entire scope of Miantonomi's career in diplomacy with the English, the overall impression emerges of a patient, highly intelligent man, eminently capable of taking in the complexities of dealing with foreigners with markedly different customs and ideas from his own. If the history of his diplomacy with the English displays anything, it shows a sustained effort to respond to requests and charges judiciously and reasonably, and an inclination to resolve disputes amicably.

It seems fair to say Miantonomi would have avoided open warfare with the English at all costs. His pan-Indian alliance, writes historian Neal Salisbury, "would have been less likely to result in violence than in an effective institutional counterweight to expansion by Connecticut and Massachusetts Bay, and in the long run stabilization of Indian-European relations in and around . . . Rhode Island."[38]

Pressed in on from all sides and keenly aware of the stark underlying dynamic of Indian-English politics, Miantonomi undoubtedly did try to build a diverse Indian coalition to act as a brake on the ambitions of the English, but he was clearly unable to do so. Ironically, Miantonomi had decided to pursue a strikingly similar strategy to that of the colonial governments, seeking strength and security in unity. The Puritan pursuit of such a policy, at least in Puritan eyes, was entirely justified by God's sanctification of their enterprise, and by the natural inclination of the heathen to dissembling and treachery. The pursuit of this same policy by a Narragansett Indian, though, was impermissible because, in the Puritan mind, it had to be motivated by malign intentions rather than self-interest—or, better put, self-preservation.

Miantonomi was put to death not so much for the reasons enumerated in the record—they were peripheral—but because he steadfastly refused to govern the Narragansetts as "dependents within the English system."[39] He had refused to do so because, unlike Uncas, or Wyandanch, who would go the route of Uncas in 1644, in fully accepting English jurisdiction and domination, Miantonomi could see the end result of such a policy in his mind's eye, and it was not pretty. As the English grew more unified and numerous, Indian societies would be pushed to the margins, politically, commercially, and geographically, or would disappear altogether. This was a fate Miantonomi was determined to resist at all costs, and he paid for it with his head.

THE MEANING OF MIANTONOMI'S DEATH

The execution of Miantonomi, writes Alan Taylor, "confirmed the long odds facing Indian visionaries who sought to transcend enmities in favor of a common union against the newcomers."[40] It also sent a strong message to every Indian community in the vicinity of the Puritan colonies: any effort to consolidate Indian power under a single leader would be considered a direct threat to the security of the English. Hence, it would not be tolerated.

In putting their marks to the 1636 treaty of alliance and friendship, Miantonomi and Canonicus fully expected postwar relations with the English to be marked by the reciprocity and respect that had prevailed before the war. Yet not long after the Pequot conflict sputtered to an end, a much-disillusioned Miantonomi found himself asking his closest English friend, "Did ever friends deal so with friends?"[41] Already, he sensed the sea change in Puritan-Narragansett relations wrought by the Puritans' new commercial and military domination.

That Uncas had executed Miantonomi, their much-revered prince, enraged the Narragansetts and only hardened their commitment to reversing the gains the Mohegan sachem had made at their expense. Miantonomi's death kept alive the bitter hostility between the two most powerful southern New England native peoples for decades, testifying to the success of the English "expedient imperialist principle of divide and rule."[42]

As the Narragansetts pondered how to carry on in their grief, Roger Williams had just arrived in London and was already hard at work seeking relief from Puritan oppression for Rhode Island's dissenters and the Narragansetts in the form of a parliamentary charter. Williams's chances of success in this venture were slender indeed, but that wasn't about to deter him from trying.

Chapter 6

To London

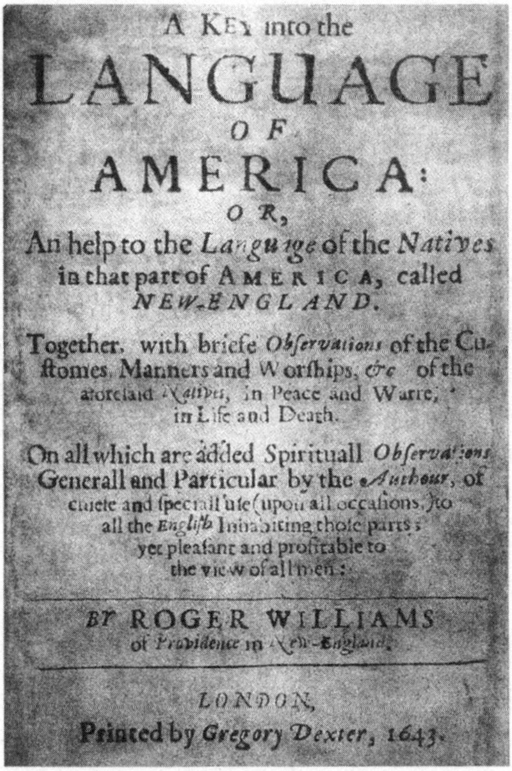
A KEY into the
LANGUAGE
OF
AMERICA:
OR,
An help to the *Language* of the *Natives*
in that part of AMERICA, called
NEW-ENGLAND.
Together, with briefe *Obſervations* of the Cu-
ſtomes, Manners and Worſhips, *&c.* of the
aforeſaid *Natives*, in Peace and Warre,
in Life and Death.
On all which are added Spirituall *Obſervations*
Generall and Particular by the *Authour*, of
chiefe and ſpeciall uſe (upon all occaſions,) to
all the *Engliſh* Inhabiting thoſe parts;
yet pleaſant and profitable to
the view of all men:
BY ROGER WILLIAMS
of *Providence* in *New-England.*
LONDON,
Printed by *Gregory Dexter*, 1643.

The cover of the first edition of Williams's classic ethnography, *A Key into the Language of America*. The book remains an invaluable source of insight and information on the culture of the southern New England Indians.

On his way east across the Atlantic Ocean, Roger Williams arrived in the thriving town of New Amsterdam, nestled on the southern tip of Manhattan Island, in late February or early March 1643.

He reached Manhattan just in time to witness the outbreak of war between the Dutch and the Weckquaesgeek Indians. The Dutch hoped to collect tribute from the Weckquaesgeeks in exchange for protection and had been bullying them into submission for some time. But the Dutch authorities had gravely underestimated Indian resolve. As Williams later reported of those turbulent days, Governor William Kieft "questioned not to finish [the war] in a few days, but before we weighed anchor, their bowries were in flames. Dutch and English were slain. Mine eyes saw their flames at their towns, and the flights and hurries of men, women and children."[1] Among the slain at Pelham, just north of Manhattan Island, were Anne Hutchinson and several of her children. They had moved to New Netherland from Portsmouth about two years earlier.

Indians were very much on the mind of the founder of Providence at that time, especially the Narragansetts, who remained locked in torturous dispute with Boston, Hartford, and the Mohegans. Talk of war to humble Miantonomi was heard everywhere in the orthodox colonies. Military action against the Narragansetts would inevitably bring a Puritan army down among the towns on Narragansett Bay. The Puritans would declare martial law over all of Rhode Island. It might well lead to the dismemberment of the outcast colony, and the destruction of the Narragansetts as a political force in the region. Only a legally binding charter from the king or Parliament establishing political unity among the Rhode Island towns, and jurisdiction over the territory of the Narragansett, could prevent the area from being swallowed up by its orthodox neighbors. Obtaining that document was Williams's chief mission in returning to London.

The charter Williams envisaged would be no easy trick to secure because it had no precedent. Williams wanted a colony grounded on the radical ideas he had been working out since coming to the New World: religious liberty for all comers, no matter how eccentric their beliefs; complete separation of church and state; democratic government, in which magistrates derived their powers not from God, as Puritan political theory had it, but from the consent of ordinary citizens; and respect for Indian political rights.

In the Rhode Island towns, a kind of rudimentary democracy already obtained pretty much by default. Decisions were made by majority rule of the towns' freemen, disputes were settled by arbitration, and officers were elected by popular vote of the freemen.

By 1643, issues of church and state authority had brought civil war to England, and the cause of religious toleration had gained many adherents as a practical political expedient, a way to accommodate the welter of sectarian views on what constituted true religion. However, even the most liberal voices found Williams's notion of a government with *no* regulatory powers over religious belief to promise little beyond blasphemy and the breakdown of social order and propriety. Yet Williams believed deep in his bones that religious *liberty*—not mere toleration—was the only road to true civil prosperity and peace. History proved it to be the case. And he believed that the truth of God, insofar as it could be gleaned by poor men and women born of flesh and sin, was best sought through the unfettered exercise of the individual conscience.

Since none of Williams's extant writings offer an explanation of how he planned to go about securing Rhode Island's charter, we are left to piece together his strategy by examining the events and circumstances surrounding his efforts. From the outset the founder of Providence recognized the necessity of publicizing the orthodox order's excesses and abuses of authority. In addition, he had to clarify—and to sell—his alternative vision of a society based on what he had begun to call "soul liberty," and explain a paradox in a way few people in seventeenth-century England were likely to find credible: that Christian faith was most likely to prosper in an environment where other faiths were permitted to flourish, unimpeded by the strong arm of the state.

To do so would challenge his considerable powers of persuasion.

He could not accomplish his task alone. He needed to build on his contacts of a handful of influential London friends to make many new ones. And he would have to write—write at length, with passion and commitment—about what he knew best: New England orthodoxy's faulty assumptions about church, state, and the Indians of America.

Since Williams had first sailed to America, the constitutional struggle between King Charles I and a Parliament dominated increasingly by Puritans and the rising merchant class had only grown more bitter and entrenched. Parliament had been dismissed by King Charles I in 1629, though he continued to levy taxes on his own authority and imprison those who refused to pay. These acts were but two of many flagrant violations by the king of the hard-won Petition of Right, which guaranteed a wide variety of civil liberties to all Englishmen and had been reluctantly ratified by the king in 1628. Williams's old mentor Sir Edward Coke was that document's principal author.

Meanwhile, Archbishop William Laud had intensified his campaign against the Puritans. The fortunes of the king and his church, however, began to falter in 1640, when Charles launched an ill-advised war to force Scotland to accept the *Book of Common Prayer* and the episcopacy of bishops. A well-disciplined Scottish army routed the king's troops, occupied northern England, and forced the king to pay the cost of occupation until a suitable peace was brokered. Short of funds, Charles was forced to recall Parliament.

The leaders of the Long Parliament (1640–53) were determined to rein in Charles's abuses of authority. Parliament passed a series of laws strengthening its own powers at the king's expense, in exchange for agreeing to levy taxes desperately needed by the crown. The parliamentary leadership aggressively pursued the leading perpetrators of religious repression. Laud was arrested and placed in the Tower of London in 1641—he would be executed at the height of the Civil War in 1645. The detested Star Chamber, which had become a grimly effective mechanism of political and religious repression, was abolished.

Incensed over what he saw as parliamentary overreaching, in January 1642 the king burst into Parliament with four hundred troops with the intention of arresting five leading members of the House of Commons for treason. But the men had been tipped off and fled just before the king's arrival. This brazen assault on parliamentary power turned many fence-sitters in the political class against the cause of the crown. Soon, the king and his supporters were pushed entirely out of London and forced to take up residence in Oxford.

In September 1642, Charles I declared war on Parliament. The English Civil War had begun, and with it, an extended period of intense debate and dispute over the nature of the church, the state, and the relation between the two. From his base in Oxford the king would prosecute the war between his "Cavaliers" and Parliament's "Roundheads."

In the summer of 1643, when Williams first arrived in London, the high level of turbulence in English politics precluded the immediate pursuit of his charter. During Williams's first few months in London, no office or commission, royal or parliamentary, exercised ultimate authority over colonial affairs. Still, Williams could begin to lay the groundwork by raising his own profile in powerful London circles as a person to be reckoned with on matters of politics and religion. Several prominent men in Parliament were known to be broadly sympathetic to his critique of the abuses suffered by dissenters and Indians at the hands of Massachusetts. Others were favorably disposed toward the founder of Providence based on what they had been told about his character by those who knew him before he had embarked for America.

One such person was Sir Robert Rich, Earl of Warwick, a close associate of Sir William Masham, Williams's former employer in Essex. Another was Sir Thomas Barrington, a respected liberal voice in Parliament with an abiding concern for colonial affairs. He knew and liked Roger Williams and would help him press his case for the new colony. Williams's greatest ally, though, was Sir Henry Vane Jr., the young former governor of Massachusetts Bay Colony. Vane had left Massachusetts Bay in disgust after the antinomian crisis leading to the banishment of Anne Hutchinson in 1637. Wise beyond his years—he was only thirty when Williams arrived in London—Vane had distinctly liberal leanings and was a recent convert to religious toleration. Sir Henry and Williams had struck up a friendship in the New World and continued to correspond after Vane's return to England. The friendship, intellectual and personal, would deepen considerably over the time Williams remained in London.

In the early 1640s, Sir Henry was a rising star in Parliament. He was instrumental in negotiating the Solemn League and Covenant with the Scots, and pushing it through the House of Commons and the Westminster Assembly, a body composed of prominent clergymen and a handful of parliamentarians meant to advise Parliament on matters of church doctrine and governance. The signing of the Covenant in September 1643 brought a powerful Scottish army of some twenty thousand men to the aid of Parliament's struggling forces, almost certainly preventing the collapse of the resistance movement to the king.

But it also brought the Presbyterianism of the Scottish church to the Church of England, which called for close association among individual churches via means of periodic assemblies, or synods. The Scots saw the decisions reached at such meetings regarding church doctrine and governance as binding on the member churches. Not surprisingly, Williams, Vane, and Oliver Cromwell, who led the Parliament's military forces, joined the great poet and tolerationist John Milton in fearing that Presbyterianism in England and Wales would usher in a "second tyranny" over both preaching and worship. "Bishops and Presbyters are the same to us," wrote Milton, "both name and thing."[2] The devil, though, was in the details, and in the coming months Williams would attend many stormy sessions of the Assembly where those details of doctrine and authority were hammered out, and in the end the Church of England never did take on the full vestments of Presbyterianism.

Here Williams put his considerable charisma and persuasive powers to good use, arguing forcefully to limit the powers of the synod on individual churches, and heralding the virtues of freedom of conscience for all believers. His efforts prompted a leading Presbyterian in the Assembly, the Glaswegian minister Robert Baillie, to remark, "My good acquaintance, Mr. Roger Williams has drawn a great number after him to a singular Independency."[3] Before too long, Williams would make his own published contributions to the swirling debates in the Assembly, including several important pamphlets and one brilliantly original, sprawling book.

But first things first. Williams needed to establish himself as an authority on *America* in the eyes of the political and intellectual elite if he was to have a fighting chance of outmaneuvering the well-funded and connected agents of Massachusetts Bay, who were already hard at work lobbying for a charter granting Boston sole jurisdiction over all of Rhode Island. Just before Williams had arrived in London, Massachusetts agents Thomas Weld and Hugh Peter had seen to the publication of a tract called *New England's First Fruits*. Written as a response to a growing chorus of critics in London over Massachusetts's failure to bring the light of God to the natives—and to forecast great progress on that front just over the horizon—the book explained away the colony's lackluster efforts to date as being due to the Indians' "infinite distance from Christianity, having never been prepared thereunto to any civility at all. Secondly, the difficulty of their language to us, and ours to them; there being no rules to learn either by."[4]

In fact, Massachusetts had diverted substantial funds from investors in the mother country designated for Indian instruction and conversion to more worldly, material projects. As of 1643, the Bay Colony had made no concerted effort whatsoever to bring the Indians around to Christianity. *First Fruits* was a transparently propagandistic, highly defensive book, and it failed to put to rest uncomfortable questions about the lack of evangelical progress in Massachusetts. It did, however, go far to reinforce the Puritan stereotype of the Indians as treacherous savages and devil worshippers who lived in a wretched state of spiritual darkness.

Williams had cobbled together on the long voyage across the Atlantic a very different book about the Indians than Weld and Peter's *New England's First Fruits*. Williams's *A Key into the Language of America* was a warmly sympathetic, closely observed introduction to Narragansett Indian language, culture, and daily life that challenged many of the bigoted ideas about the Indians that passed for conventional wisdom in seventeenth-century New England. Unlike *First Fruits*, *A Key* was indisputably the product of sustained immersion in the Indians' world by an open-minded and curious observer/participant. The renowned ethnohistorian James Axtell has observed that Williams knew the Indians "better than anyone else" in British North America.[5] He was among the first Europeans to suggest that the Indians were in some ways more Christian than Europeans who claimed to follow that faith. Few serious students of the Algonquian Indians today would disagree with Axtell. As Williams explained in his book's preface, "I have run through varieties of intercourse with [the Indians] day and night, summer and winter, by land and sea."[6]

Published by Gregory Dexter in London in September 1643, *A Key* was well received by a London audience intensely curious about the native inhabitants of the New World. The first printing sold briskly—despite being laden with printer's errors and broken type—and the volume quickly went into another. Williams's study consists of thirty-two thematic chapters, each of which begins with a set of two-column pages featuring Narragansett words and phrases spelled out phonetically in the left-hand column, and English translations in the right-hand column.

Many of the phrases in the book are presented in dialogue form, as practical questions and answers one might expect to pass between an Indian and an English speaker. The word and phrase lists are interspersed with pointed commentary and personal anecdotes. Each chapter concludes with a short poem, many of which contrast Indian mores and behaviors favorably with those of Europeans.

The initial third of the book constitutes a kind of primer to facilitate first encounters between Englishmen and Indians, with individual chapters on salutations, eating, entertaining, forms of address, and family life. The middle chapters survey the geography and natural history of Narragansett country, covering the weather, the seasons, birds and beasts, and other such topics, offering readers a richly textured picture of the Narragansetts' living world. The last third of the volume covers a variety of institutions and activities, including government, religion, games, trade, hunting, and death and burial rituals.

A Key humanized the Indian and his world with a depth of insight and empathy other books about New England's Indians lacked. "Williams's dialogues allow English readers to conceive of conversations with a far-off, fascinating people," writes scholar Jonathan Beecher Field, just as his observations conjure up an image of the Indians "as members of a civil, humane, and well-ordered society."[7]

Here among New England's natives Williams found abundant evidence that it was possible for a people to be well-mannered and humane and yet know nothing of Christianity—a jolting realization shared by few seventeenth-century Europeans. The Indians were inclined to be generous and hospitable: "There is a flavor of *civility* and *courtesy* even amongst these wild *Americans*, both amongst *themselves* and towards *strangers*."[8] When an Englishman came upon an Indian village, the natives were "remarkably free and courteous, to invite all strangers in."[9] The author had "heard of many English lost, and oft been lost myself, and myself and others have been found, and succored by the Indians."[10]

They could be more hospitable than those who claimed to answer to a higher God:

> I have known them leave their House and Mat
> To lodge a Friend or stranger,
> When Jews and Christians oft have sent
> Christ Jesus to the Manger.[11]

Williams admired the Narragansetts for their close interpersonal cooperation in everyday tasks, such as hunting, and the clearing and planting of the fields. Their form of government seamlessly incorporated elements of monarchy and basic democracy: "The *Sachims*, although they have an absolute Monarchy over the people; yet they will not conclude ought that concerns all, either laws or subsidies, or wars, unto which the people are averse, and by gentle persuasion cannot be brought."[12]

The longest chapter in the book, not surprisingly, concerns religion. Far from their being (as *First Fruits* put it) "under the devil's sway," Williams found in his many discussions with the Narragansetts a profound curiosity and respect for matters of the spirit. He includes a concise translation of the Christian version of God's making of the world in six days, reporting that he had told the story to the Indians in their own language "many hundreths of times, [and] great numbers of them have heard [it] with great delight and great convictions."[13]

The Indians believe, writes Williams, "1. That God is. 2. That he is a rewarder of those who diligently seek him." Among the Indians, Williams found what was sadly lacking among the vast majority of his brothers and sisters in Massachusetts: toleration of different religious beliefs. "They have a modest religious persuasion not to disturb any man, either themselves, *English, Dutch*, or any in their conscience and worship, and therefore say: Peace, hold your peace."[14]

In *A Key into the Language of America*, the depth of the writer's immersion in Indian culture, and his sense of the immense possibilities for English-Indian relations in the future, comes through on every page. Part of the secret of the book's success is that it resonates with expectation and hope. If the Narragansetts have much to learn from the English, so, too, do the English have much to learn from the Indians. In evoking this implicit theme, *A Key into the Language of America* stands virtually alone in the seventeenth-century literature about New England Indians.

Two months after *A Key* was published, in November 1643, Parliament was sufficiently confident of its prospects in the struggle against the king to fill the vacuum regarding oversight of the colonies. It placed authority for all colonial matters in the hands of a Commission for Foreign Plantations. The Commission, consisting of six peers and twelve commoners, was headed by Robert Rich, Earl of Warwick. Even more important for the prospects for the success of Williams's special project was the appointment of Henry Vane as one of the commissioners. Vane was the only member to have set foot in America. His voice could be expected to carry special weight in future deliberations precisely for that reason, and because of his high position in the parliamentary leadership. Williams must have been over the moon when he got word of Vane's appointment.

Over the next several months Williams pleaded, cajoled, and networked assiduously for the ten signatures required to secure the charter, with Vane as his staunchest ally. Thomas Weld and Hugh Peter pressed the case for Massachusetts's claim. The close-run contest would be waged over about four months. Meanwhile, the urgency of the matter for the Narragansett towns and the Narragansett Indians came more clearly into view. Massachusetts had decided to carry on with its campaign against the Gortonists by means other than threats.

HARRYING THE GORTONISTS AT SHAWOMET

During Williams's absence, Massachusetts had stepped up its expansionist campaign around Narragansett Bay, harrying the Gortonists at Shawomet, and attempting to intimidate the Narragansetts. In September of 1643, the Gortonists had been ordered by Massachusetts to defend their ownership of Shawomet in light of Pomham's claim that Miantonomi had forced him to sell "his" land there, and to answer complaints about their alleged mistreatment of the local Indians under Pomham and Socononoco.

The Gortonists quickly responded: they denied that Massachusetts had jurisdiction in Shawomet. They were English subjects, and only answerable to an English court. In a hotly defiant letter dated September 12, signed by Randall Holden but written on behalf of all the Gortonists, Holden denounced Pomham and his claim to Shawomet and leveled a series of countercharges against his Indians. Probably with Massachusetts's surreptitious encouragement, and unquestionably with a sense of entitlement due to their cozy arrangement with Boston, the Indians around Shawomet had engaged in no end of mischief over the previous summer, killing the Gortonists' livestock, and robbing several homes in broad daylight. Both Sococonoco and Pomham had been caught stealing from the Gortonists' households. Other Indians had on occasion thrown rocks at members of the sect as they worked in the fields.

The Gortonists turned down flat Massachusetts's offer of safe passage to go before the General Court in Boston. Again, Randall Holden penned a formal response. The Holden letter was composed in the classic style of Gorton himself, which is to say it contained hefty doses of verbal nose-thumbing, invective, and sarcasm. Holden castigated the high-handedness and hypocrisy of the Massachusetts General Court: "To the great and honoured Idol General now set up in the Massachusetts, whose pretended equity in distribution of justice unto the souls and bodies of men is nothing else but a mere device of man, according to the ancient custom and sleights of Satan, transforming himself into an angel of light, to subject and make slaves of that species or kind that God has honored with his own image."[15] The Massachusetts magistrates were "full of pride and folly." The Bay Colony was the "kingdom of darkness and the devil," and the Gortonists demanded "when we may expect some of you to come up to us, to answer and give satisfaction for some of these foul and inhumane wrongs you have done . . . to us, your country-men."[16]

The General Court quickly fired off a response, informing Gorton and his people that it would take them up on their offer to come to Shawomet, but not in a manner the Gortonists were likely to find congenial. Troops would be sent. They would demand satisfaction for the Gortonists' many crimes and blasphemies. The cost of this expedition, it was made clear, would be borne by the Gortonists. The Court desired to convince the Gortonists of the "evil of their way." If they did not alter their wayward course, the letter went on ominously, "we then shall look upon them as men prepared for slaughter."[17]

In due course, the expedition made its way south. A party of Providence men offered to arbitrate the dispute once the Massachusetts force reached that town, but the Massachusetts delegation was in no mood to tarry with the Rhode Island riffraff. As Winthrop revealingly reported in his *Journal*, "They [the Providence men] were no state, but a few fugitives, living without law or government, and so [it was] not honorable for us to join with them."[18] In other words, what could Providence settlers possibly know about justice, proper government, or religion?

Gorton and eight of his acolytes, preparing for the worst, holed themselves up in a blockhouse near what is now Warwick Neck, overlooking Narragansett Bay. The Massachusetts troops took the house under siege for several days, attempting on occasion to fire their muskets into the embrasures of the blockhouse, more with a view to prompting the surrender of the inhabitants than to killing them. Gorton and company held their own fire, but refused to budge. Finally, after a few days and a failed attempt by the Massachusetts troops to set the house alight, the Gortonists surrendered. They were summarily placed under arrest and hauled off under armed guard to face justice in Boston.

Strangely, once the Gortonists came before the General Court, there was no mention of charges concerning the defendants' treatment of the Arnold contingent. Nothing was said of the complaints from Pomham or any other Indian. Nor was the critical issue of Gorton's deed for Shawomet mentioned—at least not according to the extant sources. Had the Gortonists' heinous blasphemies directed toward the General Court blotted out all concern they had for the civil and criminal violations they had allegedly committed? Perhaps they had. Theology was a deadly serious business in Massachusetts.

But a more likely cause for the tight focus on theology rather than legal issues was that on the crucial deed question, at least, the law was on the side of the Rhode Islanders, and the learned men of Massachusetts well knew this was the case. Colonial courts had generally ruled that the principal sachems of a tribe had every right to sell lands where their minor sachems dwelled. After a lengthy and combative discourse between Gorton and the authorities tightly focused on Gorton's theological beliefs, the General Court rendered a verdict: "Upon much examination and serious consideration of your writings, with your answers about them [in court] we do charge you to be a blasphemous enemy of the true religion of our Lord Jesus Christ and his holy ordinances, and also of all civil authority among the people of God, and particularly in this jurisdiction."[19] The Court sentenced Gorton and six others to be confined in irons and to do hard labor for an unspecified amount of time. The guilty parties were dispersed to various Massachusetts towns to serve out their sentences.

However, public backlash over the severity of the sentences, and the Gortonists' continued attempts to spread their subversive ideas even while in irons, led to their release in March 1644. Another factor in the liberation of the blasphemers surely was the nagging sense of the General Court that the Commission for Foreign Plantations would not look favorably upon the Gortonists' persecution on religious grounds. So Samuel Gorton and company were summarily banished from Massachusetts, and from Shawomet, on pain of death.

The Gorton affair made it plain, as one English historian put it, that the "New England Puritan had indulged his desire to force his own profession of faith on his fellow-man till it had become a morbid passion."[20] The General Court, though, had not heard the last from Samuel Gorton. A bit more than a month after his release, after settling back in Portsmouth on Aquidneck, where he and his followers were welcomed with open arms, he met with Canonicus and Pessacus. Gorton and his friends the Indians had a mutual interest in keeping Massachusetts out of their territory, and out of their affairs. Both had been victims of Massachusetts's arrogant abuse of its authority, of its imperial overreach. The Gortonists had lost their land and their homes at Shawomet—at least for the time being. The Narragansetts had lost their great sachem, the ransom they had paid to spare his life, and the right to exploit former Pequot hunting grounds to which they believed they were entitled.

Gorton assured the sachems and their counselors that, in time, higher authority would right such injustices and rein in the haughty Bostonians. That authority was none other than King Charles I and the common law of his kingdom. Massachusetts since its inception had zealously asserted its unfettered independence, denying *even to its own freemen* the right to appeal to the crown. On several occasions the General Court had dealt out draconian punishment to citizens who appealed to the king for redress of what they saw as unjust treatment. The voices of the oppressed had been heard across the sea. As early as 1637 the king had made an attempt to revoke the Bay Colony's charter for such abuses, but the rising tide of revolutionary conflict with Parliament had sidetracked the effort.

The Gortonists' rights under common law had been flagrantly violated by Massachusetts. They stood trial, after all, "in a court where their prosecutors were also judges and jurors."[21] Gorton's very survival had, he felt sure, been due indirectly to the power of the crown and English law. Most of the judges wanted to put him to death for heresy, but fear over the repercussions of doing so prompted the Court to deliver a less severe sentence.

As the sachems and Gorton discussed the history of their travails with their Puritan oppressors, an inspired idea bubbled to the surface. It may have originated with the sachems. It may have originated with Gorton. No matter who thought of it first, all agreed it had promise. The sachems would submit their allegiance to King Charles of England, thereby gaining his protection from abuse and intimidation at the hands of other English subjects—namely, the United Colonies, and Massachusetts Bay in particular.

Gorton and his advisers drew up a deftly written deed of submission to the king for the Narragansett confederation. In a document dated April 19, 1644, the sachems agreed "to consent, freely, voluntarily, and most humbly to submit, subject and give over ourselves, peoples, lands, rights, inheritances, and possessions . . . unto the protection, care and government of that worthy and royal Prince" King Charles I. Having "just cause of jealousy and suspicion of some of His Majesty's pretended subjects [i.e.,

Massachusetts]," they would not yield "over ourselves unto any, that are subjects themselves in any case; having ourselves been the chief Sachems, or Princes successively, of the country, time out of mind."[22] Within the deed, the sachems deputized none other than Gorton and three of his followers to ensure the "safe custody, careful conveyance, and declaration hereof unto his grace."[23]

When the alarmed authorities in Boston learned of this document and confirmed its authenticity, they quickly called on the Narragansetts to send emissaries to Boston to explain their outrageous act. Pessacus and Canonicus, though, had had quite enough of Boston, at least for the time being. A few weeks earlier, Wahose, a messenger from Pessacus, had traveled to Boston on a diplomatic mission. He met with Governor Winthrop, offering a traditional ceremonial present, and then asked, yet again, if the English would remain neutral should the Narragansetts initiate war against Uncas to revenge the death of Miantonomi. Winthrop told Wahose that even if Pessacus sent a thousand fathoms of wampum and a thousand skins, the English would make war on the Narragansetts if they dared to attack Uncas.[24] It was a harsh and humiliating rebuke.

So the sachems wrote a letter back to the General Court. They would not come to Boston. They demurred on the grounds that "our occasions at this time are very great; and the more [so] because of the loss . . . of our late deceased brother." They queried why it was that Boston did not wish them to seek revenge against so "inhuman and cruel an adversary" as Uncas. They made it clear that, while they hoped for cordial relations in the future, if any great disagreement between the two parties should arise, "neither yourselves, nor we are to be judges; and both of us are to have recourse, and repair unto that honorable and just government" of England.[25]

After receiving this unwelcome missive, the Court sent two messengers to the sachems to inquire as to why "they had done as they wrote, and why they would countenance and take counsel from such evil men, and such as we had banished from us, and to persuade them to sit still, and to have more regard to us than such as Gorton."[26] Pessacus let the messengers wait in the soaking rain for two hours before greeting them. He met with them in an ordinary wigwam rather than his own quarters—yet another diplomatic slight. The Narragansett sachem asserted his people's right to determine their own course of action. They were, said Pessacus, subjects under the same king as the English, and not obliged to defer to the authority of Massachusetts. Further, he informed the Massachusetts emissaries that the Narragansetts planned to initiate a series of raids against Uncas, and soon.

In late 1644, Samuel Gorton and Randall Holden sailed for England to seek redress for their grievances, as well as those of the Narragansetts, from the Earl of Warwick and the Commission for Foreign Plantations. They had a signed copy of the deed of submission in their luggage for presentation to the king. Whether King Charles I ever laid eyes on it is doubtful. He had a great many pressing worries, being in the midst of a convulsive civil war. But the Narragansett deed of submission would come to the rescue of the Indians and the colony of Rhode Island. Unfortunately, it would take another twenty years and a different English king to put it into full effect.

WILLIAMS CONTINUES THE OFFENSIVE

By early 1644, Williams found himself busily engaged by the municipal government of London in supervising the collection of wood to heat city hearths—the coal supply to London from the north of England had been cut off by the king's forces. A man of seemingly boundless energy, Williams also found time to write, publish, and lobby for Rhode Island's charter. He hoped his writings would forward his cause with the Commission by raising his profile, but he wrote, too, for the higher purpose of shaping the direction of thinking in the English-speaking world on an issue that mattered as much to him as to any Englishman: religious liberty.

Mr. Cotton's Letter Examined and Answered, published in early February 1644, was a direct response to the publication in London of John Cotton's defense of Massachusetts's decision to banish Williams from Massachusetts Bay back in 1635. Where and when, Williams asked, did the government of Massachusetts gain authority to banish him from the *civil* community because he took issue with the ordinances of the *church's* practice in the colony? Why had he been—in his own words—"denied the common air to breathe in, and a civil cohabitation upon the same common earth" as other settlers simply for following the dictates of his conscience?[27]

Cotton had flatly denied that Massachusetts fused church and state power in banishing the dissenter. But the two were clearly intimately intertwined, "otherwise," wrote Williams, "why was I not permitted to live in the world, or commonweal, except for this reason, that the commonweal and church is yet but one, and he that is banished from one, must necessarily be banished from the other also."[28]

The thrust of Williams's argument led to vexing questions for which Cotton and Massachusetts had no good answers: Where in the New Testament did Christ persecute those who followed their own conscience in matters of belief? If Christ were to appear in New England, would He have banished people whose notions of worship differed from those of the established order? Williams evoked several powerful metaphors in this pamphlet that he would use again and again in later works in defense of the separation of church and state. He spoke of the spiritual and civil dangers of opening "a gap in the hedge or wall of separation between the garden of the Church and the Wilderness of the World."[29]

Mr. Cotton's Letter appeared in bookstalls only a month or two after news of Miantonomi's execution and the arrest of Samuel Gorton and his followers reached London—and the Commission for Foreign Plantations. Surely these unhappy developments across the Atlantic went some way toward confirming the impression among the commissioners that the United Colonies, spearheaded by Massachusetts, were abusing their authority in their dealings with both the Narragansetts and the English dissenters of Rhode Island.

A week or so after *Mr. Cotton's Letter* appeared, Williams weighed in with another pamphlet—this one directed at the Westminster Assembly, and its plan to impose a Presbyterian form of organization on the churches of England. Although it was published anonymously, *Queries of the Highest Consideration*'s radical defense of the complete separation of church and state, and Williams's prolix style, left no question as to its authorship. Where in the New Testament, asked Williams, had Christ given any king or civil power the authority to determine the ordinances of His church? During the reigns of all the English monarchs from Henry VIII through Charles I, conformity to the Church had been required of all Englishmen, but the nature of the Church and the manner and style of worship had changed under every monarch. The state's enforcement of the whims of the monarchs in matters of religion amounted to nothing less than spiritual corruption.

Besides, hadn't enforced worship led to constant bloodshed in the name of a God who stood for peace? "We query whether the blood of so many hundred thousand Protestants, mingled with the blood of so many hundred thousand papists" since the Reformation "be not a warning to us their offspring?"[30] *Queries* concluded that religious persecution was a violation of the Christian spirit, that the human soul was violated by enforced worship, and that religious warfare in defense of the "true" church had been the chief disturber of the civil peace for centuries.

While Williams had been scribbling away writing pamphlets, he continued to lobby for the charter by every means at his disposal. Probably he pressed everyone in his growing circle of admirers to weigh in with their own influential contacts, with a view to shaping the outlook of the commissioners. Meanwhile, Vane and Warwick busied themselves trying to bring the skeptics among the decision makers around to the idea of granting Williams the sort of charter he felt he needed.

About a month after the publication of *Queries*—on March 14, 1644—the great seal of the state of England was affixed to a "Free Charter of Civil Incorporation and Government" for the colony of "Providence Plantations, in the Narragansett Bay, in New England." The charter granted

> to the inhabitants of the towns of Providence, Portsmouth, and Newport, . . . full power and authority to govern and rule themselves, and such others as shall hereafter inhabit within any part of the said tract of land, by such a form of civil government, as by voluntary consent of all, or the greater part of them, they shall find most suitable to their estate and conditions; and, for that end, to make and ordain such civil laws and constitutions, and to inflict such punishments upon transgressors, and for execution thereof, so to place, and displace officers of justice, as they, or the greater part of them, shall by free Consent agree unto. Provided nevertheless, that the said laws, constitutions, and punishments, for the civil government of the said plantations, be conformable to the laws of England, so far as the nature and constitution of the place will admit.[31]

Williams must have been elated—and relieved—beyond measure, for he had achieved an astonishing victory. He had gotten precisely what he wanted for the struggling, besieged towns of Narragansett Bay and gained a strong measure of protection for the Narragansetts as well, insofar as the charter included their territory within Rhode Island's jurisdiction. The experiment would go forward, anchored on the rock of unambiguous parliamentary authority. Nowhere else in the English-speaking world were people given such broad latitude to construct a community precisely as they saw fit, without outside interference or proscription.

Even after Parliament's rising fortunes in the struggle against the king led to the formation of Lord Rich's Commission, the odds against the establishment of a colony based on religious liberty, majority rule, and a strictly civil form of democratic government were long indeed. Massachusetts had stronger and more numerous allies in Parliament than Williams; its argument for territorial expansion in view of its rapidly expanding population and influence was certainly compelling.

How, then, did Williams gain his prize? The language of the preamble to the charter hints strongly that prior possession of the land in question, and peaceful relations with the Indians, factored into the equation:

> . . . whereas diverse well-affected and industrious English inhabitants of the towns of Providence, Portsmouth, and Newport in the tract aforesaid, [had] adventured to make a nearer neighborhood to, and society with, the great body of the Narragansetts, which [might] in time, by the blessing of God upon their endeavor, lay a surer foundation of happiness to all America.[32]

Surely, too, *A Key into the Language of America* had inspired confidence among the commissioners that under Williams's enlightened direction, the strained relationship between New England's most powerful Indian tribe and the English could be expected to take a more congenial course. Besides, Massachusetts Bay's recent initiatives against the Narragansetts and the Gortonists went far

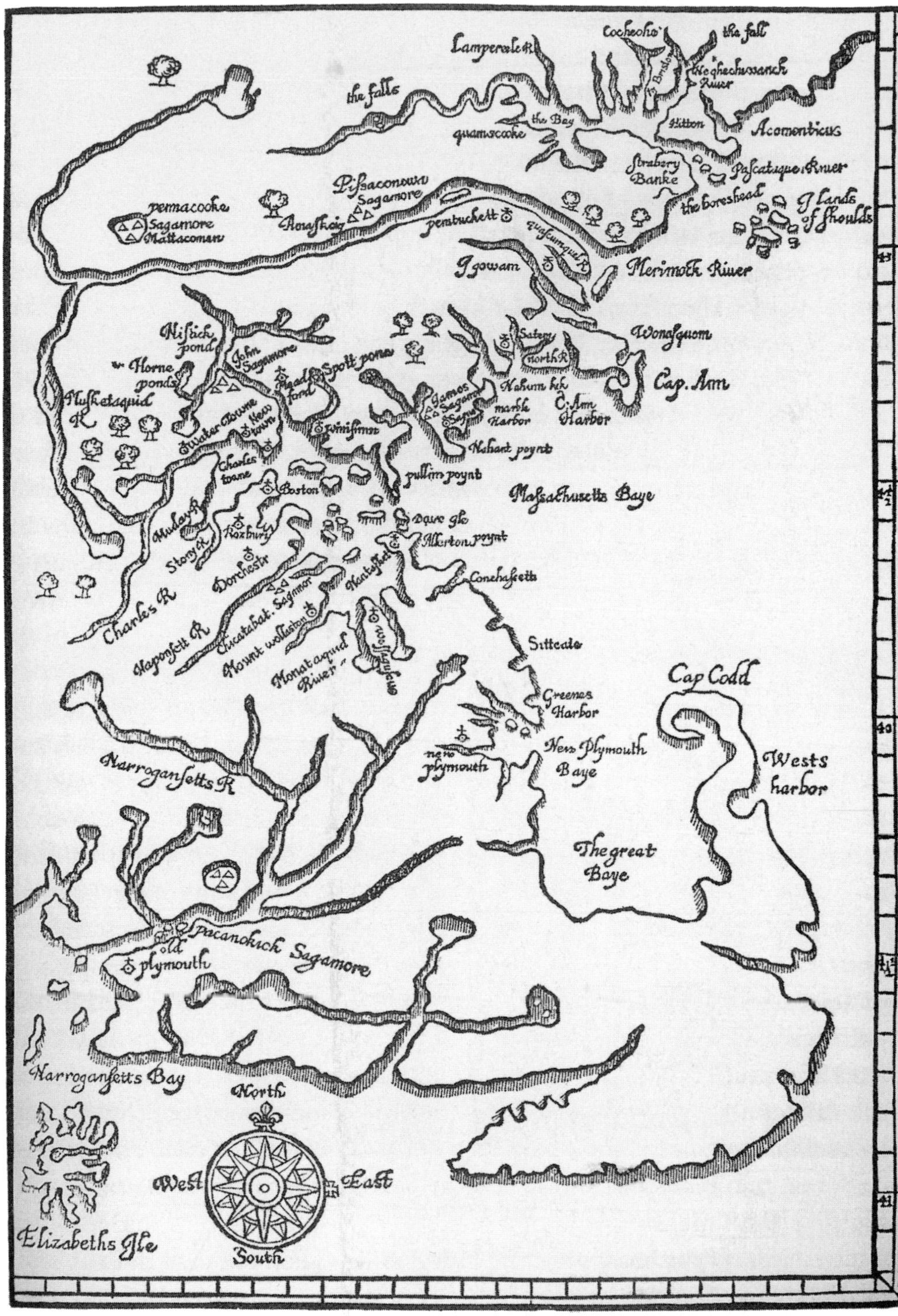

The map that appeared in William Wood's classic book *New England's Prospect*, the first truly reliable account of what life was like in New England during the earliest years of settlement.

2

Unknown nineteenth-century artist's interpretation of Roger Williams's initial landing in Providence in April 1636. The Indians are standing on Slate Rock, Rhode Island's answer to Plymouth Rock. In 1877, Providence workers accidentally blew up the rock while trying to expose it in its entirety.

3

A portrait of John Winthrop, the longtime governor of Massachusetts Bay Colony, and Williams's confidant and mentor. Winthrop urged Williams to settle among the Narragansetts after his banishment. The two Puritans conducted a lively and historically significant correspondence for many years.

4

An artist's rendering of Roger Williams, though what he looked like is anyone's guess. He never sat for a portrait. Either he was excessively modest, or he simply couldn't spare the time.

5

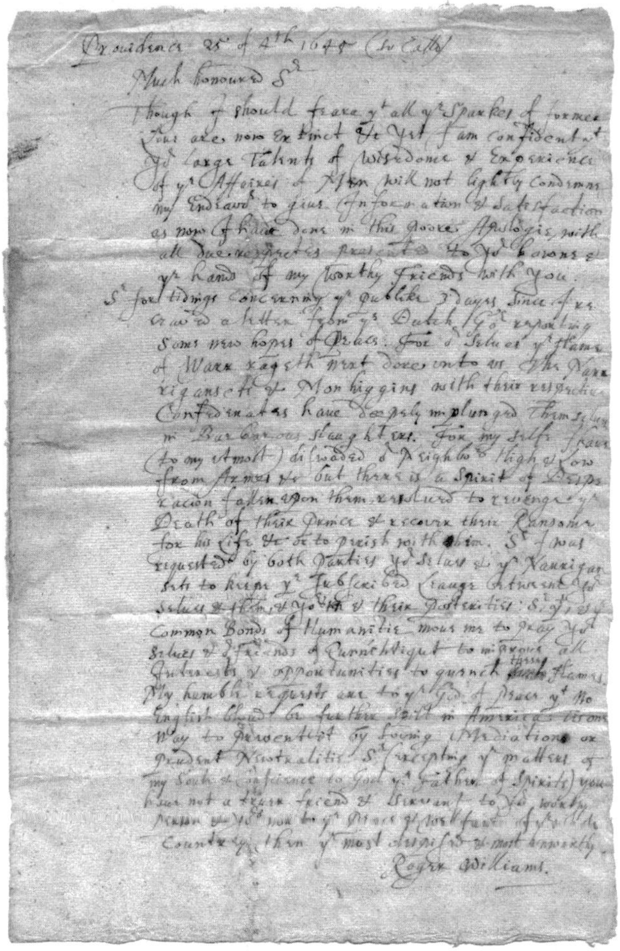

Providence 25 of 4th 1645 (so calld)

Much honoured Sir

Though I should feare that all your Sparkes of former Love are now Extinct &c yet I am confident that your large Talents of Wisedome & Experience of the Affaires of Men will not lightly Condemne my Endeavors to give Information & Satisfaction as now I have done in this poore Apologie, with all due respects presented to your Lovinge hand & my worthy friends with you.

Sir For tidings concerning the publike 3 dayes since I receaved a letter from the Dutch Governor reporting some new hopes of Peace. For your selves the flame of Warre rageth next doore unto us. The Narrigansetts & Monhiggins with their respective Confederates have deeply imbrued themselves in barbarous slaughter. For my selfe I have (to my utmost) dissuaded our Neighbours high & low from Armes &c but there is a Spirit of Desperacion fallen upon them resolved to revenge the Death of their Prince & recover their Ransome for his Life &c or to perish with him. Sir I was requested by both parties your selves & the Narrigansetts to keepe the subscribed League betweene your selves & them, & your & their posterities. Sir, the Common Bonds of Humanitie move me to pray your selves & friends of Qunnihticut to improve all Interests & opportunities to quench these flames. My humble requests are to the God of Peace that no English blood be further spilt in America: from any way to prevent it by loving Mediations or prudent Neutralitie. Sir (excepting the matters of my Soule & Conscience to God the Father of Spirits) you have not a truer friend & servant to your worthy person & yours nor to the Peace & welfare of your whole Country then the most despised & most unworthy

Roger Williams.

The last of Williams's many extant letters to John Winthrop. Williams begins by apologizing for some unknown breach in their friendship, and goes on to offer advice on how Massachusetts should respond to the outbreak of fighting between the Narragansetts and the Mohegans. Indian-English relations is a dominant theme throughout Williams's correspondence.

6

A historically accurate portrait of a Native American sachem, believed by some authorities to be Ninigret's son, the Niantic sachem Ninigret II. The Niantics were allowed to live in peace after King Philip's War in their own territory because they had remained neutral in the fighting.

7

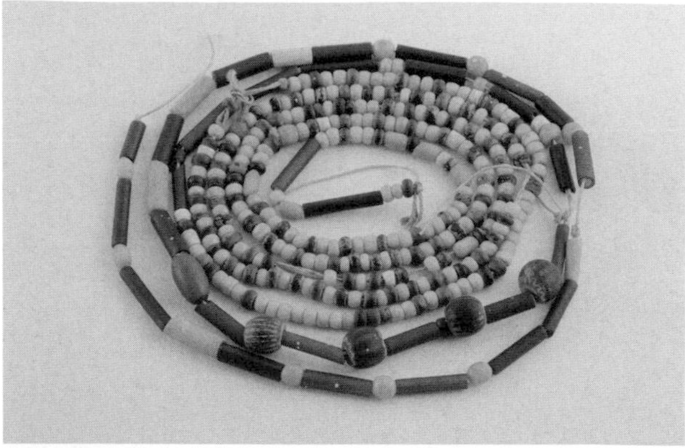

8

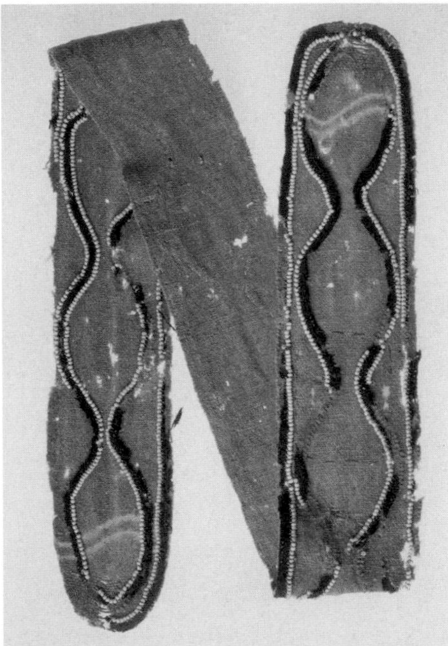

Wampum, minted in the twentieth century, and a variety of mid–seventeenth century artifacts, including a decorative sash, an eel trap, and a basket, all Wampanoag in origin; a soapstone pipe; and a beautifully carved wooden bowl. All artifacts were found by archaeologists in Rhode Island. The increasing availability of European goods led to the decline of traditional Indian manufacturing in the late seventeenth century.

9

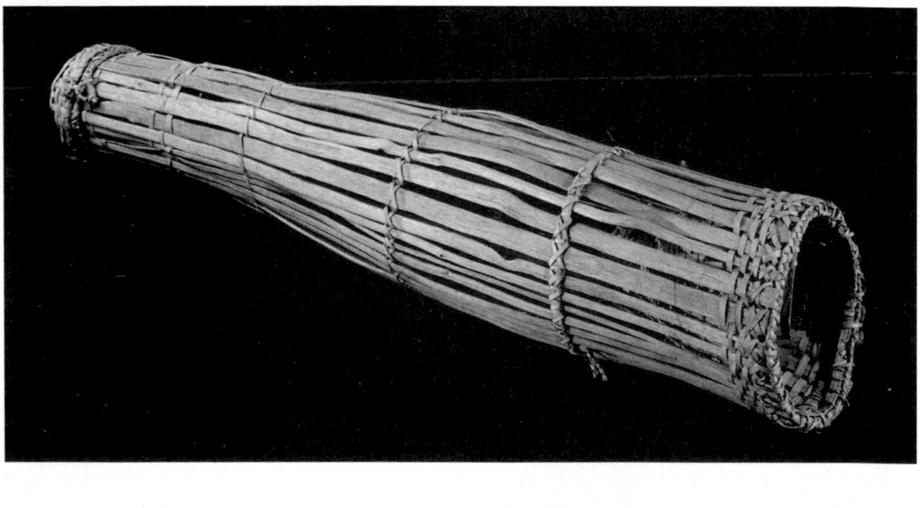

10

11

12

13

John Winthrop Jr., Connecticut's urbane and enterprising London agent, obtained a royal charter for the colony in 1662 that included the Narragansett Country within its boundaries. John Clarke of Rhode Island persuaded royal officials to void Connecticut's initial charter and to include the Narragansett country within the boundaries of Rhode Island.

14

ROBERT Earl of WARWICK
and Lord RICH of LEEZ. &c.
47

Robert Rich, who presided over the commission that granted Rhode Island the 1644 charter.

15

Sir Henry Vane Jr., Williams's close friend and the only commission member to have visited America.

17

King Charles II, who granted Rhode Island's 1663 charter, and sent out royal commissioners to New England to address myriad complaints from English settlers and Indians alike against Massachusetts.

16

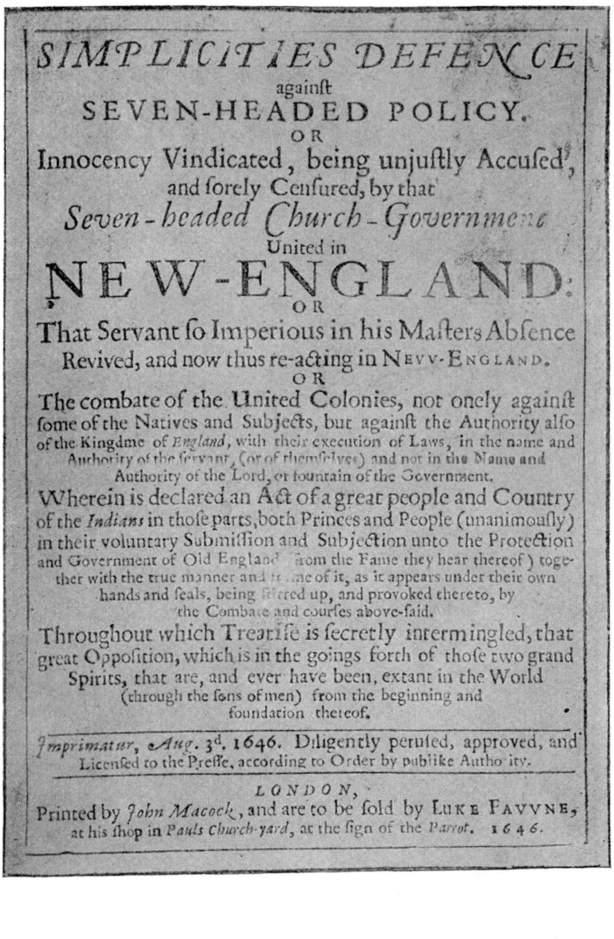

SIMPLICITIES DEFENCE
againſt
SEVEN-HEADED POLICY.
OR
Innocency Vindicated, being unjuſtly Accuſed, and ſorely Cenſured, by that
Seven-headed Church-Government
United in
NEW-ENGLAND:
OR
That Servant ſo Imperious in his Maſters Abſence Revived, and now thus re-acting in NEVV-ENGLAND.
OR
The combate of the United Colonies, not onely againſt ſome of the Natives and Subjects, but againſt the Authority alſo of the Kingdome of *England*, with their execution of Laws, in the name and Authority of the ſervant, (or of themſelves) and not in the Name and Authority of the Lord, or fountain of the Government.
Wherein is declared an Act of a great people and Country of the *Indians* in thoſe parts, both Princes and People (unanimouſly) in their voluntary Submiſſion and Subjection unto the Protection and Government of Old England (from the Fame they hear thereof) together with the true manner and [illegible] of it, as it appears under their own hands and ſeals, being ſtirred up, and provoked thereto, by the Combate and courſes above-ſaid.
Throughout which Treatiſe is ſecretly intermingled, that great Oppoſition, which is in the goings forth of thoſe two grand Spirits, that are, and ever have been, extant in the World (through the ſons of men) from the beginning and foundation thereof.

Imprimatur, *Aug.* 3d. 1646. Diligently peruſed, approved, and Licenſed to the Preſſe, according to Order by publike Authority.

LONDON,
Printed by *John Macock*, and are to be ſold by LUKE FAVVNE, at his ſhop in *Pauls Church-yard*, at the ſign of the *Parrot*. 1646.

Samuel Gorton's most famous book, *Simplicities Defence Against Seven-Headed Policy*, published in 1646 in London, detailed the injustices inflicted against the Shawomet settlers by the Bay Colony.

18

No one today has any notion of what King Philip—alias Metacomet—or Roger Williams looked like, but many artists over the centuries have created idealized portraits of both men. Here are two fine examples: The illustration of Philip is by a nineteenth-century artist and the statue of Williams is located on the main campus of Roger Williams University in Bristol, Rhode Island.

19

to confirm it was committed to a reckless policy of bullying its neighbors. The Gortonists, Rhode Island's many other dissenters, and their Indian friends plainly needed parliamentary protection; they were on the verge of being overrun.

Confidence in Williams stemmed from more than his work among the Indians. In London, as in Salem and Plymouth, Williams's integrity, intelligence, and charisma were quickly recognized, even among his ideological opponents. Robert Baillie, the Presbyterian clergyman from Glasgow, assailed Roger Williams for his "extreme mistakes" in matters of church governance, but Baillie made note as well of "the man's great sincerity though in an erroneous way, and of his disposition which is without fault as I conceive. . . . I would be loath in any point of fact to call his testimony into question . . . and have thought him fitted with many good endowments for eminent service to Christ."[33] Probably most of the eleven signers of the Providence Plantations charter had come to feel similarly about Williams, at least so far as "eminent service" was concerned.

Finally, Williams's most recent biographer has surmised that Williams pitched his vision of the new colony before the commissioners as "a test, an experiment" in a new form of governance, a new way of structuring society. "It was safely isolated from England. If the committee granted a charter . . . all England could watch the results."[34]

The charter's grant of "full power and authority" to the people to govern themselves according to majority rule was extraordinary, considering the general reputation of Rhode Island as a repository of heretics and riffraff. In fact, as of 1644, the colony of Rhode Island was the only place in the Western world where unfettered religious liberty and majority rule flourished.

In securing the new charter, Roger Williams had trumped the best efforts of Weld and Peter to secure jurisdiction of Rhode Island for Massachusetts Bay. No doubt under intense pressure to produce some sort of claim to Rhode Island, Weld sent back to Boston a "Narragansett patent," dated November 10, 1643, bearing the signatures of nine commissioners and presented it as a legitimate document. But it was not. The Narragansett patent was fraudulent: it had never been formally enrolled on the Commission's agenda for discussion, bore no great seal, and was dated on a Sunday. The English government did no business on the Lord's Day. As we shall later see, these egregious defects in the document failed to dissuade the Massachusetts General Court from deploying the document as a weapon in its long war against Rhode Island's sovereignty.

THE BLOUDY TENENT

Before returning to America, Roger Williams had one more contribution to make to the transatlantic debates swirling around the great questions of religious freedom and the nature of good government—and it was hefty. In late spring he finished the manuscript for *The Bloudy Tenent of Persecution for cause of Conscience, discussed, in a conference between Truth and Peace.* The prose is often turgid and the syntax difficult to follow, for *The Bloudy Tenent* was a hurriedly written book by an author with a penchant for run-on sentences. "These meditations," wrote Williams, "were fitted for public view in change of rooms and corners, yea, sometimes in variety of strange houses, sometimes in the fields, in the midst of travel where [the author] hath been forced to gather and scatter his loose thoughts and papers."[35]

But *The Bloudy Tenent* is also profound, universally recognized today as a classic Christian defense of religious liberty and democratic government. Williams's argument for freedom of conscience and strict separation of church and state is rooted in Scripture, but well supported by arguments drawing on history and general experience.

The Bloudy Tenent's core premise is that "it is the will and command of God, that since the coming of His Son the Lord Jesus, a permission of the most paganish, Jewish, Turkish, or antichristian consciences and worships, be granted in all nations and countries."[36] Christ in his time on earth "never appointed the civil sword for either antidote or remedy" of error concerning those who refused to accept Him as the son of God.[37] The only weapons employed by the Prince of Peace in matters of belief were gentle persuasion and love.

The orthodox Puritan belief that civil leaders possessed divine authority to make judgments about men's souls was a dangerous misconception, Williams argued. Only Christ's church had divine authority, and that authority extended to spiritual matters only. Magistrates must restrict their activities to protecting the bodies and goods of all members of the community and leave their souls to the church, and God.

All too often, the defense of religious orthodoxy by civil powers had a worldly, political end in view. While it was true, as the authorities of Massachusetts preached, that God had granted the leaders of ancient Israel civil and religious powers, wrote Williams, the Massachusetts authorities failed to recognize that, with the birth of Christ, God had dissolved His covenant with Israel and had never established a new covenant with another nation. That included England, no matter how deeply its Puritans believed otherwise.

Since the incarnation—the arrival of Christ on earth as both man and God—only individual men gathered together in discrete churches could be said to be in covenant with God, and the ministers of those churches, explains Edmund Morgan in his brilliant book on Williams's thought, "were forbidden by their founder to propagate or defend His religion by force. Israel could send forth its armies to smite the heathen. But no body of men who now employed force in defense of religion could claim the name Christian. Force could be exercised only in support of false, unchristian religions."[38]

Drawing on recent English history, Williams elaborated at length on an argument he had made in *Queries of the Highest Consideration*. Every monarch since Henry VIII had defined Christian faith and worship according to his or her own dictates, subjecting what was divine and eternal to the distortions and prejudices of the current moment. Full knowledge of the mystery of Christ and His church should instill humility and tolerance: "The experience of our fathers' errors, our own mistakes and ignorance, the sense of our weaknesses and blindness in the depths of the prophesies and mysteries of the kingdom of Christ, and the great professed expectation of light to come which we are not able to comprehend, may abate the edge, yea sheath up the sword of persecution toward any."[39]

Religious persecution had led to countless wars and great bloodshed throughout history. The elimination of religion from the sphere of civil government that Williams imagined offered the blessed promise of civil peace. The only thing government could do, should do, regarding religion was to protect citizens from coercion in matters of the conscience so they could pursue God's truth as they saw fit. "The Puritan tended to think of truth as a visible treasure in need of protection," observes scholar Timothy Hall, while "Williams saw it more frequently as a jewel in need of discovery."[40]

The Bloudy Tenent boldly challenged the conventional wisdom that civility and good government were unobtainable without enforced acceptance of Christian belief by Christian rulers. Many successful societies and governments had been created and maintained by non-Christians, Williams argued. All peoples had a capacity to identify a set of social norms and values, a kind of universal morality, permitting them to distinguish right from wrong. The last six commandments God had delivered to Moses, none of which concerned religion per se, constituted "the law moral and civil." And that law was intended for all men to follow, regardless of their faith.[41]

This was not to say every society should follow a uniform code of law or ethics. The members of every civil community must deliberate and come to their own conclusions on specific laws and standards of behavior. Williams expected those laws and codes to reflect the different backgrounds and perspectives of the populace. Civil government *alone* bore responsibility for establishing the boundaries of socially acceptable, ethical behavior, though religious piety and church attendance had a salutary effect on how people lived their day-to-day lives.

For civil government to work, it was essential that freedom of conscience be vigilantly protected. As Williams explained in a pamphlet he wrote in the early 1650s, it was "the duty of the civil magistrates to suppress all violences to the bodies and goods of men . . . and to provide that not one person in the land be restrained from or constrained to any worship, ministry, or maintenance, but peaceably maintained in his soul, as well as corporal freedom."[42]

Civil government ultimately derived its powers not from the authority of God, or divinely appointed rulers, but from the will of the ordinary members of the community:

> The sovereign, original and foundation of civil power lies in the people. . . . And if so, than a people may erect and establish what form of government seems to them most meet for their civil condition: It is evident that such governments as are by them erected and established, have no more power, nor for any longer time, than the civil power or people consenting and agreeing shall betrust them with. This is clear not only in reason, but in the experience of all commonweals where the people are not deprived of their natural freedom by the power of tyrants.[43]

Here *The Bloudy Tenent* anticipates the thinking of the great English philosopher John Locke, whose work had such a profound effect on the political worldview of the founding fathers of the

United States. Many scholars believe Locke's seminal treatises on government bear the influence of Williams's *Bloudy Tenent*, though Locke never cites Williams's work by name.

The Bloudy Tenent reached conclusions so radical for the mid-seventeenth century that even tolerationists found it outrageous. Just a few weeks after its publication on July 15, Parliament ordered the book burned by the public hangman. If the state were to permit religious error to flourish as *The Bloudy Tenent* proposed, opined Robert Baillie, then why not let men and women do as they wished in more mundane matters? Crime and vice were bound to flourish if people were permitted to follow the dictates of their own conscience without correction from their ministers. Baillie and the vast majority of other English divines and political thinkers thought Williams's "soul liberty" was a recipe for the breakdown of social order. Moreover, such liberty, by opening the door for depravity, was sure to bring the wrath of God down on England and her people.

On August 9, several members of Parliament rose to condemn Williams's book, calling attention to the terrible dangers of tolerating blasphemy. But the work had made an indelible mark. Between 1644 and 1649, at least 60 pamphlets directly addressed Williams's arguments in *The Bloudy Tenent*, and more than 120 quoted his book.[44]

By the time *The Bloudy Tenent* was in the bookstalls, though, Williams was on the roiling Atlantic, sailing back to America, mulling over the implementation of the charter, and longing to see his wife and family. A triumphant Williams disembarked in Boston on September 17, 1644, and proffered the following letter of safe passage to the authorities there, along with a copy of his treasured charter. The letter was signed by a number of prominent men in Parliament's struggle against the king, including Oliver St. John, William Masham, Thomas Barrington, and the former mayor of

London, Isaac Pennington. It testified to the high standing in which Roger Williams was held among people of substance, and read in part:

> Taking notice, some of us of long time, of Mr. Roger Williams his good affections and conscience, and of his sufferings by our common enemies and oppressors of God's people, the prelates, as also of his great industry and travels in his printed Indian labours in your parts (the like whereof we have not seen extant from any part of America) and in which respect it hath pleased both houses of parliament to grant unto him and friends with him a free and absolute charter of civil government for those parts of his abode, and withal sorrowfully resenting, that amongst good men (our friends) driven to the ends of the world, exercised with the trials of the wilderness, and who mutually give good testimony each of other, as we observe you do of him, and he abundant of you, there should be such a distance; we thought it fit . . . to profess our great desires of both your utmost endeavours of nearer closing.[45]

The governor of Massachusetts, John Endicott, an old friend and admirer of Williams's, read the letter, but after seeking the advice of other colony authorities, decided not to revoke the order of banishment. Williams would be allowed to pass through Massachusetts to Providence unmolested. That was all, but that was quite enough.

Word spread quickly among the Narragansett towns that their emissary had at last returned to American shores, and that his mission had been a brilliant success. If legend has it right, men, women, and children, Indian and English alike, began to gather along the western banks of the Seekonk River to welcome Roger Williams home. As he crossed the Seekonk, he was met by fourteen canoes full of grateful well-wishers from the Providence side and ushered to the shore of the town he had founded, where he was embraced and cheered. He appeared to one observer that day to be "elevated and transported out of himself."[46] The hard work of building an experimental colony—and fending off a Puritan colossus that did not want that colony built—was about to begin.

Chapter 7

Rumors of War, Unity at Last, 1644–57

E. Boyd Smith's 1920 imaginative reconstruction of Roger Williams's return to Providence with the colony's first charter. Granted by Parliament's Commission for Foreign Plantations, the charter almost certainly prevented the Puritan colonies from annexing Rhode Island in the mid–seventeenth century.

The unrelenting hostility of the New England oligarchy toward Rhode Island and the Narragansetts, coupled with the weakness of the colony's government, ensured that the 1640s and 1650s would be turbulent years in Williams's haven "for persons distressed of conscience." The initial steps taken by the Narragansett Bay towns toward unification under the new charter were halting, sporadic, and often challenged by the Puritan establishment. Rhode

Island's first constitutional convention—in essence, a general assembly consisting of all the freemen in the four towns—met for the first time in November of 1644, elected a handful of colony officers, and established basic principles of government.

No minutes of the debates, no documents charting the decisions worked out in this early exercise in direct democracy, have survived. One of the few facts that the earliest secondary sources seem to agree on is that Roger Williams was elected "chief officer" of the colony. From late 1644 until November of 1647, the colonial government met only a handful of times at irregular intervals, and then, it seems, only to respond to imminent crisis.

Ironically, the reactions of Rhode Island's hostile neighbors to the colony's first efforts to form a government under its new charter are far better documented than the effort itself. The governor of Plymouth, William Bradford, sent off a letter of protest to the Commission for Foreign Plantations, arguing strenuously that parts of the Rhode Island mainland, and all of Aquidneck and Conanicut (modern Jamestown) Islands, fell within Plymouth's borders. Bradford dispatched magistrate John Brown to Aquidneck to inform the officials there that "a great part of their supposed [colony] government is within the line of the government of New Plymouth," and to forbid the Rhode Islanders from exercising authority inside its jurisdiction.[1] The letter apparently prompted no response from the commissioners.

From the outset, Massachusetts acted as if Williams's charter were a work of fiction. It continued to maintain its jurisdiction over Pawtuxet and Shawomet, and to keep a sharp eye out for ways to expand its presence around Narragansett Bay. Connecticut, for its part, was willing to let the rabble of heretics run their own show on Aquidneck, and in Providence and Shawomet, but it cast a covetous eye on all the lands south of Shawomet inhabited by the Narragansett and Niantic Indians. Disputes over jurisdiction of the Narragansett country would go on continuously for the better part of a century.

Massachusetts, though, did more than any other colony, or any internal dispute—and there were plenty of those—to prevent the emergence of effective government in Rhode Island. Under an administration led by Williams and a handful of others who shared his commitment to rudimentary democracy, the fledgling colony threatened to become a beacon for dissenters, and a repository of critics of the New England Way. The Boston magistrates watched with alarm as the Narragansett towns slowly drew in more and more undesirables, just as its own government was coming under steadily increasing pressure from influential Puritan clergy and parliamentarians in England to ease up on religious persecution and imperial overreach.

Meanwhile, the simmering disputes between the Narragansetts and the United Colonies threatened to break out into general war on several occasions during these years. Naturally, the volatile relationship between the Puritans and the Narragansetts was an abiding concern for Williams and the other leading men of Rhode Island. They were allies of the Narragansetts and well aware that war between those two parties would have disastrous repercussions for the colony as well as the Indians who dwelled within its borders.

THE NARRAGANSETTS VERSUS THE MOHEGANS

When we last left Pessacus and Canonicus, it was late May 1644—a few months before Williams returned to Rhode Island with the charter. The sachems had just confirmed their formal submission to King Charles and declared themselves free of the constraints on their actions concerning inter-Indian affairs imposed by the Hartford Treaty of 1638. They intended to make war on Uncas to exact retribution for Miantonomi's death, as required by Indian tradition. As the Narragansett messenger Wahose had explained to Governor Winthrop in Boston in February 1644, Miantonomi's

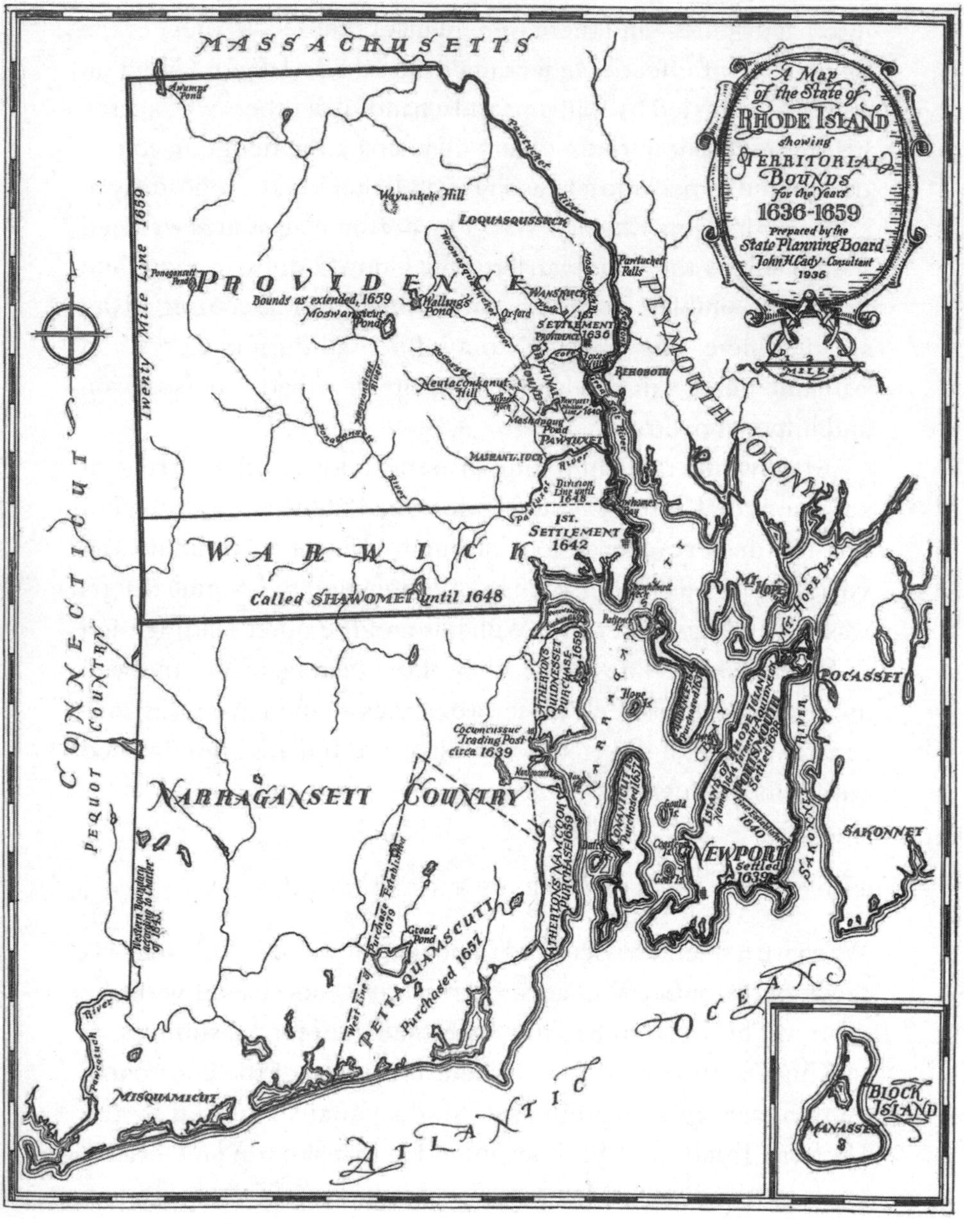

John Hutchins Cady's meticulous map of Rhode Island, 1636 to 1659, showing territorial boundaries and major land purchases.

soul wandered alone in the spirit world. He could not rest—nor could his people—until retribution had been exacted.[2]

In late May or early June, the sachems proved as good as their word. Powerful Narragansett raiding parties began to menace Mohegan villages. In a single raid on a Mohegan village, Narragansett warriors killed six Mohegans, including four high-ranking men of the tribe. A handful of Narragansett tributaries in Connecticut joined in harassing Mohegan hunting bands; others pledged their resolve to join in the fighting should the Narragansetts initiate a general war.

With Uncas remaining on the defensive late into the summer, the commissioners of the United Colonies called upon the Narragansett sachems and Uncas to attend a conference in Hartford in September. Pessacus, widely considered the leading Narragansett sachem in the years immediately after his brother's execution, was too disgusted with the English to go himself, so he sent a delegation of minor sachems. These emissaries strenuously pressed the case against Uncas, reiterating the demand for the return of the 160 fathoms of wampum the tribe had paid the Mohegans to spare Miantonomi's life.

Predictably, the commissioners did not record the substance of the Narragansett testimony regarding the ransom. They merely indicated that they themselves "did not find any proof of any ransom agreed." This statement reveals the Puritans' deep bias against the Narragansetts, for they were well aware that Miantonomi's status as a leading sachem meant the tribe would have done everything possible to save his life. Nonetheless, the Mohegans and Narragansetts agreed to remain at peace, at least until "after the next planting time."[3]

The commissioners' refusal to pressure Uncas for repayment of the ransom only hardened already strong beliefs among the Narragansetts of blatant English favoritism toward the Mohegans. The truce was short-lived. In the spring of 1645, Narragansett and

Niantic raiders once again crossed the Pawcatuck and attacked several Mohegan villages. Ninigret had arranged for several bands of Montauk warriors to cross the sound and join in the raids. In early June, almost a thousand Narragansett and Niantic warriors crossed the Pawcatuck and fought a daylong engagement, inflicting heavy casualties on Uncas's fighters. More raids followed. Sensing that momentum in the conflict was with the Narragansetts, several Pequot bands in eastern Connecticut joined in the attacks against their former Mohegan minders.

According to one reliable source, Uncas's bands were forced to repair to the comparative safety of the large, palisaded Mohegan fort at Shantok near Norwich, Connecticut. There, they were besieged for about a week by the Narragansetts.[4] Uncas sent for help from his English friends in Hartford, and both Connecticut and New Haven colonies sent out forces to prevent their ally's demise. The arrival of English cavalry appears to have caused the Narragansett forces to break off the siege and return to their home territory. In late June, Williams penned a letter to Winthrop, imploring the authorities to mediate the dispute with a measure of impartiality:

> For ourselves the flames of war rage next door unto us. The Narragansetts and Mohegans with their respective confederates have deeply implunged themselves in barbarous slaughters. For myself I have (to my utmost) dissuaded our neighbors high and low from arms, but there is a spirit of desperation fallen upon them, [they are] resolved to revenge the death of their prince and recover their ransom for his life etc. or to perish with him. Sir, I was requested by both parties your selves and the Narragansetts to keep the subscribed league between your selves and them . . . that, and the common bonds of humanity, move me to pray [to] yourselves and our friends of Connecticut to improve all interests and opportunities to quench these flames.

> My humble requests are to the God of Peace that no English blood be further spilled in America. One way to prevent it [is] by loving mediation or prudent neutrality.[5]

With Uncas on the defensive, the commissioners of the United Colonies met in an emergency session in Boston in late July. Messengers were again dispatched to the Narragansett sachems, imploring them to call a halt to the fighting and promising them a fair hearing to air their grievances. Pessacus and Ninigret demurred—rather abruptly, it seems, and it's not hard to see why. The commissioners and the General Court in Boston had often promised the Narragansetts a fair hearing, but their words were invariably belied by their actions. Ninigret was deeply frustrated with English favoritism and meddling. According to Winthrop's account of the meeting, the Niantic chief was

> resolved to have no peace without Uncas his head [i.e., until Uncas was killed], it mattered not who began the war, they were resolved to continue it, the English should withdraw their garrison from Uncas, or they would take it as a break of former covenants [i.e., the 1636 treaty of friendship between Massachusetts and the Narragansetts, the Hartford Treaty of 1638], and would procure as many Mohawks as they the English should affront them with, that they would lay the English cattle on heaps as high as their houses, that no English man should stir out of his door to piss, but he should be killed.[6]

The commissioners ignored Williams's advice, as they usually did when he advocated respect and fair-mindedness over intimidation in dealing with the Narragansett Indians. Instead of "loving mediation" or "prudent neutrality," the commissioners raised the iron fist. The United Colonies declared war on the Narragansetts and the Niantics. An army of three hundred troops was raised, under the command of Major Edward Gibbons. His orders were to "prosecute with force of arms the said Narragansetts and Niantics . . . until you may (through the Lord's assistance) have subdued them or brought them to reason."[7]

A long, detailed justification of the decision to declare war, written by Winthrop, was entered into the official United Colonies records. In keeping with many earlier Puritan documents, the "Declaration of Former Passages and Proceedings betwixt the English and Narrohiggansets" failed even to acknowledge that the Rhode Island Indians had a legitimate grievance with either the Puritans themselves or the Mohegans. Writing as if the United Colonies had bent over backward to conciliate the Narragansetts, Winthrop opined that the commissioners "cannot but exercise force, when no other means will prevail, to reduce the Narragansetts and their confederates to a more just and sober temper."[8]

Gibbons and a small advance party traveled by horse to Providence in the hopes of resolving matters peacefully before initiating an attack. The Puritan commander attempted to secure Benedict Arnold to serve as translator. Arnold was not to be found, but Roger Williams was more than willing to be of service. This was a good thing all around, for the Indians did not trust Arnold as a translator. They did trust Williams, and he proved adept, yet again, at defusing a highly volatile situation.

He again advocated negotiation and compromise as the only way to avert a war that was likely to have catastrophic consequences. Canonicus and the other sachems, well aware that their allies the Mohawks were not about to join them in a full-fledged war against a powerful English army—that had been a bluff—agreed to come to Boston to negotiate a settlement.

Pessacus, Mixan, Canonicus's eldest son, and Aumsaaquen, one of Ninigret's most trusted men, along with a large retinue of their warriors, arrived in Boston a few days after Williams's intervention. If the Narragansetts thought they might be able to work out a reasonable compromise, they were very much mistaken. The commissioners read the Narragansetts' decision to talk in Boston as an indication of weakness. They intended to make the most of it.

The Narragansett delegation laid out its extensive list of grievances against Uncas. The commissioners, once again, were having none of it. The Narragansetts had been a continual source of frustration and expense to the United Colonies, to say nothing of what they had cost Uncas in their recent incursions. After many hours of heated negotiations, the commissioners made it clear that the Narragansetts faced a stark choice: a costly and humiliating settlement—or an English invasion of Narragansett country.

With great reluctance, the sachems chose the settlement. Under the terms of the agreement, the Narragansett confederation agreed to pay reparations of *two thousand fathoms* in four installments over two years—a sum that appears to be considerably larger than any other indemnity levied against an Indian polity by the English in New England in the seventeenth century. The best estimate we have for determining the number of individual workdays it would take to produce such a quantity derives from a report by the Dutch in 1654, which calculated that it took a skilled Indian minter about ten full days of work to produce a single fathom. Thus, it would take about twenty thousand individual workdays to produce two thousand fathoms.[9]

In addition, the Narragansetts agreed not to sell any of their lands without the consent of the commissioners, and to forfeit all hunting and fishing rights in the Pequot country forever. Future disputes with Uncas or any other Indians had to be put before the commissioners of the United Colonies for consideration. In other words, the commissioners were dismissing out of hand the Narragansetts' contention that as subjects under the same king, the commissioners had no legal standing to exert authority over them. Finally, four sons of Narragansett sachems were to be held hostage until the reparation payments were completed.

This harsh "agreement" had a number of interlocking purposes: it was meant to hamstring Narragansett diplomatic and military activity; to diminish the confederation's prestige among potential tributaries; to break the tribe's resolve to resist Puritan encroachment on their autonomy; and finally to fill the coffers of the United Colonies at the Narragansetts' expense. The treaty of August 27, 1645, bears a strong resemblance to the armistice imposed on Germany at the end of World War I, in that it placed punitive demands on the vanquished party, thereby exacerbating its grievances rather than laying the groundwork for a stable peace. It was designed to humiliate and humble. As if to throw salt in the wounds, the United Colonies announced that they would allocate one hundred fathoms of the reparations paid by the Narragansetts directly to Uncas, in recognition of their collective failure to provide him with timely aid during his recent travails.

Pessacus was later heard to remark that the Narragansetts had been coerced into signing the 1645 treaty at the point of a gun and therefore did not regard it as binding. That statement goes far in explaining the diplomatic strategy the Narragansett sachems would take over the coming years in dealing with the English. The chief architect of that strategy, though, was clearly Ninigret, not Pessacus or Mixan. Among all the Narragansett sachems in the seventeenth century after Miantonomi, Ninigret seems to have most fully grasped the essence of the Puritans' expansionist designs, and how the Narragansetts could best counter them, given their limited resources and the steadily growing power of the United Colonies. He showed few signs of being intimidated by Puritan military might. His future actions tell us that he believed the tribe had little choice but to adopt the Puritan diplomatic tactic of deliberately failing to make good on promises made at the conference table—if those promises did not work to the tribe's long-term advantage.

What exactly did this mean in practice? Insofar as it was possible, the terms of the treaty of 1645 would be passively resisted, ignored, and on occasion defied. Incremental payments on the massive fine would need to be made to avoid a Puritan invasion. But they could be made on a much more forgiving schedule than the one specified in the agreement. Far better to allocate scarce wampum to purchasing firearms and gifts for various Indian bands to forge new alliances than to turn over large installments in a timely fashion to the United Colonies.

Ninigret was confident that he could buy more time to make the payments. Despite the treaty's prohibition, Narragansett and Niantic hunting parties would continue to be dispatched to the Pequot country—the tribe had earned that right by its participation in the Pequot War. Meanwhile, the Narragansett confederation would continue by various means to extract retribution from Uncas, and to strengthen its diplomatic and trade ties with old and new allies.

WHO SHALL RULE IN RHODE ISLAND?

While Pessacus and the other sachems traveled to Boston to sign the August 1645 agreement, a letter arrived for Williams at his Providence address from the General Court of Massachusetts. Curt and to the point, the letter revealed in no uncertain terms that the government of Massachusetts was willing to engage in a bit of outrageous duplicity in order to secure control over radicals and Indians alike around Narragansett Bay:

> We received lately out of England a charter from the authority of the high court of Parliament bearing the date 10th December 1643 whereby the Narragansett Bay and a certain tract of land wherein Providence and the island of [Aquidneck] are included which we thought fit to give you and other our countrymen

> in those [parts] notice that you may forbear to exercise any jurisdiction therein otherwise to appear at our next General Court . . . to show by what right you claim any such Jurisdiction for which purpose yourself and others your neighbors shall have free liberty to come and stay and return as the occasion of the said business shall require.

The General Court was finally putting into play Peter and Weld's "Narragansett patent" in an attempt to derail the Rhode Islanders' efforts to form a proper colony government under their new charter. There can be no question whatsoever that the Massachusetts General Court knew the Rhode Island charter of 1644 was legitimate and their own document blatantly fraudulent in the eyes of the government of England, but it hardly mattered. God, after all, was on Massachusetts's side, even if Parliament was on Rhode Island's.

Shortly after receipt of the General Court's letter, dated, ironically enough, on August 27, *the very same day* the agreement between the Narragansetts and the United Colonies was executed, Williams fired off a "righteous and weighty" response to John Winthrop—a document long lost—to which Williams "never received least reply," from his old friend or any other Massachusetts official.[10] Two months after sending its "cease and desist" directive to Williams, the Massachusetts General Court wrote to its magistrate, Benedict Arnold, in Pawtuxet, requesting that he negotiate with Pomham at Shawomet for ten thousand acres of land in the area for an entirely new town under Massachusetts Bay jurisdiction. The Court expressed the hope that the purchase would be close to "the place where Gorton and his company had erected three or four small houses . . . (for it was a great concernment to all the English in these parts, that a strong plantation should be there as a bulwark, etc., against the Narragansetts)."[11]

Massachusetts's designs for the new town in and around Shawomet were foiled initially not by the inchoate colony government of Rhode Island, but by Plymouth Colony, which claimed Pomham's lands rightly belonged to the Wampanoags, and therefore fell under *their* jurisdiction, per their agreement with that tribe. Then, in September 1646, another obstacle arose to frustrate Massachusetts's expansionist designs on Narragansett Bay. The advance guard for the Gortonists, Randall Holden, returned from London to Boston bearing two official letters from the Commission for Foreign Plantations. One was a letter of safe passage for Holden, permitting him to travel through Boston to Shawomet, where he and others of his company were to be permitted to "inhabit and abide without interruption."[12]

The second document was broader in its intent, and far more problematic in the eyes of the Massachusetts authorities. In summary, said the Commission for Foreign Plantations, Gorton and Holden had put forward a strong case against Massachusetts's unjust treatment of the Gortonists. Based on the evidence presented, the commissioners wrote,

> the tract of land called the Narragansett Bay . . . was diverse years since inhabited by those of Providence, Portsmouth, and Newport, who are interested in the complaint, and that the same is wholly without the bounds of the Massachusetts Patent granted by his majesty. We . . . pray and require you to permit and suffer the petitioners and all the late inhabitants of Narragansett Bay . . . to live and plant upon Shawomet and such other parts of the said tracts of land within the bounds mentioned in our said charter, on which they have formerly planted and lived without extending your jurisdiction to any part thereof, or otherwise disquieting them in their consciences, or civil peace, or interrupting them in their possession.[13]

The only good news for the United Colonies was that the commissioners were prepared to hear evidence contrary to the version of events presented by the Gortonists before the committee. But that was boilerplate language in all official correspondence from the London commissioners regarding colonial disputes. Naturally, the Massachusetts General Court was greatly alarmed by the Gortonists' triumph, and quick to rise to the challenge.

In December 1646, the Court sent Edward Winslow off to London with copies of all the relevant documents in the Gorton case, along with an exceptionally well-oiled, crafty letter signed by Governor Winthrop addressed to the Warwick commission. The letter spelled out the General Court's best (albeit tortuous) arguments in defense of its past treatment of Gorton and his followers, and against the general practice of permitting rogue settlers to seek redress for their grievances against the colonial courts in English ones.

Further, it defended the system of justice in Massachusetts in light of the avalanche of criticism leveled against it by Gorton and a growing chorus of individuals in both England and America. Allegations that the colony exceeded its authority, engaged in extensive religious repression, and was dismissive of English common law were, wrote Winthrop, entirely false and unworthy of the commissioners' attention.

As for Gorton, Winthrop pleaded that Boston had no recourse but to extract him from Shawomet by force. The "wrongs and provocations" of his party against the colony were "prejudicial to our liberties granted us by the . . . charter." Gorton had taken "such liberties as neither our charter, nor reason or religion will allow."[14] To make matters worse, wrote Winthrop, Gorton and company threatened the local Indians, who had turned to the Bay Colony for protection of their very lives.

Winthrop argued that permitting persons convicted by the Massachusetts courts to seek redress in English courts was prejudicial to the course of justice, as well as to the colony's "well being in this remote part of the world." Besides, Winthrop opined, Parliament could rest assured that "our care and endeavor also hath been to frame our government and administrations to the fundamental rules" of England, "so far as the different condition of this place and people, and the best light we have from the word of God, will allow."[15]

Never mind that "the best light we have from the word of God" conflicted with actual English statutes time and time again! Winthrop closed with a plea to the authorities "to confirm our liberties, granted us by charter, by leaving delinquents to our just proceedings."[16]

Sadly for Massachusetts, and happily for Rhode Island, nothing ever came of Winslow's efforts. The commissioners heard his case and informed him that if Plymouth Colony could produce proof that its charter extended to Shawomet or elsewhere in Providence Plantations, "this fact would much alter the state in question."[17] No such proof was forthcoming. By 1648, Samuel Gorton had returned to take up his old residence in Shawomet, joined by several of his disciples. There they stayed, renaming the town Warwick in honor of their benefactor at a crucial hour—Robert Rich, the Earl of Warwick. Gorton went on to play an important role in the early history of the colony of Rhode Island. He even became a friend and colleague of his old adversary from Providence, Roger Williams.

THE COLONY GOVERNMENT BECOMES MORE FIRMLY ESTABLISHED

In the late 1640s, Rhode Island remained a struggling frontier outpost of four towns with a population of only 750 people in the heart of a rapidly expanding Puritan empire of about 18,000. The town of Providence, Rhode Island's original settlement, was exceptional for the principles upon which it was founded, but little else. The small farming and fishing village had few craftsmen and an undeveloped harbor and hinterland. Five or six of the original thirteen families had moved south to Warwick and Pawtuxet. Each of those two settlements consisted of only ten to fifteen households. The Williams family remained in its modest home on Towne Street, near the little spring that supplied all 180 of Providence's residents with fresh water. Roger's brother, Robert, and his family now lived a few doors down from the founder's dwelling. All the residents, so far as we know, were people of quite modest means.

Providence was a one-street town. Until the early 1650s, when the inhabitants began to hire carpenters to build classic "stone-ender" homes of stone foundations, the homes were constructed by the townsmen themselves from rough-hewn beams, with roofs of thatch or bark, and dirt floors.

Fifty-two long, narrow lots (1,600 to 3,000 feet, east to west; 100 to 135 feet, north to south) ran in a row along Towne Street (now North and South Main) for just over a mile. Each lot extended up the steep hill to the east, to a rough, rutted path, later to be called Hope Street. Most of the houses were at the base of the hill, facing the Moshassuck River in the north, which emptied into the town cove, and the Great Salt River to the south.

Atop the hill were the town common lands. On the west side of the Great Salt River—today's downtown Providence—lay flat, fertile lands for the grazing of pigs, cattle, and sheep, and the farming of vegetables. Remarkably, Providence in 1647 had but one public edifice and no village green. John Smith's grist mill at the north end of town on the Moshassuck served as an informal gathering point, as well as a venue for town meetings and religious services. Not until 1649 did the town fathers appoint a constable. Until 1660 there wasn't even a bridge connecting the east and west sides of the settlement at Weybosset Point. The men who worked the fields on the west side had to cross by boat from Towne Street.

Newport, though founded three years later than Providence, quickly eclipsed the original settlement in population and commercial activity. By 1650, about three hundred people dwelled there. Among them were a handful of merchants of considerable means who hired tenant farmers to raise herds of sheep and cattle on excellent farmland in Newport and invested in the nascent coastal shipping business. Skilled artisans tended to settle in Newport rather than Providence because of its bustling harbor.

In May 1647, two and a half years after Williams had returned from the great metropolis of London with the original charter, the Rhode Island freemen—the fully vested landholders, who then numbered only about 150 men—finally convened in Portsmouth to lay the foundations for a proper colonial government. As was the case with the 1644 gathering, no formal records of the convention's deliberations have survived, but the results of their negotiations—a code of laws, and a basic description of the original form of the colony government—were put down on paper and, much later, gathered together and published in *The Records of the Colony of Rhode Island and Providence Plantations*.

Each town sent a delegation of ten men to Portsmouth to conduct business on its behalf. The impressive productivity of the May meeting, which was carried out over only three days, makes clear that the town delegations had convened several times at irregular intervals during the previous few months to discuss first principles, hash out compromises, and work on draft documents. The convention in Portsmouth established an experimental, strictly secular form of government that was very much a reflection of the character of the tiny population of the colony: religiously heterodox, staunchly individualistic, and deeply distrustful of centralized authority.

Town identity in Rhode Island preceded colony identity, and under the original framework, each town held veto power over legislation duly passed by the colony's legislative body, a General Assembly consisting initially of the entire body of the colony's freemen. Due to the unwieldiness of this exercise in direct democracy, the Assembly within a short time placed authority in the hands of a representative General Court of twenty-four commissioners, six from each town, to carry out the colony's legislative functions.

The colonial government's form and structure clearly bore the stamp of the leading delegate from Providence, Roger Williams. Not only was Williams the most prominent and influential citizen of the colony, but he had also thought longer and harder about the nature of government and society than any other settler in Rhode Island. Moreover, Williams's ideas on these weighty topics were congenial to Newport's leading political figure, Dr. John Clarke.

Williams believed government was a strictly *civil* institution, meant to protect the bodies and goods of citizens. Its purpose was to establish a framework for the smooth functioning of a secular community, in which, as the final paragraph of the code of laws put it, individual citizens could "walk as their consciences persuade them, everyone in the name of his God."[18]

In Rhode Island, officeholders didn't have to pass any religious or social litmus tests other than being property owners. Williams thought it foolish to restrict office holding to Christians, let alone Christians of one denomination or another, for people's religious beliefs had nothing to do with their ability to serve their community in public office. The church, after all, was a sacred garden, while government's purview was "the wilderness of the world." There, in the mundane world of politics and commerce, wrote Williams,

> we know of many excellent gifts wherewith it hath pleased God to furnish many, enabling them for public service to their countries both in peace and war (as all ages and experience testifies) on whose shoulders he hath not yet pleased to shine the face of Jesus Christ: which gifts and talents must all lie buried in the earth, unless such persons may lawfully be called and chosen to, and improved in public service, notwithstanding their different or contrary conscience and worship.[19]

To deny non-Christians the right to hold office, to vote, to own land, was wrong in the eyes of Christ, and wrong for Rhode Island, for a pragmatic reason: the colony had no upper class, no gentry to whom the people could look to for leadership. It needed contributions from all its citizens, which well before the end of the seventeenth century included one of the first communities of Jews in North America, and a considerably larger number of Quakers. The Quakers were drawn to the colony because they were persecuted pretty much everywhere else in British North America, and in England. In Massachusetts, four Quakers were hanged simply for preaching their own faith within the colony's borders.

Keeping religion altogether out of the business of government had another great benefit, as Williams saw it. Many, if not most, of the conflicts in the world over the centuries had been sparked by rulers attempting to force a particular kind of religion on their own people, other peoples, or both. Williams assumed the type of government a particular society adopted should reflect its particular customs, inclinations, and ways of life, and that the members of that society had a right to change that government as they saw fit. There was no "right" form of government.

These beliefs, taken together, help explain why Williams was able to get on so well with the Indians. He accepted their form of government and society as entirely legitimate, and worthy of respect, because *it worked for them*.

Through various statutes the colony's founders zealously guarded the citizenry from the kind of abuses by magistrates, ministers, and other officeholders that seemed to them so prominent a feature of life in the orthodox Puritan colonies.[20] The form of government was famously described by the founders as "DEMOCRATICAL: that is to say, a Government held by the free and voluntary consent of all, or the greater part of the free inhabitants."[21]

The first paragraph of a four-part colony bill of rights echoed the words of the Magna Carta: "That no person, in the colony, shall be taken or imprisoned, or be disseized [i.e., denied] of his lands or liberties, or be exiled, or any other otherwise molested or disturbed, but by the lawful judgment of his peers, or by some known law, or according to the letter of it, ratified and confirmed by the major part of the General Assembly lawfully met and orderly managed."[22] The original Rhode Island code of laws, observes Yale historian Charles Andrews, was the first such code in America "to embody in all its parts the precedents set by the laws and statutes of England. . . . Unlike those of the Puritan colonies, [they] were founded not on the word of God but on the statutes of parliament."[23]

Rhode Island's original government, based as it was on the idea that government derived all its power from the consent of the people, majority rule, and protection of the individual's rights from violation by the state or church, clearly anticipates the cluster of political ideas we associate with the founding fathers of the American Revolution generation, although the Rhode Islanders' rationale for such a government was quite different from that put forward by Jefferson and Madison more than a hundred years later.

On the ground in seventeenth-century Rhode Island, this experimental system of governance led to chronic dysfunction, internal dispute, and chaos. Liberty and license trumped order and discipline time and time again. Men elected to office refused to serve. The towns refused to pay taxes levied by the colony government, and on several occasions, new settlers banded together against the "old order" within the towns, establishing their own officers and town meetings. Government in Providence seems to have been particularly mired in chaos, produced by an endless series of disputes over land ownership and distribution.

The colony government was weak throughout the entire century, but virtually powerless during much of its first decade. A major source of the problem, as historian Sydney James points out, was that the "towns designed a government to be superior over them more in a theoretical than a practical sense."[24] The island towns wanted legislation to be passed by majority vote of all the colony's freemen, while Providence and Warwick, with smaller populations than the island towns, wanted a representative system. Individuals at Pawtuxet refused to recognize the legitimacy of the new government; Massachusetts continued to exercise jurisdiction there.

Yet another threat to the functionality of the colony government stemmed not from the structural weaknesses embedded its 1647 foundations, but from William Coddington. That Massachusetts refugee and a coterie of a dozen or so supporters, the wealthiest men in all of Rhode Island, were from the outset hostile to unification with their poorer relations on the mainland, preferring to run their own affairs as they saw fit. In turn, Coddington's authority was strenuously challenged in Newport by a faction led by the physician and Baptist preacher John Clarke. Clarke's supporters were committed to the new colony government, but were not entirely in sync with the views of the mainland towns as to how government should function.

In 1648, Coddington secretly petitioned the United Colonies to admit Portsmouth and Newport, themselves united under an island government since 1640, as an independent colony within the New England Confederation. Since Plymouth still claimed that Aquidneck fell within its jurisdiction, the commissioners of the United Colonies demurred. Not to be deterred, Coddington sailed to London, where he maneuvered successfully to obtain a commission from the Council of State, which then functioned as the executive department of the parliamentary government, to serve as governor for life of Aquidneck Island.

The potential dismemberment of the colony as a result of Coddington's extraordinary position, as well as a desire to secure additional legal protection for the Narragansetts against a United

Colonies invasion, forced Williams once again to brave an Atlantic crossing. For the second and last time, the founder of Providence sailed to England, this time joined by John Clarke and his wife. With the indispensable help of both Henry Vane and Cromwell, Clarke and Williams convinced the Council of State, the successor to the Commission for Foreign Plantations, to annul Coddington's commission on April 7, 1652.

Williams stayed on in London for another two years, publishing several new works on the issues and institutions that had preoccupied him throughout his adult life, including *The Bloudy Tenent yet More Bloudy*, and working closely with Clarke to defend the integrity of the colony and the Narragansetts against further encroachment by its powerful neighbors. As we shall see later, Clarke deserves most of the credit for ensuring Rhode Island's independence once the Interregnum came to an end and a new king, Charles II, assumed the throne in 1660. He was to remain in England on behalf of the young colony until 1663.

Coddington was successfully stripped of his office, but this hardly ushered in a period of tranquillity and smoothly functioning government. Until 1654, two discrete administrations—one for the island, one for the mainland—continued to operate. Such scraps of documentary evidence that remain suggest the two colony governments were in effect shadow administrations, exerting almost no influence over events in the towns, while the towns themselves were riven with factionalism. "When the tension between liberty of conscience and good order grew into conflict," writes historian Bruce Colin Daniels, "it was invariably settled on the side of liberty by the first generation of settlers."[25]

These developments were surely a source of grave concern to the founder of Providence. So contentious was Rhode Island's first town that news of its troubles was widely known among men of influence in London, as well as throughout the English colonies. On Williams's return to Providence in 1654, he brought with him a letter from Henry Vane to the people of Providence, imploring them to resolve their differences and pull together as one. Many historians believe Williams drafted the letter for Vane's signature, but we will never know for sure:

> Loving and Christian Friends,
>
> . . . I hold myself bound to say to you, out of Christian love I bear you, and for his sake whose name is called upon by you and engage in your behalf. How is it that there are such divisions amongst you? Such headiness, tumults, disorders and injustice? The noise echoes into the ears of all, as well friends as enemies, by every return of ships from those parts. Is not the fear and awe of God amongst you to restrain? Is not the love of Christ in you, to fill you with yearning bowels, one towards another, and constrain you not to live to yourselves, but to him that died for you, yea, and is risen again? Are there no wise men amongst you? No public self-denying spirits, that at least, upon the grounds of public safety, equity and prudence, can find out some way or means of union and reconciliation for you amongst yourself, before you become a prey to common enemies, especially since this state, by the last letter from the Council of State, gave you your freedom, as supposing a better use would have been made of it than there hath been?[26]

The letter might well have been written to all the towns in Rhode Island. It was a clarion call for action and unity. Around the time of the letter's arrival, the men of Rhode Island began to make a concerted effort to restore unified government to the colony. For the first time in several years, the full General Court, with delegations from all four towns, met in Warwick in 1654. Among the first acts was the reestablishment of the 1647 code of laws, which had fallen by the wayside amid all the tumult and near anarchy in the colony. In September, Roger Williams was elected colony president—a post he was to hold until 1657.

On Williams's watch the government of the colony finally began to function with a modicum of efficiency and coherence. Here Williams's well-earned reputation as a mediator and conciliator, so much in evidence in his dealing with the Indians, came into play. He built widespread support behind a platform designed to strengthen the powers of the central government in relation to the towns. In May 1655, the Assembly granted the commissioners of the General Court the right to assess general taxes and appoint officials to ensure they were efficiently collected. The following year the General Assembly passed a bill declaring that no colony law could be "obstructed or neglected under pretence of any authority of any of the town charters."[27]

As Massachusetts, Plymouth, and Connecticut continued to press in on the English towns and the Indians around Narragansett Bay, a sense of urgency set in among the colony leaders. If the towns did not pull together, and fast, the prospect that each would be devoured by grasping neighbors loomed large. Under such circumstances, "ringleaders of cliques and contentious groups were threatened with transfer to England for trial, lesser offenders were told they would be fined or whipped, if they continued in their course of opposition."[28] In March 1656, the strength and prestige of the colony government received an unexpected boost when a contrite William Coddington formally submitted "to the [colony] as it is now united, and that with all my heart."[29]

WAR LOOMS ON THE HORIZON . . . AGAIN

As the government of Rhode Island struggled to unify the Narragansett towns and defend itself from encroachment, it was forced to confront daily the possibility of open warfare between the Narragansett confederation and the United Colonies. In the decade following the signing of the 1645 treaty, Ninigret continued to test the patience of the United Colonies commissioners, in both word and deed. Called on to explain late indemnity payments, suspicious meetings with the Mohawks and Pocumtucks, and a series of raids against the Long Island Indians, the Narragansett sachem was by turns defiant, apologetic, angry, conciliatory, contrite, cooperative, and defiant all over again.

Sometimes Ninigret seemed to make a genuinely sincere effort to appease the wrath of the oligarchs. But mainly he baffled and frustrated them and carried on in the best interests of the confederation. Ninigret seemed to have a sixth sense, knowing exactly how far he could go in resisting Puritan demands before the English would resort to violence.

By these methods he preserved a remarkable degree of Narragansett autonomy throughout the 1650s and 1660s. Not until September 1654 did the United Colonies, in utter frustration, finally declare war against the wily Niantic, "finding by experience," as the official records of the United Colonies put it, "that forbearance and lenity of the Colonies doth but increase his insolency and our danger."[30]

But little of consequence, and no bloodshed, was to come out of this "war." Ninigret emerged from this new trial with an enhanced reputation among those who resented Puritan arrogance and overreach, Indian and English alike. Having said that, "forbearance and lenity" were much in evidence when Ninigret made his first solo diplomatic mission to Boston in early August 1647. The deadline for complete payment of the two thousand fathoms was approaching, and the Indians had paid only about four hundred fathoms. At the opening session of the proceedings, Ninigret protested once again, railing against the injustice of the 1645 treaty. Where, he no doubt asked, was the 160-fathom ransom Uncas owed the tribe? The commissioners were as usual unmoved by such entreaties. They had heard it all before, and the matter had been resolved—at least as they saw it—when the Narragansett sachems put their marks to the August 27, 1645, treaty.

The next day, a more contrite Ninigret appeared before the panel, joined by several members of his retinue. He was, he said,

> resolved to give the English satisfaction in all things. I will send some of my men immediately to Narragansett and Niantic, to raise the wampum now due to them, and hope to hear what they will do in three days. In ten days I think the wampum will arrive, and I will stay here until it comes. . . . But if there should not enough at this time be raised, I desire some forbearance as to time, as I assure you that the remainder shall shortly be paid, and you shall see me true to the English henceforth.[31]

Ninigret remained in Boston. Two weeks passed. The messengers returned, bearing the less-than-princely sum of two hundred fathoms. Ninigret, unfazed, begged for the commissioners' forbearance. He was sure that if he himself returned to Narragansett along with the four Narragansett children the commissioners had been holding as hostages, he could collect a considerably larger sum. The commissioners agreed, but were quick to add that if they did not receive an additional one thousand fathoms within twenty days, they would send an armed force into Narragansett country to "take course to right themselves."[32] Further, the commissioners expected the remainder of the payment to be in their possession just after planting time in 1649.

Off went Ninigret with the hostages. Over the next two years, he and the Narragansett sachems sent additional payments, but in such minuscule amounts that by the fall of 1649 only eleven hundred fathoms had been paid in total.

Meanwhile, Ninigret and the confederation pressed forward with other business. The Niantic chief made energetic and sustained efforts to curry friendship with several bands of Pequots operating between the Weekapaug Brook (in Westerly, Rhode Island) and the Thames River, and to support their struggles to remain free from Uncas's grasp. He set up his nephew Wequashcook as sachem over one Pequot band near Weekapaug and enlisted their help in several incursions against Mohegan settlements.

In the summer of 1648, a large force of Narragansetts and Niantics gathered together with their Pocumtuck and Mohawk allies at the main Pocumtuck village near Deerfield, Massachusetts. Their apparent aim was to develop a plan to attack Uncas, probably by a series of raids on the Mohegan's major villages, in hopes of encouraging a number of his many tributaries to align themselves with other Indians.

The commissioners were informed of this gathering by—who else?—Uncas. Again, the Puritan authorities accused Ninigret of diverting substantial sums of wampum owed to them to his Indian allies and warned him that no good would come of it if he continued this practice. The commissioners also sent Lieutenant Humphrey Atherton to parley with Ninigret at Cocumscussoc. They wanted to know the purpose of the big gathering in Pocumtuck country.

Once again, Ninigret, with a bit of help from Roger Williams, assuaged the commissioners' doubts about Narragansett intentions. Williams told Atherton that Ninigret was indeed sincere in his claim that it was Sequassen, the Wangunk sachem, who had entertained the idea of enlisting Mohawk aid in gaining revenge against Uncas for repeated attacks on the Wangunks, but then, fearing English retribution, had decided against the venture. In his talks with Atherton, Ninigret defended his people's presence at Pocumtuck as little more than a ritual gathering of allied tribes—it was nothing more than traditional Indian statecraft—and promised to make good on the overdue payments as soon as possible. Atherton grudgingly accepted the response and returned to Boston.

Two years passed. During that time, the Narragansetts made but a few more token payments on their indemnity. The United

Colonies once again commissioned Humphrey Atherton to pay a visit to Narragansett country to expedite payment. In October 1650, Atherton and twenty armed men arranged through Williams to meet with Pessacus and Ninigret about three miles from Williams's trading house. Atherton now demanded 508 fathoms in total: 308 fathoms were owed in arrears, and the commissioners attached an additional charge of 200 fathoms to cover the cost of mounting his expedition into Narragansett country.

As Williams recounts the story, after agreeing to meet with the sachems and himself with only one or two of his soldiers present, Atherton showed up with his entire force and threatened to arrest Pessacus and Ninigret and take them by force to Boston if the Narragansetts failed to produce the entire payment due. It was a reckless act, for the sachems were attended by more than fifty well-armed Indians. These warriors weren't about to stand by idly while their sachems were carted off by a platoon of Englishmen. Williams was incensed by Atherton's betrayal. As a result of his rash actions, the entire gathering found itself "on the ticklish point of a great slaughter."[33]

Williams's exceptional diplomatic skills saved the day yet again. He prevailed upon Atherton and his troops to stay with him at Cocumscussoc, while the sachems agreed to procure a substantial quantity of wampum and return within four days. Sure enough, a party of Indians showed up at the trading post within the allotted time, bearing 380 fathoms of white wampum. It wasn't the full balance owed, but it was a significant installment nonetheless.

Williams then persuaded Atherton to support a petition he prepared for the court of deputies in Boston, arguing that the best course of action for all considered was to accept this substantial payment, write off the remainder of the debt, and at long last put the matter to rest. A short time later, the Massachusetts court declared the indemnity paid in full.[34]

The Narragansetts' stubborn refusal to defer to colonial authority continued to vex the Puritan oligarchs in the early 1650s. Ninigret raised the ire of the authorities in Connecticut by sending hunting parties into the eastern reaches of the Pequot country. In 1650, Uncas claimed Ninigret had hired a Narragansett man to assassinate him, a far-fetched accusation on the face of it. In any case, Uncas's list of Indian enemies seemed to grow with each season, as he tried to extend his rule over numerous Connecticut villages. Ninigret was hardly the only sachem in the region with a motive for dispensing with the ambitious Mohegan chief.

Ninigret was again summoned to Boston by the United Colonies commissioners, but after he made a strong case that the supposed assassin had been tortured by the Mohegans until he agreed to claim the Narragansetts had hired him, the commissioners let Ninigret return home in peace. Here, as in the past, part of the secret of Ninigret's success in dealing with harassment from the Puritans was his steadfast refusal to be intimidated. He had the necessary poise to go into the lion's den and keep his cool, and his reason.

In the winter of 1652–53, Ninigret journeyed to Manhattan and established some sort of informal alliance with Governor Peter Stuyvesant of New Netherland. This raised suspicion of a conspiracy among the English because the English and the Dutch were at war on the high seas, thanks to English efforts to close their colonial ports to Dutch traders. Connecticut and Plymouth authorities proposed mounting a preemptive strike against the Narragansetts, but Massachusetts wisely demurred for lack of hard evidence of a Narragansett conspiracy.

They were surely right to do so. Only about five thousand Dutch were in New Netherland, and they had their own problems managing relations with the local Indian population. They were hardly in a position to mount an attack on the English in New England, with or without Narragansett help. It does seem, however, that Ninigret obtained a substantial number of firearms from the Dutch, and that he planned to put those to good use in his campaign against Uncas.[35]

The catalyst for the next crisis between the Narragansetts and the United Colonies was a resurgence of the chronic conflict between the Niantics and the Montauks. Ascassasotic, a minor Montauk sachem at the eastern end of Long Island, was at the center of the controversy. The sources do not agree precisely on the sequence of events, but the gist of the story is clear.

In the fall of 1653, Ascassasotic's men drew first blood, killing a Niantic man hunting in Connecticut near Long Island Sound. Ninigret sent a substantial war party by canoe into Montauk territory. The Niantic war party ambushed a group of Montauks, killing a number of men, and taking a dozen women hostage. The Montauks called on the commissioners of the United Colonies for help. Thomas Stanton was sent to recover the prisoners at Ninigret's village.

Tempers flared during the meeting. Stanton struck one of the Niantic warriors after being told that the Niantics simply did not care that the commissioners wanted the prisoners returned—it wasn't any of their business. Stanton was roughed up a bit for his efforts by several Niantic warriors.

Ninigret was then called upon by the commissioners to explain himself. As for the Long Island Indians, he exclaimed, they "had slain [one of his] sachem's sons and sixty other of his men; and therefore he will not make peace with the long islanders but desires the English would let him alone. . . . If your governor's son were slain and several other men, would you ask council of another nation [as to] how and when to right yourselves[?]"[36] It was yet another refrain of the enduring Narragansett grievance: the English should stay out of intertribal conflicts and let the Indians resolve them of their own accord.

The United Colonies refrained from sending an expedition against Ninigret at the time, hoping that stern warnings of English retaliation would lead the Narragansetts to cease and desist. Winter passed uneventfully, but in the spring of 1654, Ninigret picked up where he had left off, harassing Ascassasotic's people throughout the summer in a series of raids on their villages. The commissioners assembled in September 1654, and the Niantic prince, always "proud and insolent in his carriage," was again prominent on the agenda. He had gone too far on Long Island and needed reining in. The time had come for concerted action.

War was formally declared against Ninigret and the Narragansetts by the commissioners in September 1654. An advance party was ordered to go ahead of an army of about three hundred troops, with the hope of obtaining satisfaction from Ninigret without resort to violence. The advance force, some twenty cavalry and forty foot soldiers under Major Simon Willard of Massachusetts, made its way to Ninigret's village with these demands: Ninigret must surrender the Pequots he had adopted into the tribe; they belonged under the jurisdiction of the English, in accordance with the treaty of 1645. He was to cease making war on the Montauks and must agree to pay the costs of raising the army about to be deployed against him, as well as the costs associated with preparing and maintaining defenses against his predations on Long Island.

Even in the official records, with their marked penchant for bias in all matters relating to the Narragansetts, it's clear the expedition turned out to be an embarrassment bordering on a fiasco for the United Colonies. Willard's efforts at negotiation were tentative, hampered as they were by extended delays in the landing of ammunition and horses on the coast near the Niantic's village, and Willard's general lack of command presence in dealing with the Indians.

Once Willard and his men reached the Indian settlement, they were told by Niantic warriors that Ninigret was utterly disillusioned with his treatment at the hands of the English. He had gone off to a swamp some fifteen miles away and did not wish to engage in face-to-face negotiation. Before too long, though, Ninigret consented to meet with four English officers at his encampment in the swamp and communicate through them to Willard. The Puritan officer agreed to this proposal, and off to the swamp went his emissaries.

Why, Ninigret wondered aloud to these men, would the English not let him alone? Why were they so prejudiced against him and his people? During his first meeting with Willard's representatives on October 17, Ninigret made it clear he had no intention of halting his attacks against the Long Island Indians.

On the next day, Ninigret reluctantly agreed to turn over the few Pequots he had with him in the swamp at the moment, as well as a few more who were then out on a hunting expedition. Although he was pressed several times to promise to stop harassing the Montauks, and to indemnify the United Colonies for the cost of raising the current expedition against him, he refused to do so. And that is where Willard and Ninigret left the matter.

Thus, Willard and his men departed the Narragansett country and headed back to Boston with precious little to show for their efforts. The authorities were not well pleased with the results. Major Simon Willard was severely reprimanded (in writing) for failing to achieve the expedition's objectives. Willard's humiliation was compounded by Ninigret's failure to turn over any additional Pequots, despite his promise to do so. Nor did he pay further tribute demanded of him for harboring those Indians.

This was the first and only military expedition mounted directly against Ninigret, which seems surprising considering his persistent reluctance to comply with English demands generally, and treaty obligations in particular. Plaintive cries for military assistance came into Boston from the Montauks at several junctures in 1655 and 1656 in the wake of Niantic raids on their villages. The English must stop Ninigret, said the Long Island Indians, or they feared they would be forced into servitude to the Narragansett confederation. Over the next several years, the United Colonies requisitioned funds for a variety of defensive measures to aid the Montauks, including the maintenance of an armed sailing vessel to attack Narragansett canoes as they crossed Long Island Sound. And it was agreed that should Ninigret undertake future attacks on the Montauks on land, English militia should come to their aid.[37]

Ninigret and the Narragansetts had won another round in the ongoing struggle to preserve their autonomy. But the Puritan oligarchs' will to prevail was strong, and they had a new, clever strategy in mind to bring the stubborn Narragansetts to heel at last.

Chapter 8

A Royal Charter, and New Troubles in Narragansett Country, 1657–65

Unknown artist's portrait of Newport's physician-preacher, John Clarke. Against all odds, Clarke secured Rhode Island's justly famous royal charter of 1663, which marked the first time in history that a monarch had guaranteed a people's right to practice the religion of their choice without any interference from the government.

The establishment of a reasonably stable colony government in Rhode Island in no way dampened the zeal of the orthodox Puritan colonies to extend their jurisdiction over the lands around Narragansett Bay, and to dominate the stubbornly independent Narragansett confederation. As a second generation of settlers came of age in the midst of a population boom—first-generation Puritan families had an average of between seven and eight children—the price of land suitable for farming in southern New England, particularly land along the coast and navigable rivers, soared.

Now, more than ever, Puritan speculators and magistrates alike set their sights on Narragansett Indian country. Rhode Island contained some "five thousand acres of rich silt loam and more than seventy thousand acres fit for general farming . . . and excellent for grazing."[1] Much of the best farmland lay on the west coast of the Bay, south of Warwick in Narragansett country. A coterie of well-to-do investors from Massachusetts and Connecticut, many of whom had played leading roles in the governance of those colonies, intended to gobble up as much of the Narragansetts' land as possible, and soon. The prospects for this group, known as the Atherton Company, or the Narragansett proprietors, looked reasonably bright. They reckoned that Rhode Island's government remained too weak, too preoccupied, or both, to interfere with their schemes. The Narragansett confederation's leadership was considerably less unified than it had been under Canonicus and Miantonomi, and the tribe now found itself perennially strapped for funds. The value of wampum had precipitously declined as Dutch manufacturers flooded the market with low-quality beads. The tribe's most valuable asset by far was land.

In 1657, the sachems sold Conanicut Island to William Coddington and a handful of Rhode Island investors. The next year, they sold a substantial tract of land around the southeasternmost point on the mainland, Point Judith, to a consortium of five Rhode Islanders. The Narragansetts retained the rights to hunt and fish on selected portions of these lands, and the sale seems to have been encouraged by the colony government largely to preempt large purchases by Massachusetts investors—including the Atherton Company—with malign intentions.

Meanwhile, the governments of Plymouth, Massachusetts, and Connecticut continued to lay claim to parts of Rhode Island, as its boundaries were loosely defined in the 1644 charter. Land lust now joined religion and Indian relations as a major source of conflict between Rhode Island and the United Colonies.[2] Whether the Indians and the government of Rhode Island would be able to defeat the latest Puritan strategy of conquest would depend in large measure on the ability of Rhode Island's able agent in London, John Clarke, to persuade King Charles II and his ministers that an experimental plantation founded as a haven for the oppressed deserved the right to exist unmolested by the Puritan Goliath. It wouldn't be an easy trick.

With the restoration of the monarchy in May 1660, all the New England colonies faced the prospect of renegotiating the terms of their authority and status as outposts within the realm. Rhode Island's charter of 1644 had been granted under parliamentary authority alone and was thus subject to challenge or abrogation by the king at any time. Quick to recognize its vulnerability, the government of Rhode Island formally declared its loyalty to the new king in October 1660—the first of the New England plantations to do so.

Even before the restoration, it was borne in on the leading men of the colony that preparations must be made to secure a royal charter confirming the colony's extant boundaries, as well as its fundamental principles of religious liberty and democratic government. Unfortunately, the colony government's preoccupation with internal disputes, and a chronic shortage of funds, led to near-disastrous delays in Clarke's pursuit of his mission.

Connecticut had no charter at all. Its leaders, too, recognized the necessity of obtaining a royal charter as soon as possible. To achieve that end, Connecticut sent its urbane and well-connected governor, John Winthrop Jr., to London with clear instructions and ample funding. When Connecticut's charter was formally approved by the Privy Council in the spring of 1662, Clarke was utterly astonished to find out that the entire Narragansett country fell within Connecticut's boundaries. He somehow had to persuade the king and his lord chancellor, the Earl of Clarendon, that the boundaries in Connecticut's new charter must not be allowed to stand, for they rested on a shaky legal foundation, and threatened the survival of Rhode Island as an independent colony. We'll return to this story later in the chapter.

The land grab campaign in Narragansett country by the Atherton Company began in earnest in 1659—a year before the restoration of King Charles II—with the full, albeit masked, support of the commissioners of the United Colonies. Leading the charge was the irrepressible Major Humphrey Atherton of Massachusetts, one of the United Colonies' most trusted and experienced military officers, and principal of the Atherton Company.

Atherton was quite familiar with the many blessings of the Narragansett country, having led several expeditions to intimidate the Narragansetts for failing to adhere to directives or pay off indemnities according to schedule. Atherton had commanded the force that had arrested Samuel Gorton and his followers and brought them to Boston to answer charges in 1644. A former assistant governor and speaker of the house in the General Court of Massachusetts, Humphrey Atherton was comfortable wielding power, and he took special relish in wielding it over the Narragansetts. He had long dreamed of establishing his own plantation in the heart of Narragansett country and, in the mid-1650s, sought out the services of Roger Williams to help broker a large purchase from the sachems. Well aware of Atherton's cynical designs, the founder of Providence turned him down flat.

Undeterred, Atherton and his fellow speculators in the summer of 1659 cozied up to Cojonoquant, the younger brother of Miantonomi, and for the absurdly modest sum of three hundred fathoms of wampum purchased two extensive tracts of choice land abutting the western shore of Narragansett Bay. Quidnessett, just to the north of Williams's Cocumscussoc, extended some six miles in length and one and a half to three miles in width. Namcook, just to the south of the trading post, was a bit larger. It ran ten miles in length and was a mile and a half wide. Taken together, the two tracts comprised most of contemporary eastern North Kingstown—some of the most fertile farmland in all of New England.

Rumor had it that Cojonoquant had been plied with drink before being persuaded to put his mark to the deeds. His credentials to sell the land were at best questionable—he was a generally ineffective minor sachem with an abiding fondness for alcohol. Even if he'd been sober as a judge, one thing was certain: the sales were in direct violation of Rhode Island's 1651 and 1658 laws prohibiting the purchase of Indian land without the express consent of the colony government.

Letters of protest were issued by Rhode Island to the commissioners of the United Colonies, to the General Court of Massachusetts, and to Atherton. No replies were forthcoming. Roger Williams a decade later would describe the Atherton purchases memorably as "an unneighborly and unchristian intrusion upon us, as being weaker, contrary to your laws as well as ours, concerning purchasing lands without consent of the General Court."[3]

Believing that the Narragansetts were attempting to extricate themselves with the aid of their Rhode Island allies from the swindles they had suffered at Quidnessett and Namcook, the commissioners of the United Colonies pursued what the British military historian B. H. Liddell Hart famously called "the indirect approach." In September 1660, they levied a fine of 595 fathoms of wampum on the Narragansetts for various alleged offenses. These included several Narragansett raids on the Mohegans and the Montauks; the firing of musket shots into the trading house of Jonathan Brewster, a purveyor of firearms and shot to the Mohegans; and the killing of several Montauk Indians during a skirmish on Gull Island off the coast of the north fork of Long Island. Yet again, the United Colonies commissioners were attempting to punish the tribe for engaging in traditional warfare and coercive diplomacy with other Indian powers. But they were also surreptitiously lending a helping hand to the Atherton speculators.

In his inimitable fashion, Ninigret tried to put this new dispute with the United Colonies off for another day. He had said years earlier that the English "talked much but did little," and his experience over the previous twenty years in jousting with them had gone far to confirm that belief.[4] The sachems offered to attend the first meeting of the commissioners in 1662 to give satisfaction for this new litany of offenses.

"Having plentiful experience of [Ninigret's] frequent breach of promise," the commissioners were having none of it.[5] They sent emissaries to the Narragansetts within a few days and demanded that the Indians make full restitution to the governor of Connecticut within six months. If such payment failed to arrive on time, the General Court of Connecticut was empowered "to send a convenient company of men under some discreet leader to force satisfaction of the sums aforesaid."[6]

The threat of military intervention had by this time lost a fair amount of credibility in the eyes of the Indians, so the commissioners took the novel step of demanding that the sachems take out a mortgage on their *entire territory* as a bond to guarantee timely payment of the fine.[7] On September 29, 1660, Ninigret, Pessacus, and Scuttup, a grandson of Canonicus, put their marks to a mortgage, agreeing to forfeit "all our whole country with all our rights and titles thereunto" if the tribe failed to pay the fine on time.[8]

A great deal was riding on the Narragansetts making the payments. They had put about four hundred square miles of territory up as collateral, and there were many demands for limited tribal funds. Then, in just a couple of weeks, the other shoe dropped. Major Atherton and his partners, finding the Narragansett sachems "in a very sad condition, not knowing how to discharge their engagement to the commissioners," stepped into the breach and paid the fine to Connecticut on their behalf. Atherton's gesture of "help" was not entirely disinterested—quite the reverse. Before he paid the fine he prepared a new "Deed of Mortgage" for the Indians' signature, in which the sachems agreed to assign ownership of the four hundred square miles of real estate to the Atherton Company if they failed to repay the loan, in addition to a hefty service charge (!), within six months.[9]

As Atherton fully expected—and hoped—the Narragansetts failed to make full payment within the specified time. The company then foreclosed on the mortgage and, following a brief ceremony held at Pettaquamscutt Rock, took formal possession of the lands of the Narragansetts in the spring of 1662. By the terms of the mortgage, however, the Indians had been granted several years to vacate the area, so no effort was made to enforce their removal, and life went on pretty much as normal for the Narragansetts.

No conclusive evidence of collusion between the commissioners' persecution of the Narragansetts and the Atherton Company's machinations has thus far been found by historians in the extant documents. The clever Puritans weren't so naive as to leave an obvious paper trail. All that can be said is that the close personal and business ties between the Atherton Company and the commissioners, and their shared cynical objectives regarding the Narragansetts, together make a compelling circumstantial case that there was collusion aplenty.

The most plausible explanation for the bizarre mortgage transfer from the United Colonies to the Atherton Company is that the commissioners realized soon after they had secured the initial mortgage that the king would be sorely tempted to declare the

United Colonies' foreclosure on such an exploitive mortgage null and void, but far more hesitant to do so if a private corporation held the mortgage and did the foreclosing. The commissioners knew all too well that King Charles II took a dim view of the Puritan oligarchs' exploiting English dissenters and Indians alike. (In just a few years' time, King Charles II would declare the United Colonies an illegal institution, but did precious little to prevent it from functioning afterward.)

Besides, it seems highly likely that Williams and Gorton had already penned letters on behalf of the tribe to the new monarch, calling to his attention that the Narragansetts had formally subjected themselves to the king's protection way back in 1644, but the United Colonies had consistently ignored that claim and continued to maintain that the tribe was subject to its authority. It seems equally certain from the events that follow that the king had been informed in those letters of the fraudulent sales of Quidnessett and Namcook, as well as the outrageous Atherton mortgage foreclosure.

If Williams and Gorton did indeed write to the king on the Narragansetts' behalf, their letter(s) have not survived. But in a 1670 letter to John Mason that addresses the machinations of the United Colonies and the Atherton Company in Rhode Island, Williams lamented the "depraved appetite after great vanities, dreams and shadows of this vanishing life, great portions of land, land in this wilderness, as if men were in as great necessity and danger for want of great portions of land, as poor, hungry, thirsty seamen have, after a sick and stormy, a long and starving passage. This is one of the great Gods of New England, which the living and the most High Eternal will destroy and famish."[10]

Why, one might well ask, would the Narragansetts have signed these mortgages? We can only speculate. The most likely answer is that they were deliberately misled about the dire implications of the documents they had signed and believed that, based on extensive past experience, once they'd signed the documents, the English authorities would leave them alone and let them go about their business. The extant documents provide no clue as to who translated the deeds; it's inconceivable that Williams was involved.

Even if they understood what they were signing, the Indians probably believed they could renegotiate more favorable terms later without too much difficulty. That had been how things had worked out more than once in the past.

As for the Atherton mortgage foreclosure, the sachems may have been aware that the colony of Rhode Island viewed it for what it was—an illegal act designed to swindle the Indians out of their most treasured asset—and would do all in its power to prevent Atherton and his associates from taking possession. Rhode Island appointed a committee to confer with the Atherton proprietors over the legality of their purchases, even as those proprietors began to install tenants and livestock on a few farms within the confines of Quidnessett and Namcook. Major Atherton died in September 1661 of injuries sustained from falling off his horse, but his partners pressed their Narragansett claims on a number of fronts, and on none more vigorously than in the halls of Westminster, London.

The proprietors wrote at length and often to Connecticut's London agent, John Winthrop Jr., imploring him to obtain a royal charter for Connecticut that would include within its bounds the entire Narragansett country. They conspired with their confreres among the commissioners of the United Colonies, too, trying to sort out strategies to foil Rhode Island's efforts to challenge their recent acquisitions and void the Atherton foreclosure.

In February 1662, Lord Clarendon, the king's chief minister, told John Clarke and Winthrop that the crown was willing to consider the petitions of both Rhode Island and Connecticut for charters. Clarke's efforts to secure the charter had been needlessly delayed by a lack of funds, preventing him from obtaining prompt legal advice and from filing the necessary preliminary petitions.

Rhode Island's agent wanted to negotiate directly with Winthrop to resolve any disputes between neighbors.

As Clarke tells it, Winthrop initially consented to working cooperatively, but while the Rhode Island agent awaited additional instructions from the colony government and some much-needed cash, Winthrop, in Clarke's words, "turned away and refused the motion [to work together] and grew stranger and stranger, thereupon I grew jealous of him and plied my business with double diligence."[11]

By May 10, the reason for Winthrop's "strange" behavior became clear: he had deftly employed his considerable contacts within the king's court, and even more considerable slush fund, to fast-track a Connecticut royal charter to approval. In keeping with instructions from Hartford and plaintive requests from his partners in the Atherton Company, the charter set the eastern boundary of Connecticut not at the Pawcatuck River—where the Rhode Island charter of 1644 had it, and Clarke had fully expected it to be—but at the western edge of Narragansett Bay, extending as far north as the southern border of the town of Warwick. In other words, the new charter granted Connecticut legal jurisdiction over the Narragansett country in its entirety.

Luckily for Clarke, Rhode Island, and the Narragansett Indians, Winthrop's claim for Connecticut's jurisdiction over the Narragansett country rested on quicksand. All he had to back it up was a *copy* of an obscure 1632 deed of conveyance from the Earl of Warwick to Lord Saye and Sele and his partners for a tract of land running from Narragansett Bay 120 miles southwest to the New Netherland border, and an unsubstantiated claim that this deed had been purchased in 1642 by the government of Connecticut.

No record of the deed, or the patent that should have accompanied it, could be found in the archives in London. So in effect, Winthrop lacked the legal documentation to back the deed. However, he did have several close friends on the Privy Council who were willing to attest to his good character and worthy intentions, including Lord Saye and Sele himself, who was very old and could not remember anything at all about the 1632 deed of conveyance. But Lord Saye and Sele was the Lord Privy Seal, meaning he kept the king's personal seal for the purposes of royal authorization, and *that*, in the chaotic days following the Restoration, counted for a great deal. If Lord Saye and Sele wanted Winthrop to get a charter, he would assuredly get one, and he did.

On May 14, four days after the Connecticut royal charter had passed the seals, Clarke made an urgent appeal directly to the king for "a speedy dispatch of a good and ample charter for the colony of Rhode Island . . . and that the charter lately granted unto my neighbor Mr. Winthrop may again be reviewed by your Majesty, for as much as thereby he hath injuriously swallowed up the one half of our colony."[12] When fully briefed on the details of the situation by Clarke, the Lord Chancellor Clarendon had to admit the Rhode Islander had a point.

Accordingly, he withheld the new Connecticut charter, forbidding its distribution, and arranged for the dispute between the two colony agents to be arbitrated by Robert Boyle, Samuel Maverick, and Sir Thomas Temple. They couldn't resolve the matter, so another board was appointed—this one with five members. Arbitration dragged on for about a year. Finally, in April 1663, after tortuous negotiation and much hand-wringing, the two colony agents made a private agreement to set the border between the colonies where it had been (at least in the eyes of the Rhode Island authorities) since 1644, and where it now stands—at the Pawcatuck River.

But there was a quid pro quo. To gain the crucial concession, Clarke had to agree to permit the Atherton proprietors, who allegedly owned the tracts at Quidnessett and Namcook, the option of choosing Connecticut jurisdiction over that of Rhode Island. Clarendon believed that the compromise agreement was unlikely to be accepted by either the governments or the peoples of either colony, given the stakes and the emotions the issue of the border evoked. Accordingly, he decided the only way to straighten out the mess was to send a royal commission to New England to investigate the situation thoroughly on the ground and make some binding determinations in the name of the king.

The royal charter for the colony of Rhode Island finally passed the seals on July 8, 1663. In addition to considerably strengthening the hand of the colony magistrates at the expense of the town representatives, the charter guaranteed the right of its citizens to travel and conduct business anywhere in the realm. The colony government was granted the right to appeal to the king directly in intercolony disputes. Henceforth, armed forces from neighboring colonies could not enter Rhode Island territory without consent of the colony's government. "In other words," writes historian Sydney James, "Massachusetts was not to arrest any more heretics outside its borders, and theoretically, the United Colonies were to stop intimidating the Narragansetts."[13]

All of this went down badly with the Puritan oligarchs. Equally galling to the Puritan fathers was the king's endorsement of Roger Williams's bold idea—put into words in the text of the charter by his friend John Clarke—that the citizenry of Rhode Island "hold forth a lively experiment that a most flourishing civil state may stand and best be maintained, and that among our English subjects, with a full liberty in religious concernments," and that "no person within the said colony, at any time hereafter, shall be any wise molested, punished, disquieted, or called into question, for any difference in opinion in matter of religion which do not actually disturb the civil peace" of the colony. A year or so before his death, Roger Williams wrote with great pride that "our charter excels all in New England or the world, as to the souls of men."[14]

Rhode Island had endured more than a quarter century of attacks from imperious neighbors on its territory, jurisdiction, and the moral standing of its "heretic" population. Now an English king had bestowed his imprimatur on the struggling experiment on Narragansett Bay. At a boisterous meeting in Newport on November 24, 1663, virtually all the freemen in the colony gathered along with the new colony officers, who had been named by the king in the text of the charter.

Together they listened intently as the charter was read aloud by Captain George Baxter, whose ship had carried the precious document across the Atlantic. Rhode Island's struggle for respect and survival was hardly over, but a great prize had been won.

Clarendon's concern that the compromise worked out in London by Clarke and Winthrop would not win acceptance by the respective colony governments proved entirely correct. When the Rhode Island charter arrived in November 1663, its language indicated that, notwithstanding the boundary definitions in Connecticut's earlier charter, the border between the two colonies stood at the Pawcatuck. But it contained no reference at all to the right of the Atherton proprietors to choose Connecticut as their jurisdiction rather than Rhode Island.

Rhode Island magistrates soon attempted by force to get the Atherton tenants to accept their jurisdiction, and the tenants abruptly called for protection from the government in Hartford. So began litigation and arbitration over jurisdiction in the Narragansett country that would not be resolved conclusively until 1742. (In the end, the crown awarded full and unfettered jurisdiction to Rhode Island.)

Meanwhile, the government of Connecticut considered Winthrop's concession on the boundary issue invalid because he had negotiated the compromise *after* he'd obtained a legal charter for Connecticut—thus, his authority as their agent had formally expired. While all parties awaited the arrival of the royal commission, the Atherton proprietors voted to place their properties at Quidnessett and Namcook under the jurisdiction of Connecticut and appointed magistrates to administer their settlement, which they named Wickford.

Thus, Connecticut had laid the seeds of its own settlement in the heart of Narragansett country. Rhode Island's legislature declared Connecticut's jurisdiction in Wickford, as well as in Misquamicut (modern Westerly, Rhode Island), where another small cluster of Connecticut families had settled, null and void, but it could do little else except await deliverance from the royal commissioners.

In July 1664, four royal commissioners, Colonel Richard Nicholls, Sir Robert Carr, Colonel George Cartwright, and Samuel Maverick, arrived in Boston—the first of several New England ports of call. Their chief mission, plainly put, was to judge the New England colonies' general level of allegiance to the crown, and to sort out the most pressing disputes among the colony governments, and between the colonies and the Indians.

But their primary concern was Massachusetts, for that colony, in addition to its long history of repression and intolerance, had shown a decided reluctance to accept the primacy of royal authority since the Restoration. In addition, the crown had been inundated with petitions from Quakers, Baptists, English traders, and Indian sachems seeking relief from abuse at the hands of the Bay Colony's government. The commissioners were invested with "full power and authority to hear and receive, and examine, and determine all complaints and appeals in all causes and matters, as well military as criminal and civil."[15]

In Boston, they received a frosty reception from a Massachusetts government overtly hostile to any royal intrusion whatsoever into their affairs. The Massachusetts magistrates, who had continued to refuse the king's 1662 request to permit all persons in good standing to take communion in their churches, or to grant religious dissenters the right to vote, took a resolutely defiant stance. The magistrates claimed their own charter had already given them "full and absolute power of governing all the people of this place, by men chosen from among themselves, and according to such laws as shall from time to time see meet to make & establish, being not repugnant to the laws of England."[16] The commissioners could do little but file detailed reports about Massachusetts's defiant stance toward the royal prerogative, then move on to their next stop.

In Rhode Island, it was an entirely different story. There the commissioners were warmly welcomed as liberators. They were brought fully up to speed concerning the machinations of the United Colonies and the Atherton Company in the Narragansett country. Pessacus passed along to the commissioners a petition from the Indians that complained of "violence and injustice from the Massachusetts, amongst others that they had caused them to be fined, and then [the Atherton Company] took their whole country in mortgage."[17] Along with that document, he handed them a copy of the Narragansetts' 1644 submission of jurisdiction to King Charles I.

After extensive review of these documents, among other petitions, the commissioners at long last formally confirmed the acceptance of the Narragansetts' submission to royal authority in an elaborate ceremony at the main Narragansett village. The sachems laid down muskets and bows and arrows "at his Majesty's feet" and presented the commissioners with two exquisitely crafted hats of wampum and two war clubs for the king, "and a feather mantle and porcupine bag for the Queen." The king's representatives, in turn, presented the sachems with two handsome coats "in acknowledgement of the great affection" for the king the sachems had expressed after the granting of Rhode Island's 1663 charter.[18]

Taking the 1644 deed of submission, as well as some convincing testimony from several Rhode Island colonial officials, into account, the commissioners removed the entire Narragansett country from colonial control altogether—at least in theory. It was declared henceforth under the jurisdiction of the king, to be called the King's Province. Until further notice, crucially, it was to be administered exclusively by Rhode Island magistrates.

Henceforward, whenever the United Colonies attempted to impose fines or legal judgment against the tribe, the Narragansett sachems invariably asserted that their status as subjects of the king put them on an equal footing with each of the New England colonies as a separate polity, under its own government. The tribe owed allegiance to the king, but only friendship to the governments of the other colonies, not submission, for they, too, were subjects of the king.[19] Naturally, the orthodox colonies steadfastly refused to accept this bold assertion and continued to treat the sachems and their people as inferiors, and subjects.

As for the exploitive schemes foisted on the Narragansetts by the Atherton Company, the commissioners issued the following proclamation:

> Whereas, Major Atherton and others of his Majesty's Colony of the Massachusetts pretend a mortgage of a great part of the said [Narragansett] country, we order and appoint that whenever either of the Sachems known by the name Pessacus or Ninigret . . . do pay unto any one of the persons laying claim to the same mortgage the sum of seven hundred and thirty-five fathoms of [wampum], the said mortgage shall be void.
>
> . . . And whereas there is also two purchases pretended to be of two great tracts of land [called Quidnessett and Namcook] by the same Major Atherton . . . We, his Majesty's Commissioners, having heard the whole business, do declare said purchases to be void, and order and command that the said purchasers shall quit and go of the said pretended purchased lands, and shall not keep any cattle of any sort upon said land by pretense of said purchases after [September 1665].[20]

The sachems and the magistrates of Rhode Island were ecstatic, as one might expect. The mood in Hartford and Boston was bleak, but the oligarchs were not about to throw in the towel. Indeed, the royal commissioners' rulings were viewed as little more than temporary setbacks by the Puritan expansionists.

In the wake of the commissioners' rulings, Massachusetts leaders noted an alarming turn for the worse in the deportment of the Narragansett Indians. While "the savage natives bordering upon this and other [of] his majesty's colonies . . . have been principally awed by Massachusetts," the magistrates now found "that awe turned into contempt by their unwonted, proud, and insolent words and deeds."[21]

When the commissioners returned to Boston in May 1665, they censured the Massachusetts authorities for their failure to give due respect to the king and his agents, and for their mistreatment of the Narragansetts, among other things. The magistrates' response to the opening of the commissioners' court was to print a declaration stating that *the court itself* constituted a flagrant violation of the Massachusetts charter, and the magistrates could not bring themselves to consent to its rulings.

After several weeks of wrangling, the royal commissioners grew tired of butting heads. As they prepared to depart Boston, they prepared a lengthy list of changes they expected to be made in the Bay Colony's *Book of General Laws & Liberties*. The book's title page should acknowledge the king as the "fountain" of the colony's liberties; every reference to the General Court as the chief judicial power in the colony must acknowledge that it was "under his Majesty." To the delight of both the Narragansetts and the government of Rhode Island, the commissioners went so far as to deny Massachusetts's right to join with other colonies in a confederation such as the United Colonies, or to exercise power through such an organization.

In one of their final missives to the Massachusetts authorities, the commissioners told them, since "you will make use of that authority which [the king] hath given you to oppose that sovereignty which he hath over you, we shall not lose more of our labors upon you, but refer it to his majesty's wisdom."[22]

Taken together, the commissioners' rulings of 1665 and the advent of Rhode Island's royal charter probably prevented the United Colonies from launching an expedition to enforce their authority by force over the Narragansetts and their lands in the mid-1660s. Comforted by the knowledge that in the eyes of the king they were his subjects alone, and enjoying his protection from an alliance of Puritan colonies the king's commissioners had declared to be without legal standing, the Narragansett tribe would continue to conduct business as an autonomous entity over the next few years, with minimal oversight from a handful of Rhode Island magistrates.

But their days of peace and freedom were numbered. Rather than challenge Massachusetts's defiance of royal authority head-on, the king chose to take a far more conciliatory tone in his dealings with the Holy Commonwealth than any of the royal commissioners would have expected, or the Narragansett Indians would have liked. Although the Confederation of New England ceased meeting regularly for a few years as a result of the commissioners' prohibition, it would reemerge as the chief vehicle for the destruction of Indian political power and autonomy in the coming decade. Not even the king could save the Narragansetts from the looming catastrophe of total war.

Chapter 9

"In a Strange Way": King Philip's War

Paul Revere's engraving of King Philip of the Wampanoags. Philip initiated the conflict that bears his name, but he didn't exercise control over the trajectory of the conflict for very long.

On June 24, 1675, the chief sachems of the Narragansetts—Pessacus, Ninigret, Quinnapin, and Quaiapen, the sister of Ninigret—met with Roger Williams and three emissaries from the General Court of Massachusetts on the shore of Worden Pond, twelve miles southwest of Cocumscussoc. A crisis was at hand.

Metacom—known to the English as King Philip—the son of Massasoit, great sachem of the Wampanoags, was on the verge of war with Plymouth Colony. Massachusetts and Plymouth had rapidly dispatched representatives to the major Indian tribes in the region. They wanted assurances from their sachems that their warriors would not join Metacom in an uprising, if, indeed, one was in the offing.

Would the Narragansett confederation remain at peace?

According to Williams's account, the sachems were well aware of the crisis. They reported that "they had not sent one [warrior], nor would: that they had prohibited all their people from going on . . . [to Philip's] side: that those of their people, who had made marriages with [the Wampanoags] should return or perish there: That [if] Philip or his men fled to them yet they would not receive them but deliver them up unto the English."[1]

This was all reassuring news to Williams and the emissaries from Massachusetts. But it was not the whole story. In fact, the Narragansetts were deeply conflicted about whether to join Philip's uprising. Ninigret was by now in his late sixties. He had wrestled with the problem of ascending English power for decades and had in recent years found himself in weighty discussions of the English problem not only with his fellow Narragansett sachems and Philip, but with sachem Robin Cassacinamon of an independent band of Pequots near New London, and, astonishingly, even with Uncas.

Ninigret had turned the subject over and over in his mind and had concluded that the strength of the English in the region in numbers and military power meant that war was likely to end in catastrophe for the Indians. The Niantics, at least, would play no part in any uprising. He urged his fellow Narragansett sachems to remain neutral should full-scale war erupt.

Pessacus had long deferred to Ninigret in Narragansett diplomacy. He, too, was getting on in years and wished the confederation to remain at peace. Ninigret's younger sister, Quaiapen, appears to have been in close communication with Philip throughout the early 1670s about the increasingly aggressive stance of the English and had come to share his resentment over the Puritans' domineering arrogance—and his belief that war was the answer.

The only way to preserve Narragansett autonomy and honor, Quaiapen believed, was to humble the English in battle and force them to take a more respectful stance toward all the Indians in the region. Most of the younger generation of males in the Narragansett confederacy shared her sentiments. They had a burning desire to strike at haughty English officials who had become openly dismissive of Indian assertions of dignity and autonomy. By the third week in June, several dozen Narragansett warriors had made their way to Mount Hope in support of Philip, though they had done so against the wishes of the tribal government.

A few days after the rendezvous at Worden Pond, Williams expressed doubts about the intentions of his Narragansett friends in a letter to Connecticut governor John Winthrop Jr. Philip had sent the Narragansetts three English heads. These grim trophies of war had been turned away as a sign of Narragansett refusal to join in the hostilities, but Pessacus told Williams he was skeptical of his ability to restrain the young men of the tribe from striking out against the English.[2] Meanwhile, Williams reported, a hundred armed Narragansett warriors had marched into Warwick, striking a menacing pose, but hurting no one.

Just what was all the trouble in Plymouth about? The Indian uprising, known today as King Philip's War, was the result of a slow but steady deterioration in English-Indian relations generally, but in Plymouth, the situation was particularly acute. The first violence was sparked by the Plymouth government's execution of three of Philip's men on June 8, 1675, for the murder of a prominent Christian Indian named John Sassamon.

In January 1675, Sassamon, a model convert who had briefly attended Harvard College and served as a preacher in the Christian Indian community at Natick, had informed Governor Josiah Winslow that the Wampanoags were planning an imminent uprising against the English. Reports of such plots were not uncommon, and the governor seems to have taken no immediate action upon receiving the news, even though Sassamon was clearly sincere when he remarked that he feared for his life in revealing the plot.

He was right to be afraid. At the end of January, Sassamon's body was discovered under pond ice about fifteen miles southwest of Plymouth by a group of Indians. They buried the body, but a witness later came forward claiming he had seen three Wampanoag Indians kill Sassamon and place him under the ice. An inquest was launched by the magistrates. The body, when exhumed, showed unmistakable signs of foul play—the head was badly swollen and the neck had been broken. The witness, a Christian Indian named Patuckson, identified the killers as Tobias, one of Philip's chief counselors; his son, Wampapaquan; and another Wampanoag man named Mattashunnamo.

The record has far too many gaps for us to ever know for sure who killed Sassamon, but the circumstantial evidence makes a compelling case that Philip had ordered his execution. Sassamon had, after all, accused Philip of an offense for which the sachem might well have been executed by the English authorities. What's more, several years earlier, Sassamon, while serving as Philip's scribe, had deviously inserted himself into Philip's will as beneficiary of a large plot of land and been caught in the act. He had been forced to flee Mount Hope and seek protection from the English authorities overseeing the Christian Indian communities.

Philip flatly denied any personal culpability for Sassamon's death—at least to the Plymouth authorities. Moreover, he was utterly incensed that Plymouth intended to prosecute the case under English law. Since no English people were involved as victims or alleged perpetrators, and the crime had happened on Indian territory, the case should have been left for the Wampanoags to adjudicate. The magistrates, who had let few opportunities to humble Philip or disparage his authority slip by since he had assumed power, were having none of it. The three suspects were tried by a jury of twelve Englishmen, "assisted" in their work by six praying Indians who had no vote in the matter, and summarily found guilty. They were hanged on June 8.

The trial raised an issue in Philip's mind that had come to symbolize Plymouth's flagrant disregard for his authority: the colony's active support of missionary efforts among the Wampanoags. It had begun in earnest in 1667, when the minister John Cotton Jr. began to preach to Plymouth's Indians regularly. Two of the key figures in the trial, Sassamon and Patuckson, were Christians. Philip despised the missionary program, as it inevitably led to the defection of Indians from his sachemdom, and from the traditional Indian way of life. The missionary program had a direct effect on Philip's pocketbook, and his power.

Over the next week signs of impending rebellion were everywhere. Lieutenant John Brown of Swansea, an English town just above the Mount Hope peninsula that was Philip's seat, reported on June 11 the frightening presence of sixty well-armed Indians. They were there, an Indian told Brown, to prevent the English authorities from arresting Philip. Coweset, Narragansett, and Pocasset warriors had been flocking to Philip's village for several days, said the Indian, prepared to join in his defense. Meanwhile, Wampanoag women and their children were already making their way via canoe to the Narragansett country, where they would be safely out of harm's way—for the time being, at least.

An adventurous carpenter-farmer by the name of Benjamin Church, the first white settler in Sakonnet Indian territory, had established a friendship with the Sakonnet squaw sachem, Awashonks. When Church, who was to play a prominent role in the looming conflict, heard that trouble was in the wind, he rode out to Awashonks's village (in what is today Little Compton, Rhode Island), only to find six of Philip's men in war paint, eager to persuade the Sakonnet chief to join Philip in the uprising. They brazenly threatened to attack nearby English farmsteads to provoke the English forces into attacking her people, leaving her little choice but to join in the uprising.

Not a man easily intimidated, Church accused the Wampanoags of being "bloody wretches [who] thirsted after the blood of their English neighbors" and counseled Awashonks that she'd be well advised to look to the Plymouth Colony government for protection from such bullying.[3] The governor of Plymouth was sure to protect her and her people if she swore allegiance to Plymouth. Awashonks weighed Church's advice and dismissed it. Within a few days, she and her warriors would be swept up in the whirlwind, throwing their lot in with Philip's forces.

Church next rode to the Pocassets, whose territory was just to the east of Mount Hope, in the vicinity of the modern town of Tiverton. There he learned from the Pocasset sachem, Weetamoo, that many of her warriors had deserted her, against her will. They had gone to Mount Hope to join with Philip. War, she feared, was inevitable. Church advised Weetamoo and her remaining followers to canoe from the Pocasset country to nearby Aquidneck Island in Rhode Island, where they would be safe, and wait for word from him. He was on his way to talk to Governor Winslow and would report back with instructions. Before Church had a chance to return, he was recruited into Plymouth's forces to lead a reconnaissance and raiding company of friendly Indians and English volunteers.

On June 14, Governor Winslow dispatched a conciliatory message to Metacom, indicating that the colony had no intention of undertaking further prosecutions for Sassamon's murder. The Wampanoag sachem was off the hook. The message did little to assuage the sachem's resolve, or his anger. He refused to meet directly with

Plymouth authorities, but agreed to entertain a peace delegation from Rhode Island, led by Deputy Governor John Easton.

Easton, whose colony had a long history of equitable dealings with Indians, described the meeting as friendly. He proposed to assemble a panel of arbitrators, including a sachem of Philip's choosing and representatives of the United Colonies, to resolve the crisis before it got out of hand. Metacom's experience with English arbitrators in the past left him cold to this proposal. The Wampanoag sachem insisted that Easton and his delegation listen to their grievances, and although Easton was at first reluctant to go over this ground, it's clear that, in the end, he did just that. Taken together, Metacom's statements to Easton and his delegation provide a good summary of the sachem's rationale for going to war.

The Indians, said Philip, resented the English authorities for interfering in matters of justice that concerned only Indians. They had a "great fear" of missionary work because Christian Indians often lied to their sachems and were disloyal. "If 20 of their honest Indians testified that an Englishman had done them wrong, it was as nothing. . . . If but one of their worst Indians testified against any Indian or [a sachem] when it pleased the English, that was sufficient." Still another grievance was that Englishmen repeatedly claimed they had purchased more land than had actually been agreed and then used fraudulent documents to prove their case. Englishmen plied Indians with liquor to swindle them of land.

"They said . . . when the English first came [Massasoit] was as a great man and the English as a little child, he constrained other Indians from wronging the English and gave them corn and showed them how to plant." The English "should [now] do to them as they did when they were too strong for the English," for they would rather be killed than give up their way of life.[4]

Philip was well aware of the shift in the balance of power in the region from the Indians to the English. The English authorities in Plymouth were exploiting that shift aggressively, and he was determined to put an end to it. A few days after Easton and his retinue returned to Rhode Island, on June 20, a band of Indians looted and burned several deserted homes in Swansea. Governor Winslow immediately sent orders for seventy colony troops to march to Swansea, where the inhabitants had taken refuge in several garrison houses, and secured promises of military support from Governor John Leverett of Massachusetts. At Winslow's request, Leverett sent emissaries to the Nipmucks and the Narragansetts to secure their promise of neutrality. These missions proved successful, in the short term.

On the twenty-third, a nervous English youth serving as a sentry in Swansea shot and killed a marauding Indian. The next day, a group of settlers in town who'd left the safety of their garrison house to collect some food and belongings were set upon by a band of Indian warriors. Before the night was over, nine English men and women were killed. New England was now at war.

THE ROOTS OF CONFLICT

The execution of three Wampanoags had sparked the crisis, but the roots of the conflict were deep and complex. The Wampanoags and the Pilgrims had forged an alliance in 1621 that bestowed significant benefits to each party and was the foundation of stable peace and prosperity for several decades. The English gained a legal basis for their settlement on native soil, as well as access to a wealth of knowledge about surviving in a strange, new world, including intelligence on the intentions of the many Indians peoples in the region. The Wampanoags, weakened by disease and under pressure to cede territory to the Narragansetts, gained a powerful trading partner and ally. The tribe made a considerable profit by serving as the primary intermediary for trade between Plymouth and neighboring bands of Indians.

Relations between the Wampanoags and Plymouth began

to show signs of serious strain in the mid-1660s. More so than in any other colony, Puritan expansion and prosperity seemed to come directly at the Indians' expense in Plymouth. With the market for furs and wampum in precipitous decline, the Wampanoags were forced to purchase European-made goods with cash obtained by selling the only commodity they had that was in high demand: land.

As noted in the last chapter, the value of land in New England in the 1660s was increasing rapidly, but the government of Plymouth prohibited Philip from selling land to the highest bidder on an open market. Instead, he could sell only to the colony government, and then invariably at a price well below what the market would bear. Speculators in Plymouth grew rich by purchasing large tracts of former Indian lands from the government and reselling them at double or triple the original buying price.

In the 1630s and 1640s, the Wampanoags had ample lands to accommodate the needs of Indian and Puritan alike. But the rapid rise in the English population created an almost insatiable appetite for land. By the mid-1660s, the children of the first generation of settlers were clamoring for farms for their own families. They wanted those farms as close as possible to the original settlements.

Soon after he became sachem in 1662, Philip and the Plymouth government agreed to a seven-year embargo on Indian land sales, but the tribe's urgent need for cash, coupled with the rise in demand for Indian lands, put an end to the embargo. Between 1650 and 1659, fourteen deeds to Wampanoag land were registered in Plymouth's court. Between 1665 and 1675, seventy-six such deeds were registered. "Pushed south to the neck of Mount Hope, Philip and his people were hemmed in from every side," writes historian Nathaniel Philbrick.[5]

Land was not the only bone of contention. Philip also remained bitter over the Plymouth government's suspected role in his older brother's demise. Philip's father, Massasoit, had turned over the reins of power to his eldest son, Alexander, and gone to live in the late 1650s among the Quabaugs, a band of Nipmuck Indians who were tributaries of the Wampanoags. In 1662, Alexander had refused to respond to a summons to answer the Plymouth magistrates' questions concerning his sales of lands to the town of Providence.

The magistrates sent Major Josiah Winslow out to retrieve Alexander, and to accompany him to Duxbury for the inquest. Winslow insisted that Alexander, who was ill, come to the inquest—at gunpoint. After submitting to questioning under duress, Alexander had been given a purgative by an English doctor. A few days later, the young sachem died. Philip bitterly resented the vile and insulting way Winslow had treated his brother and joined many Wampanoags in believing—incorrectly, it seems—that Alexander had been poisoned by the English authorities.

We have no way of knowing when Philip first seriously entertained the idea of leading a pan-Indian rebellion against the English. It may have been as early as 1671. In March of that year, a crisis developed when Philip refused to respond to a summons from the Plymouth court to answer a complaint about a rumored Narragansett-Wampanoag conspiracy. When Hugh Cole, an agent of the court, was sent out to Mount Hope to bring Philip in for questioning, he observed many Indians around Mount Hope "generally employed," as he put it in his report, "in making bows and arrows . . . and fixing guns."[6] Philip declined to show up for questioning. Fear of war spread rapidly through the colony.

Metacom was summoned yet again, this time urgently, to the town of Taunton. The proud sachem arrived with a band of warriors armed with traditional weapons as well as muskets, their faces painted. They were met by armed Plymouth militiamen. Taunts were exchanged. Tensions were so high that a skirmish was only narrowly averted. Under duress, and seething with humiliation, Philip signed a document acknowledging the "naughtiness in my heart." Puritan sources claim he further agreed to surrender all of his people's guns, but historians dispute this claim. The Indians at the meeting surrendered their weapons grudgingly, but hundreds of other Wampanoags retained theirs, leading to festering tensions, and on again, off again talk of war throughout the summer.

Then, on September 24, 1671, the governors of both Massachusetts and Connecticut joined Plymouth officials in a vain attempt to sort out the cluster of disagreements festering between the Wampanoags and Plymouth Colony. "The meeting," opines historian Douglas Edward Leach, "was conducted almost as though it were a criminal trial, with Philip at the bar of justice."[7] The English leveled a host of charges against Philip: he had violated the Treaty of Taunton by failing to turn over all his men's guns; he had carried himself insolently toward Plymouth's authorities by refusing to appear when called to court; he had harbored Indians who were Plymouth's "professed enemies."[8] The list went on at some length.

With the full weight of the United Colonies against him, Philip was forced to sign yet another document, this one far more humiliating than the Treaty of Taunton, for it required him—for the first time—to recognize all the Wampanoag people as subjects of Plymouth Colony. He was also obliged to surrender all the arms in the tribe's possession, pay a fine of one hundred pounds, and pay annual tribute of five wolves' heads to the colony government as a sign of that subjection.

After being forced into signing away the last vestiges of Wampanoag autonomy, Philip probably felt he had little choice but to begin to plan in earnest to go to war against Plymouth. The Wampanoag sachem soon sold off virtually every scrap of Indian land at his disposal and used the cash to surreptitiously replenish the tribe's arsenal of weapons. He also entered into extended discussions with neighboring sachems about rising up against Puritan domination.

After the humiliations of the fall of 1671, war was never far from Philip's mind, for it seems he had now concluded that without a radical shift in the balance of power between English and Indian peoples, his sachemdom was doomed. This realization, shared as it was by a good number of other sachems, and by a majority of young Indian males in their late teens and twenties among all the tribes, more than any single event or series of events, was the primary cause of King Philip's War.

In the immediate aftermath of the Swansea killings of June 24, 1675, the clang of bells and barn fires set on hills throughout southern New England alerted men to pick up their muskets and form up into trainbands—local militia units—to defend their towns. Governor Leverett of Massachusetts ordered a contingent of three hundred Massachusetts troops to join Plymouth's forces with a view to crushing the uprising near its point of origin, before it had a chance to spread to outlying settlements.

As the small colonial army cautiously made its way down through the Mount Hope peninsula on June 30, they found no hostile Indians, only the ghastly visage of a dozen or so English heads and hands mounted on poles. Philip and his warriors had given the army the slip, making a daring night crossing by canoe from Mount Hope to Pocasset country. Hopes of bottling up the rebellion early and defeating Philip within the confines of his own peninsula were now lost. In one of many early indications of the tactical ineptitude of the English, the Puritan forces lingered on Mount Hope for several days, where they built a fort in the unlikely event that the Indians would return to fight a pitched battle on their own home ground.

Then the Puritan forces committed a more serious blunder. Instead of chasing Philip with all the speed and aggression they could muster, Massachusetts's forces, which constituted the bulk of the colonial army, headed south to Narragansett country to secure yet another guarantee of neutrality from their sachems. Between the eighth and fifteenth of July, the Narragansetts engaged in tortuous negotiations at Wickford with the agents of Massachusetts, mediated by Roger Williams. Negotiations almost broke down entirely, and the Massachusetts officers found themselves on the verge of sending for the main body of their army, which was encamped near Providence, to force the issue. A confirming peace accord was reached, but both sides seemed to have been left with a distinct sense of foreboding.

The agreement of July 15 recommitted the Narragansetts to remain loyal to the English, and to regard the rebel forces as their enemies. Any Wampanoags seeking refuge among the tribe were to be turned over to the English authorities, and the English agreed to pay for any captives or for the heads of any warriors killed by Narragansett warriors. Four Narragansett hostages were yielded up to guarantee that the terms of the treaty would be observed.

That the treaty was signed not by the senior sachems but by their counselors strongly indicates that the Narragansetts felt coerced into signing and consequently did not view the treaty as binding. Meanwhile, the campaign to suppress the Wampanoag uprising foundered. While the Bay Colony troops dallied in Rhode Island, Philip's rebellion gathered momentum. The Plymouth towns of Rehoboth and Taunton fell victim to Indian raids.

Benjamin Church and his joint force of volunteers narrowly escaped annihilation in a daring foray into the hornet's nest that was the Pocasset country. Pinned down by a superior force of Indians, Church's men had to be evacuated by boat while under attack. On July 9, Indian warriors attacked Middleborough. Six days later, Mendon came under attack by Nipmuck bands that had initially pledged to remain out of the fight. It was the first of many Massachusetts towns to feel the sting of war. As news of Metacom's early successes spread rapidly among the Indian communities of southern New England, the forces of the rebellion grew in confidence and strength.

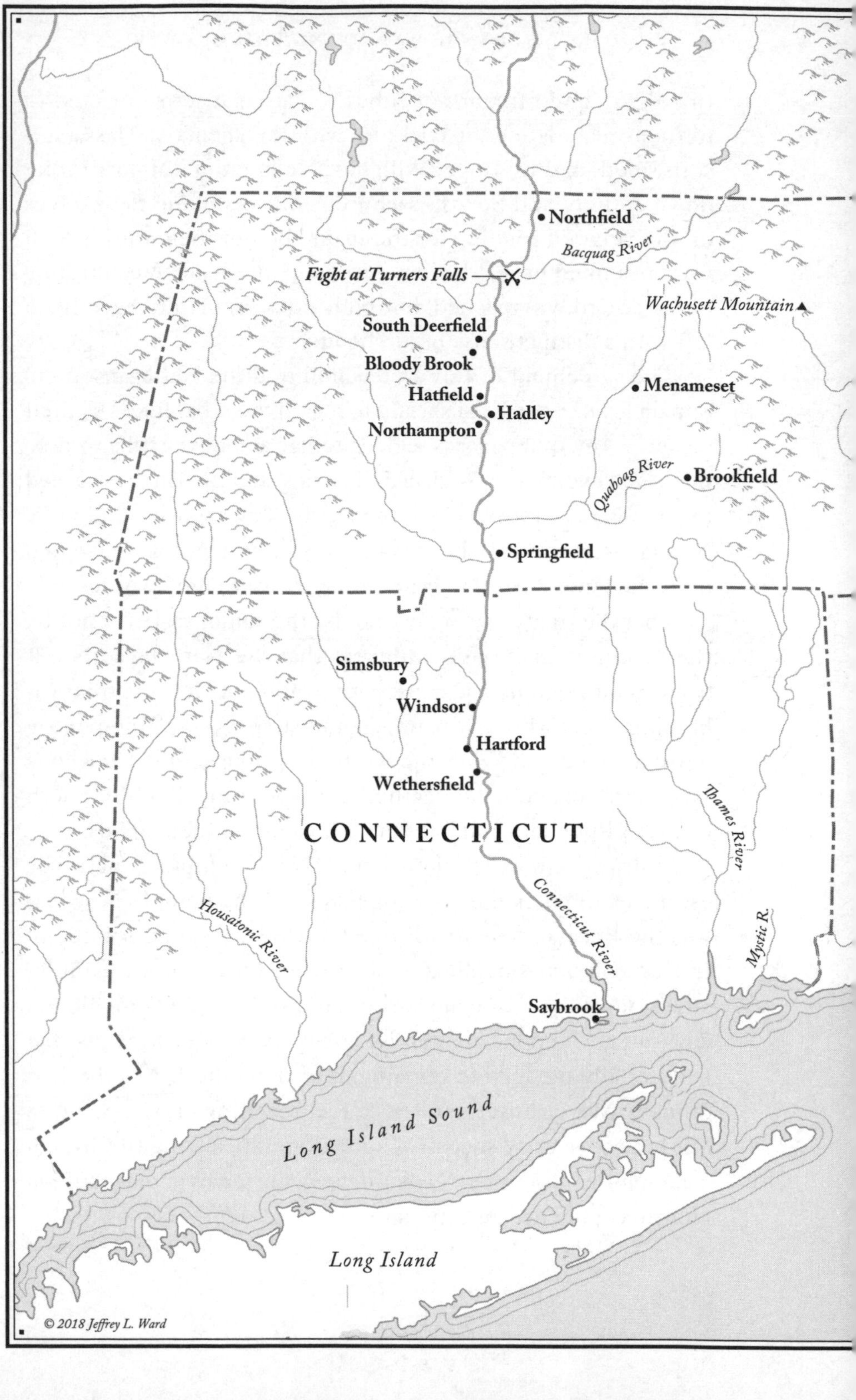
Northfield
Bacquag River
Fight at Turners Falls
Wachusett Mountain
South Deerfield
Bloody Brook
Menameset
Hatfield
Hadley
Northampton
Quaboag River
Brookfield
Springfield
Simsbury
Windsor
Hartford
Wethersfield
Thames River
CONNECTICUT
Connecticut River
Housatonic River
Mystic R.
Saybrook
Long Island Sound
Long Island
© 2018 Jeffrey L. Ward

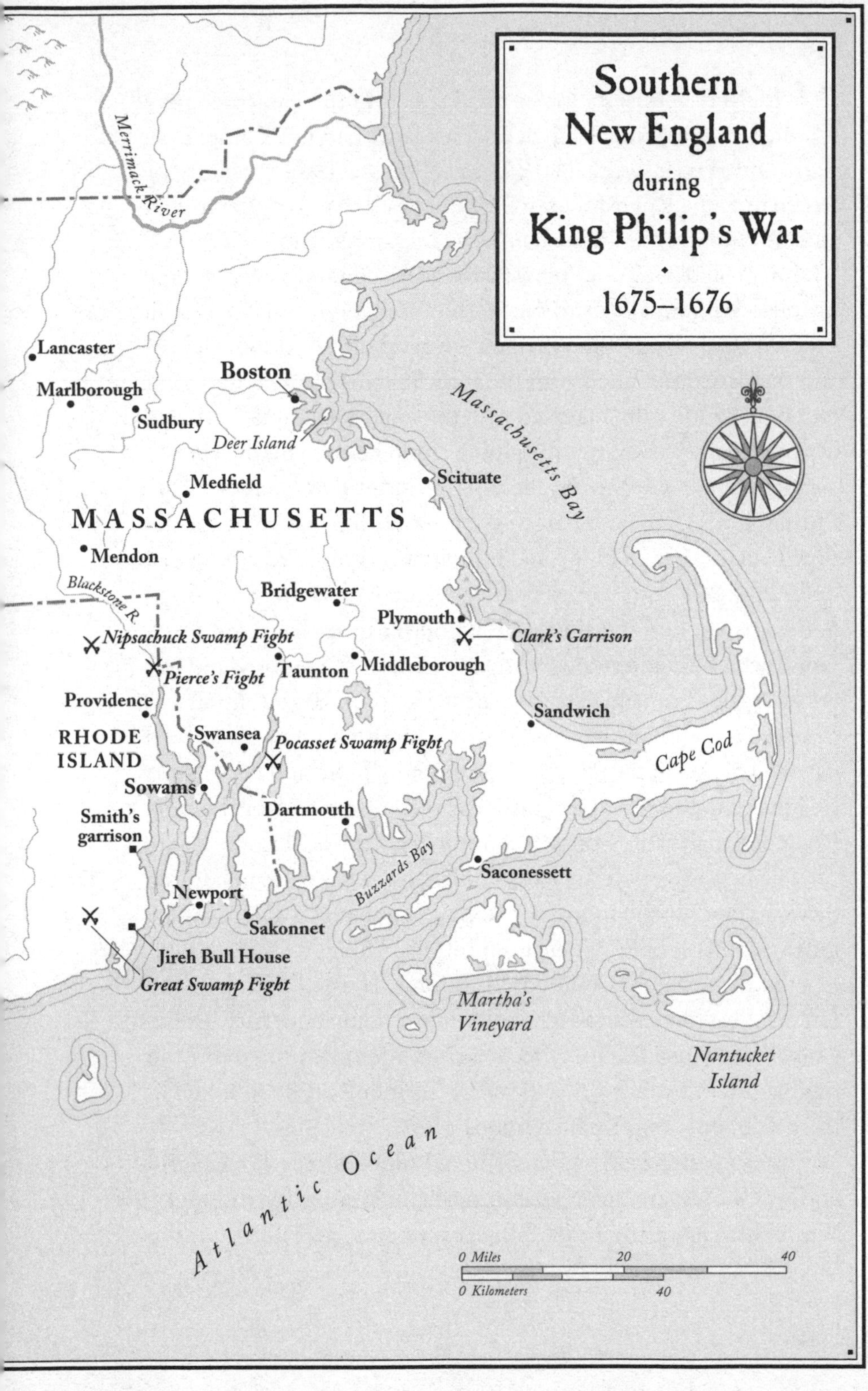
Southern
New England
during
King Philip's War
1675–1676
Merrimack River
Lancaster
Marlborough
Boston
Sudbury
Deer Island
Massachusetts Bay
Scituate
Medfield
MASSACHUSETTS
Mendon
Blackstone R.
Bridgewater
Plymouth
Nipsachuck Swamp Fight
Clark's Garrison
Pierce's Fight
Taunton
Middleborough
Providence
Sandwich
RHODE
ISLAND
Swansea
Pocasset Swamp Fight
Cape Cod
Sowams
Dartmouth
Smith's
garrison
Buzzards Bay
Saconessett
Newport
Sakonnet
Jireh Bull House
Great Swamp Fight
Martha's
Vineyard
Nantucket
Island
Atlantic Ocean
0 Miles
20
40
0 Kilometers
40

With Massachusetts forces finally back in the campaign, two hundred English troops tangled with a large band of Wampanoag warriors in a cedar swamp in the heart of Pocasset country on July 19. Seven or eight Englishmen were killed as they struggled to find an elusive enemy amid the tangle of vines, trees, and underbrush. The English troops now knew firsthand, as contemporary Puritan historian William Hubbard put it, "how dangerous it is to fight in such a dismal wood, when their eyes were muffled with the leaves and their arms pinioned with the thick boughs of trees, and their feet were continually shackled with the roots spreading every way in these boggy woods. It is ill fighting a wild beast in his own den."[9]

Now James Cudworth, the elderly, inept commander of the Puritan forces, called a halt to swamp fighting—at least for the time being—though Philip and his followers remained ensconced deep in the swamp. He sent most of the Massachusetts forces home, dispatched the bulk of Plymouth's units back to Mount Hope, which he intended to use as a base of operations, and left only a single company to cordon off the swamp. His intention was to starve the Indians into submission. After lying low for several days and nights in the depths of the swamp, Philip and his warriors stealthily slipped through the English cordon, crossed the Taunton River, and made for Nipmuck country in northwest Rhode Island.

The first of very few successful English engagements during the war's first ten months took place at Nipsachuck swamp, twelve miles northwest of Providence, on July 31. There the bulk of Philip's forces, perhaps two hundred warriors, clashed with a mixed force of Providence and Rehoboth militia, and about fifty Mohegans under Uncas's son, Oneco. Before Metacom broke off the fight and withdrew, twenty-three of his men had been killed at the cost of only two English troops' lives.

Instead of pressing on in pursuit of Philip's forces, the English and the Mohegans set up camp near the swamp for the night. While they slept, the rebel Indians slipped stealthily out of the swamp, making their way ever deeper into Nipmuck country in Massachusetts. Once again the Puritans had missed a chance to bottle up Philip's forces and contain the rebellion.

With perhaps five or six hundred warriors under three sachems, the Nipmucks would add considerable punch to the rebellion. Combined with Philip's warriors, they carried out a series of successful raids against individual farms and towns in the interior of Massachusetts in the late summer and early fall from their remote base at Menameset, near modern New Braintree, Massachusetts.

The Nipmucks' relations with Massachusetts Bay had begun to deteriorate about the same time as Philip's had with Plymouth. The declining market for furs and surplus Indian food had forced the Indians to pay off their (considerable) debts to English traders by selling extremely valuable lands east of the Connecticut River valley at substantially reduced prices. It was much the same story among the Pocumtucks and other River Indians. By late summer they, too, had joined the ranks of the uprising. Metacom's war had now become what the English had dreaded for decades: a full-fledged, pan-Indian uprising.

Central Massachusetts was the scene of many of the bloodiest clashes of the entire war. The lush valleys and fertile soil surrounding such towns as Springfield, Hadley, and Deerfield had become the breadbasket of New England. On August 2, a Massachusetts force of about thirty troops under William Hutchinson was ambushed three miles south of Brookfield. Eight soldiers were killed in the opening salvos, and Hutchinson himself mortally wounded.

After scrambling back to Brookfield, the soldiers joined sixty or so of the town's inhabitants in a terrifying two-day siege of a single garrison house by Indian bands. While the combatants traded musket fire, some Indians attempted to set the house ablaze by positioning a wagon full of hay and other combustible materials against a wall and setting it alight. Suddenly rain poured from the skies, foiling the Indians' scheme. The arrival of a large relief force from Marlborough caused the Indians to break off the fight, but the town was abandoned, the first of many in the area to be given over to the enemy.

In the wake of the Brookfield siege, an army of disparate companies from Massachusetts and Connecticut was cobbled together by the Puritan war council for offensive operations in the area of the river towns. During the last week in August, at Hopewell Swamp between Deerfield and Hatfield, two Massachusetts companies pursued a group of Indians who had fled into the swamp after local authorities demanded that they turn over their weapons. When the English force engaged the Indians in the swamp, nine English soldiers were killed.

This was neither the first nor last time that an English demand for the surrender of firearms had come to grief. Although no Englishman on record seems to have recognized the legitimacy of Philip's grievances—not even Roger Williams—several Englishmen in positions of authority attributed the rapid growth of Indian combatants to ham-fisted attempts to disarm or take into custody Indian bands that had never given even the slightest indication of hostility.

Fall 1675 was a grim time for the English of New England. The Indians carried out a long string of successful ambushes and raids. Between August 1 and November 10, all eight Massachusetts towns on the Connecticut River were attacked. Three towns, Brookfield, Deerfield, and Northfield, had to be abandoned. Two miles south of Northfield, deep in the forest, early on the morning of September 4, Captain Richard Beers lost his life along with those of half his company of thirty-six men in an ambush. Two weeks later, in one of the costliest engagements in the war to date, a supply column fell into a Nipmuck ambush five miles south of Deerfield. Only the arrival of Captain Samuel Moseley's battle-hardened volunteers saved Captain Thomas Lathrop's force from complete annihilation. As it was, Moseley's company buried sixty-four English corpses in the wake of the battle of Bloody Brook.

"As the Puritans saw it, their Bible Commonwealth was failing, consigned by God to a scourging by the forces of Satan as punishment for the sins of New England," writes historian Alan Taylor. "To vindicate their God and prove their own worthiness, the Puritans felt compelled to destroy their Indian enemies."[10] Yet, to their despair and their horror, the Indian forces proved as elusive as spirits in the wind. They struck hard and fast, only to withdraw deep into the woods, just as plodding English reaction forces began to arrive on the scene of the attack.

One reason for the extended series of English defeats was the enduring belief on the part of the Puritan military leaders that the traditional tactics and maneuvers they had learned on the battlefields of the English Civil War were inherently superior to those the "savages" employed in the forests of New England. "Because there was a lingering feeling that civilized gentlemen must not fight like savages," writes Douglas Leach, "the lives of many civilized gentlemen were lost."[11] Only the grudging adaptation of the Indians' "skulking" way of war, and the recruitment of significant numbers of friendly Indian scouts and guides by the United Colonies, would turn the tide of the conflict. And that did not begin to happen until the spring of 1676. (Later, the descendants of the colonists would adopt the same Indian tactics against British soldiers in the American Revolution.)

On the other hand, the Indians showed a keen willingness to adapt English technologies and tactics to supplement their own. They prized the relatively quick-loading and effective flintlock rifle and were generally far better shots than their adversaries because they hunted regularly, while English farmers did not. And the Indians had learned, writes scholar Patrick M. Malone,

> that the traditional restraints which had limited deaths in aboriginal warfare [before the arrival of the Europeans] were nothing more than liabilities in any serious conflict with the English

> colonists. . . . The Wampanoags, Narragansetts, Nipmucks and Pocumtucks who either joined or were swept into the war with the English and their Indian allies in 1675 followed the precedent set in the Pequot War. They waged war on all colonists, not just combatants, and they used every means at their disposal to defeat their enemies. The total warfare which the English had introduced to New England became a nightmare for the frontier towns and militia bands. Although nothing that the Indians did ever approached the horror of the Pequot fort, King Philip's war showed the English how well and how fiercely Native Americans could fight.[12]

The success of the uprising was about to lead the United Colonies to make a pivotal decision that would change the face of the war for everyone, especially the Narragansett Indians.

Chapter 10

The Narragansett War

This statue of Canonchet, the great war chief of the Narragansetts in King Philip's War, sits on the main green of the town of Narragansett, Rhode Island. Warriors under his command razed the towns of Warwick and Providence in March 1676.

When the commissioners of the United Colonies convened on November 2 to discuss the future course of the conflict, they faced a decision of the utmost gravity: What should be done about the Narragansetts? The most powerful tribe in southern New England had come under intense suspicion as the rebellion picked up momentum in the fall. Miantonomi's son, the young sachem Canonchet, and Ninigret's chief counselor, Cornman, had come to Boston on October 18 to confirm for the third time since the outbreak of hostilities the Narragansetts' commitment to remain allied to the English. They had promised to turn over all

Wampanoag refugees living among them no later than October 28. That day had come and gone, and not a single Wampanoag had been turned over.

Thomas Stanton and Richard Smith, two Englishmen in close touch with the tribe, reported that the Narragansetts received remarkably prompt intelligence on the rebels' military exploits in central Massachusetts—and seemed well pleased with the news. Meanwhile, an Indian from Plymouth who'd spent time among the Narragansetts that fall filed an ominous report: Canonchet and a large force of Narragansett warriors were planning to join the rebellion in the spring. This was yet another rumor, but one that many of the leading men in the United Colonies had good reason to believe true. If it was, perhaps the best course of action would be to launch a powerful preemptive strike while the Narragansetts' large force of warriors (estimates of their strength range from one thousand to two thousand) were still in the comparative isolation of southern Rhode Island.

About the best that can be said with certainty about Narragansett intentions in the fall of 1675 is that they remained ambivalent. Among the Narragansett sachems, Ninigret remained steadfast in his commitment to the English. Richard Smith joined Roger Williams in believing Pessacus sincerely wanted peace: "I believe that [Pessacus] of himself and some others incline to peace rather than war; but [the Narragansetts] have many unruly men, which cares not what become of them."[1]

To be sure, some Narragansett warriors had already joined Philip's uprising. But their number was small, and they had joined of their own volition, not on orders from the sachems. The vast majority of Narragansett men of fighting age remained at home, at war with no one. An Indian spy who had traveled at length with the anti-English Indians throughout the summer in Massachusetts told Puritan officials that the Narragansetts were not regarded as allies among the rebels, but as friends of the English.

The Narragansetts were, it seems, willing to go to some lengths to appease the English, but they were unwilling to turn over Wampanoag or Nipmuck noncombatants, or to engage in combat themselves against Philip's forces. Their reluctance to turn over women and children, many of whom were their kin, was reinforced by the United Colonies' "merciful" treatment of Wampanoags who had surrendered early in the conflict. They had been sold as slaves in the West Indies.

From the outset of the discussions, the delegations of both Plymouth and Massachusetts Bay were strongly inclined to confront the Narragansetts with force. Their view of the situation was nicely summed up by Daniel Gookin, a Massachusetts magistrate: "We judge they [the Narragansetts] do but juggle with us. . . . And that the . . . Narragansetts also are abroad (though they pretend a hunting) yet in conjunction with some of Philip's company."[2] Accordingly, the delegations wanted to mount a powerful expedition to force the issue: either the Narragansetts should abide by the terms of their agreements or face war. The senior Connecticut commissioner, Governor Winthrop, advocated a more moderate course of action. He thought it unwise to make "the potentest of all our neighboring heathen . . . open professed enemies because we have suspicion of them or cannot be so confident or certain of their continued fidelity."[3]

After sustained and at times heated debate, the commissioners decided that an army of one thousand men—the largest English military operation in North America to date—should be raised and sent into Narragansett country to confront the Indians. Either the Narragansetts must turn over "those enemies that are in their custody," make "reparations for all damages sustained by their neglect hitherto with security for their future fidelity," or the army was to "proceed against them as enemies."[4]

Given the unprecedented scope of the proposed invasion, and the long and frustrating history of the United Colonies' efforts to force the Narragansetts to submit to their authority, who could doubt that the sword would win out over peace? Metacom's uprising had given the United Colonies a pretext for ignoring the royal commissioners' prohibition against invading the King's Province, and they weren't about to let the opportunity slip by.

The expedition was to commence no later than December 10. The commissioners appointed Josiah Winslow as overall commander of the expedition and set troop quotas for each colony: 527 from Massachusetts, 355 from Connecticut, and 158 from Plymouth. The Massachusetts and Plymouth units were to rendezvous at Rehoboth and march overland to the advance base of operations at Smith's trading post at Cocumscussoc. Connecticut's forces, coming northeast from New London, would link up with the main army either at Cocumscussoc or at some other location in the Narragansett country, depending on what the scouting units led by Captain Samuel Moseley and Benjamin Church learned about the enemy's disposition.

By the time the main army arrived at Smith's trading post on December 13, Moseley and Church had rounded up more than thirty Narragansett prisoners. One of these men, a disgruntled Narragansett traitor named Peter, claimed to know the exact location of the main Narragansett settlement—a well-fortified palisaded village in the midst of a remote swamp, about sixteen miles to the southwest of Cocumscussoc. He agreed to serve as guide for the expedition.

Peter may or may not have tipped off General Winslow to the location of another encampment of Narragansetts under Quaiapen three miles due west of Cocumscussoc. A company or so of mounted troops launched a surprise attack against her fort on December 14. Most of the Indians fled into the surrounding woods. Seven Indians were killed, and eight prisoners taken.

The next day, a Narragansett Indian by the name of Stonewall John, with an excellent command of English, arrived at

Cocumscussoc in an apparent attempt to sue for peace, but he was turned away by General Winslow as having insufficient authority to conduct negotiations. Douglas Leach suggests that Stonewall John's actual intention may have been to gain intelligence on the size and disposition of the English forces. Just minutes after he'd left Cocumscussoc, a Narragansett raiding party killed or wounded three English soldiers in the vicinity; three more were slain a few miles from the base just hours later.

That same day, Winslow, anxious over the failure of the Connecticut force to arrive on schedule, dispatched a company to Jireh Bull's garrison house twelve miles to the south on the Pettaquamscutt River to see if they could pick up any intelligence about their whereabouts. The troopers found Bull's stone house gutted by fire, along with fifteen English corpses scattered about. This discovery, along with the attack on Quaiapen's fort, put to rest whatever slim possibility there had been for a diplomatic solution.

On the seventeenth, Major Robert Treat's Connecticut force, 300 English troops and 150 Pequots and Mohegans, finally arrived at Bull's garrison. Winslow now finalized his plan to attack the main Indian fort identified by the Narragansett traitor, Peter. The Massachusetts and Plymouth forces would march down to Bull's house on the morning of the eighteenth, link up with Treat's troops, and bivouac there for the night. At dawn they would begin their march west, to the swamp, with Peter serving as guide.

The troops moved out from Wickford in good order on the morning of the eighteenth, arriving at Bull's garrison around 5:00 p.m. The night of the eighteenth was frigid and stormy—a thick blanket of snow greeted the first risers on the morning of the nineteenth. The men had slept fitfully, if at all, in the open fields around the garrison house. Chilled to the bone, they were understandably apprehensive about the mission that lay ahead. Most had never engaged in combat, let alone combat deep in enemy territory against the largest confederation of Indians in the region.

Moreover, supply ships from Boston had failed to arrive at Cocumscussoc, and most men had only a day or two of rations with them as they departed that morning.

The army marched in column with infrequent breaks for about six hours, arriving on the outskirts of the swamp around 1:00 p.m. There the units in the van were met with desultory musket fire from Indian skirmishers. A number of the English troopers broke from the ranks, in hot pursuit of the Indians. The rest looked out on a massive, fortified Indian village in the midst of the snow-covered, frozen swamp. Extending for four or five acres, it was enclosed by a palisade wall about twelve feet high. Around the perimeter of the wall was a thick berm of earth, brush, and felled trees. Between the berm and the wall were strategically located blockhouses and flankers from which defenders could fire on any attackers attempting to scale the wall.

What appeared as the main entrance to the fort was accessed by a single long tree trunk, which crossed a moat of frozen water between the thick berm and the opening in the palisade wall. This opening was well covered by several flankers and a blockhouse. Soldiers attempting to gain entrance would have to do so in single file. Thus, they would have been easy prey for Indian muskets as they attempted to cross the moat. The entrance was quickly deemed unassailable.

Not long after the battle commenced and several companies had dispersed around the fort's perimeter, Captain Nathaniel Davenport and Captain Isaac Johnson and their companies found another entrance at a remote corner of the fort, just large enough to permit the entrance of two or three men at a time. It, too, was well covered by musket fire from a blockhouse. The English troops rushed the opening and struggled to gain entrance. Captain Johnson fell dead as he led the first push into the fort. Captain Davenport was killed just inside the fortress. Five more Puritan captains, all company commanders, would fall before the battle's end. Their men pressed forward, firing and shouting. Fifteen or twenty troops penetrated the Narragansett sanctum. Warriors quickly converged on the breach, counterattacked, and forced the English out, but a second attempt to gain entrance to the fort was successful, and a great and confused melee ensued.

For the next four hours, amid the din of musket fire and war cries of the enraged Indians, the adversaries engaged in close and desperate combat. Inside the fort, women and children hid from the flying lead inside wigwams, many of which were packed with bags and tubs of corn and other provisions for the winter. The combatants went at each other with every weapon at their disposal, including muskets, bows, war clubs, tomahawks, sabers, knives, and rocks. Meanwhile, outside the fort, English troops skulked in and around the swamp in search of their adversaries or concealed themselves in the snowy woods, holding their fire until a good target came by.

An hour or so into the fight, the irrepressible Benjamin Church, according to his own account, hastened out of the fort with his thirty-man company.

> to get a shot at the Indians in the swamp . . . He soon met with a broad bloody track, where the enemy had fled with their wounded men. Following hard in the track, he soon spied one of the enemy, who clapped his gun across his breast, made toward Mr. Church, and beckoned him with his hand. Mr. Church immediately commanded no man to hurt him, hoping by him to have gained some intelligence of the enemy that might be of advantage; but it unhappily fell out that a fellow that had lagged behind . . . shot the Indian, to Mr. Church's great grief and disappointment. But immediately they heard a great shout of the enemy . . . [Church's unit was] favored by a heap of brush that was between them and the enemy and prevented their being discovered to them . . .

> "Now, brave boys," said Mr. Church to his men, "if we mind our hits, we may have a brave shot, and let our sign for firing on them be their rising up to fire into the fort." It was not long before the Indians, rising up as one body, designed to pour a volley into the fort, when [Church's men] started up and gave them such a round volley and unexpected clap on their backs, that they who escaped with their lives were so surprised that they scampered, they knew not wither themselves.[5]

Sometime between 3:00 and 4:00 p.m., the English gained control of the interior of the fort. Despite the presence of large quantities of ground corn, meat, and other provisions, in addition to several hundred terrified Indian women and children, the English army put the fort to the torch. Benjamin Church attempted to persuade General Winslow to remain the night at the scene to tend to the wounded, but Winslow, fearing a Narragansett counterattack, ordered a march all the way back to Wickford. It was said that the first three miles of the trek back to Cocumscussoc were backlit by the flames of the burning fort.

No one knows how many Narragansetts were killed in the Great Swamp encounter. English estimates at the time varied widely. Eyewitness accounts have it that between two hundred and three hundred warriors were killed in the fighting, along with four hundred noncombatants, the latter mostly by fire. But several hundred warriors escaped the inferno with their lives and their weapons. Among them was Canonchet, the young sachem who would soon emerge as the leading war chief of the tribe. Surely, too, at least a few dozen traumatized women and children also escaped the inferno, making their way through the icy wilderness to find shelter at one of several smaller Narragansett encampments in the area, including Ninigret's inland village some seven or eight miles to the south. The English suffered more than two hundred casualties in the Great Swamp Fight—a fifth of the expeditionary force—including twenty men killed in action, and sixty who died soon after of their wounds or from the extreme weather. The vanguard of the exhausted, half-frozen column stumbled into Smith's trading house around 2:00 a.m. on December 20. Winslow's command group lost its way in the storm that continued to buffet the area and did not arrive until seven that morning. Twenty-two of the wounded had died on the march back to Cocumscussoc.

The English of New England rejoiced at the news of their army's success. To be sure, the Great Swamp Fight had dealt a staggering blow to the Narragansetts. But the English army had failed to achieve its chief objective, which was to crush the confederation's military potential. The most important result of the assault was that it brought at least a thousand angry Narragansett warriors into the fighting, bent on retribution. They were led by Canonchet, whom many contemporary sources depict as the rebellion's finest strategist and commander during 1676—"a very proper man, of goodly stature and great courage of mind, as well as strength of body."[6]

Intercolony squabbling over the provision of fresh troops and supplies, and a generally low level of military competence, kept Winslow's army from pursuing the Narragansetts on their seventy-mile march to the headquarters of the uprising at Menameset, in Nipmuck country, until January 28. By then it was too late. The Narragansetts had begun their trek during a mid-January thaw that had melted the snow and made it next to impossible for the Puritan army's Indian scouts to track their enemy's progress. In rearguard skirmishes with colonial army scouts perhaps a handful of Narragansetts lost their lives as they made their way toward Menameset. The last of the Narragansett warriors arrived at the great Indian encampment in early February.

By that date, more than two thousand Indians were concentrated in and around Menameset and Mount Wachusett in central

Massachusetts. We know from a Puritan woman captive who was at Menameset at this time that the Indian warriors there "derided the slowness and dullness of the English army in its setting out. . . . Thus did they scoff at us, as if the English would be a quarter of a year in getting ready."[7] Narragansett warriors, along with those of the Nipmuck sachems Matoonas, Muttaump, and Sagamore Sam, would join Philip's original followers in executing the February raiding campaign already planned against settlements west of Boston, including Lancaster, Marlborough, Medfield, and Sudbury.

Remarkably, a Christian Indian spy in the ranks of Philip's supporters, Job Kattenanit, warned the authorities of the first attack, on Lancaster, late in the night on February 9, just hours before the Indians raided the town. A forty-man cavalry troop arrived in Lancaster early on the morning of the tenth, but the damage had already been done. Several hundred Nipmuck and Narragansett warriors had burned most of the town to the ground, killed a dozen people, and broken through the defenses of one of the town's half dozen garrison houses.

The Indians spirited away about twenty women and children, including the wife of the town minister, Mary Rowlandson, and her young daughter, who died nine days later of wounds sustained in the initial attack. For much of the eighty-two days of Rowlandson's captivity, she was kept on the run with Indian raiding parties, making many punishing, daylong marches, and setting up temporary camps in the woods about twenty times. She worked for much of her time with the Indians as a servant to the Narragansett sachem Quinnapin, a nephew of Miantonomi's, and his family. Several weeks into Rowlandson's ordeal, her captors linked up with Philip and a band of Wampanoags. The Wampanoag chief had just returned from a failed mission to enlist the Mohawks in the rebellion.

Rowlandson's 1682 book about her experiences, *The Sovereignty and Goodness of God*—the first North American publication by a living woman—offers a vivid and penetrating view of life among the Indians as they conducted their special brand of mobile warfare:

> I was with the Enemy eleven weeks and five days, and not one week passed without the fury of the Enemy, and some desolation by fire and sword upon one place or other. They mourned (with their black faces) for their own losses, yet triumphed and rejoiced in their inhumane, and many times devilish cruelty to the English. They would boast much of their victories; saying, that in two hours' time they had destroyed such a captain, and his company at such a place; and such a captain and his company in his place . . . and boast how many towns they had destroyed, and they scoff, and say, *They had done them a good turn, to send them to Heaven so soon.*[8]

Here we have a harrowing picture of a large Indian band on the move, as the Puritan forces give chase:

> The occasion of their moving at this time, was, the English Army, it being near and following them: For they went, as if they had gone for their lives, some considerable way, and then they made a stop, and chose some of their stoutest men, and sent them back to hold the English army in play whilst the rest escaped; and then, like Jehu, they marched on furiously, with their old, and with their young: some carried their old decrepit mothers. . . . Four of them carried a great Indian on a bier; but going through a thick wood with him, they were hindered, and could make no haste; whereupon they took him upon their backs and carried him, one at a time, till they came to the Bacquag [Millers] River.[9]

Before a major attack on the town of Sudbury, Rowlandson witnessed a remarkable pre-battle ceremony:

> Before they went to that fight, they got a company together to powwow; the manner was the followeth: There was one that kneeled upon a deer-skin, with the company round him in a ring who kneeled, and striking upon the ground with their hands, and with sticks, and muttering or humming with their mouths, besides him who kneeled in the ring, there also stood one with a gun in his hand: Then he on the deer-skin made a speech, and all manifested assent to it; and so they did many times together. Then they bade him with the gun out of the ring, which he did, but when he was out, they called him in again; but he seemed to make a stand, then they called him more earnestly, till he returned again: then they all sang. Then they gave him two guns, in either hand one: and so he on the deer-skin began [speaking] again; and at the end of every sentence in his speaking, they all assented . . . striking upon the ground with their hands.[10]

Rowlandson's dual status as a sachem's servant and a Puritan captive ensured that she was treated with both great kindness and harsh cruelty. Beaten and slapped by the vain and severe Pocasset squaw sachem, Weetamoo—one of Quinnapin's three wives—Rowlandson was nonetheless shown considerable compassion by Quinnapin and Metacom, both of whom gave her food and consolation at several junctures.

From her account we know that the Indians had already begun to suffer from serious food shortages that would soon lead to widespread demoralization and desertion among Metacom's forces. Rowlandson reports that her captors were reduced to eating tree bark, bones, and plundered English provisions. Their stores of corn had been completely exhausted.

Although some isolated farmhouses and unlucky travelers were menaced by bands of Indians in the area over the following few days, the next major attack didn't occur until February 21, against Medfield, less than twenty miles southwest of Boston. Although a hundred colony troops were stationed in and around the town, the stealthy Indians entered the village proper undetected late in the evening, hid, and awaited daybreak. At dawn they began to set houses and barns alight. Before the English troops could organize themselves for an attack, the Indians withdrew across a bridge over the Charles River, but not before one of the warriors had attached a defiant note to the bridge:

> Know by this paper, that the Indians that thou hast provoked to wrath and anger, will war this twenty one years if you will; there are many Indians yet, we come three hundred at this time. You must consider the Indians lost nothing but their life; you must lose your fair houses and cattle.[11]

Four nights later, the Indians struck Weymouth on the Massachusetts coast, partially destroying the town. Arrogance and prejudice precluded the United Colonies army in Massachusetts from taking the step that would have greatly improved their military performance: recruiting friendly Indians as scouts, guides, and fighters. A new wave of desperation began to set in among the English of New England as fears grew that continued attacks would prevent farmers from preparing their fields for spring planting.

Although Philip remained in central Massachusetts with the Nipmucks for several more months, it appears that around this time a combined force of Wampanoag, Narragansett, and Nipmuck warriors returned to Plymouth and Rhode Island under the overall leadership of Canonchet. At Philip's request, Canonchet had earlier led a small party back to Mount Hope from Nipmuck country to retrieve some hidden seed corn and seen to it that the seed was delivered to Indians in the Connecticut River valley for planting.

Now Canonchet's powerful combined force would wreak havoc on the towns in Plymouth, and on the Rhode Island mainland. The campaign in the east began on March 12 with a bold strike on William Clark's garrison house near the Eel River, just three miles south of the town of Plymouth. Eleven settlers were killed, spreading a new wave of terror not far from the rebellion's original epicenter.

A few days later, most of the deserted homes at Warwick and Wickford went up in flames, including Smith's garrison house at Cocumscussoc. On March 26, five miles north of Providence along the Blackstone River, in modern Cumberland, Rhode Island, a company of sixty-five English troops with Indian auxiliaries under Captain Michael Pierce went out in search of a band of hostile Indians spotted several times the previous day. Moving along the eastern riverbank, they spotted several Indians and gave chase. Within a few minutes Pierce and his company were in deep trouble, surrounded by a force of more than five hundred Indians. Organizing his men into a circular perimeter, Pierce fought a furious battle, but the heavily outnumbered English troops were soon overwhelmed. Over the next few days, forty-two English bodies were buried near the scene of the fight. Nine of those bodies were found a short distance away. These troops had been tortured before being killed.

Providence came under attack three days later. By 1676, Rhode Island's second most populous town was home to five hundred people. All but about thirty inhabitants had fled to the comparative safety of Aquidneck Island when the town was attacked by several hundred warriors from different anti-English tribes. As the Indians began to loot and burn the homes on Towne Street, seventy-three-year-old Roger Williams emerged from a garrison house unarmed and confronted the Indians. Even at such an advanced age, as his own home burned behind him, he felt compelled to do what he had been doing for the last forty-five years—to talk, to understand, to do what he could in this orgy of destruction to bring peace. In a letter to his brother composed not long after the confrontation, he wrote:

> I asked them why they assaulted us [i.e., the people of Providence] with burning and killing who had long been kind neighbors to them. This house of mine now burning before my eyes had lodged kindly some thousands of you these ten years. They answered that we were their enemies joined with Massachusetts and Plymouth, entertaining, assisting . . . guiding them, and I said . . . neither we nor this colony had acted in hostility against them. I told them this while they were killing and burning . . . like wolves tearing and devouring the innocent and peaceable. I told them they had no regard for their wives, relations . . . nor to God whom they confessed made them and all things. They confessed they were in a strange way.[12]

Williams reminded the raiders that he had many times in the past "quenched fires" between the Indians and all three of the warring colonies. And he "did not doubt (God assisting me) to quench this [fire] and help restore quietness to the land again."[13] He urged them to consult with the sachems and come up with a peace proposal, which he would then write up and send to the commissioners in Boston.

After at first dismissing the proposal out of hand, Kutquen, a Connecticut River Indian who seemed to be in command, said they would consider Williams's proposal after they returned to Plymouth, presumably to consult with Canonchet and the other leading figures of the uprising. This, the last of Williams's documented peace parleys with the Indians, occurred almost forty years after he and his small party of followers first crossed the Seekonk to settle at the headwaters of Narragansett Bay.

Peace was not much on the mind of Canonchet, who had by now established a reputation among Indians and English alike as a leader of great tenacity and courage. On April 9, he was with a small band of Indians in the vicinity of the Blackstone River not far from Providence when Captain George Denison's combined company of English troopers and Pequots suddenly threatened to surround his band. Heavily outnumbered, Canonchet's men made a run for it. The bold Narragansett war chief made a dash across the river, but slipped on a stone and fell into the water. A Pequot Indian named Monopoide took him captive.

According to historian William Hubbard, when asked to supply information about other rebel Indians in the area, Canonchet "boasted he would not deliver up a Wampanoag, or the paring of a Wampanoag's nail; that he would burn the English alive in their houses." Later, when he was told he would be put to death for refusing to try to convince the other leading sachems of the uprising to sue for peace, he said, "he liked it well, that he should die before his heart was soft or he had spoken anything unworthy of himself."[14]

At his own request, Canonchet of the Narragansetts was executed by Oneco, Uncas's son, in Stonington, Connecticut. His head was sent to the magistrates of Hartford as a sign that victory was near. It was a devastating loss to the cause of the uprising.

By late April, with Indian food supplies and ammunition dwindling, the military and psychological balance of forces in the war had shifted markedly in the direction of the United Colonies and their Indian allies. The war in central and western Massachusetts began to sputter to an end in May. On May 19, 150 troops under Captain William Turner launched a surprise attack on a major Indian base camp at Peskeomskut (later known as Turners Falls), killing close to two hundred Indians. Most of the casualties were women, old men, and children. Not since the Great Swamp Fight had so many Indians been lost in a single attack. Turner would lose his life in a retaliatory attack, but by mid-June, Indian raids in central Massachusetts had come to an end.

The English had at last begun to adapt Indian tactics in the field. Virtually all colonial army units, and some local militia, had integrated Indians into their ranks as scouts, guides, and regular fighters. In addition, the colonial forces initiated a scorched-earth campaign, denying the Indians desperately needed food caches. Months of Indian military success had indeed produced widespread shock and even despair in the hearts of the English populace. Yet paradoxically, it had also strengthened popular resolve to vanquish an enemy seen as both traitorous and barbarous.

For the anti-English Indians it was an altogether different story. After almost a year of crisscrossing the countryside and fighting frequently, they were generally exhausted, homesick, and hungry. Indian captives reported that disease and famine had killed far more Indians than English bullets. The killing of hundreds of Indian women and children at the hands of the English army, and the confirmation of reports that hundreds of their kin had already been sold off as slaves in the West Indies, had a devastating effect on the morale of the rebel warriors.

Benjamin Church's English-Indian volunteer company had developed a reputation as a first-rate fighting force, led by a man with a rare sense of empathy for the Indians. He was now regularly taking the surrender of Indians who had simply had enough. "They were weary of fighting," explained Church, "and . . . had fought so long by Philip's instigation, but they could not tell for what end, and therefore were resolved they would fight no longer."[15]

Church had it exactly right: the widespread success of months of raiding failed to produce an achievable objective, a realizable goal to make continued sacrifice seem worthwhile. For the Indians of the uprising, King Philip's War was a conflict, writes Edmund Morgan, "with abundant causes but without a cause: it produced no real program of reform, no revolutionary manifesto, not even any revolutionary slogan."[16] The rebellion had several other fundamental weaknesses. After Philip's journey into Nipmuck country, the uprising expanded geographically, but it lacked an overarching commander and a long-term strategy. Canonchet's campaign along the coast had no strategic connection with the

Nipmuck and Pocumtuck operations in central Massachusetts, and the strikes in both of the major campaigns had a decidedly random pattern.

Nor had the long string of Indian military victories in the first ten months of the conflict induced substantive concessions from the enemy. There was no talk among the United Colonies commissioners of bringing the war to a rapid end with a promise to apportion land west of the line of English settlement for the Indians to live according to their own ways. By early summer, the only offer the United Colonies put forward to the warring tribes was for merciful treatment for those who surrendered, and that only applied to noncombatant Indians. Fighters faced execution.

The death of Canonchet was a staggering blow to the Narragansett confederation. He had been the driving force behind their war effort since the Great Swamp Fight. Late in May, the remaining Narragansett sachems sent word to Massachusetts that they wanted to talk peace. The Bay Colony sent an Indian emissary, Peter Ephraim, to meet with the sachems, but he was taken captive by Connecticut forces and kept well clear of the Narragansetts. Connecticut was about to initiate an aggressive mop-up campaign against the much-diminished tribe to lay the groundwork for a claim of jurisdiction in the Narragansett country. The last thing Hartford wanted was a wholesale Narragansett surrender to Massachusetts before it had completed its ambitious campaign.

A volunteer force of troops from New London, Norwich, and Stonington made two sweeps into the Narragansett country just east of the Pawcatuck River in June, encountering and defeating considerable numbers of Narragansetts. Far more lethal than those forays, though, was the early July expedition into Narragansett country by Major John Talcott's battalion of four hundred Connecticut, Mohegan, and Pequot troops. With specific instructions from Connecticut's War Council at Hartford to "kill and destroy them, according to the utmost power God shall give you," Talcott did his best.[17] On the morning of July 2, not far from where Michael Pierce and his force had met their end, Talcott's unit caught a large encampment of Narragansetts by surprise. How many of the Rhode Island Indians were armed combatants is unclear, but the death toll—171 men, women, and children—suggests the engagement was more of a massacre than a battle. Among the dead was the squaw sachem, Quaiapen.

The next day, Talcott learned that a substantial number of Narragansetts under the sachem Potuck were at Warwick Neck, Pomham's old stomping grounds. They were awaiting Potuck's return from Newport, where he was trying to arrange their surrender. Talcott's men attacked them nonetheless, killing or capturing sixty-seven Indians. For all intents and purposes, Narragansett resistance had collapsed by mid-July.

By then, Philip and a small number of Wampanoag fighters had returned to Plymouth, probably for no other reason than they had nowhere else to go. He may well have been hastened out of central Massachusetts by talk among the weary Nipmucks and Pocumtucks that they might gain better surrender terms for themselves and their people if they surrendered Philip's head to the authorities. After playing cat and mouse with Church's joint volunteer company for more than two weeks, Philip was tracked down to a swamp on the southwestern edge of Mount Hope peninsula. There, early on the morning of August 12, Philip met his end, killed by the musket fire of a Sakonnet Indian. A handful of skirmishes followed Philip's death, but for all intents and purposes, the Indian uprising in southern New England was over.

Chapter 11

Aftermath

Narragansett Indians gather in front of their church in Charlestown, Rhode Island, during the 1925 powwow. The church is still there today, and the powwow, held each August, is an important Narragansett ritual.

The end of the fighting brought joy and immense relief to the English in New England. God had tested them through the trial of a brutal and merciless conflict against the savages, they believed, and through God's infinite mercy, they had prevailed. But the costs were staggering. More than a thousand lives had been lost, including several hundred women and children. A dozen towns, including Wickford and Warwick, had been burned to the ground. Another forty settlements had suffered significant damage. In all, twelve hundred houses in southern New England had gone up in flames, and eight thousand head of cattle had been killed. The bustling New England economy was in a shambles.

The spirit of unity among the Puritan colonies that had blossomed in the cauldron of total war soon gave way to a series of bitter disputes over the spoils of victory and the management of the reconstruction. These conflicts inevitably led to protracted intervention by the crown in New England's political and economic affairs—interference bitterly resisted by the Puritan establishment, particularly in Massachusetts.

Royal intervention, land lust, and the dislocation of war ate away at the vitals of the Christian commonwealths. "Ironically," observes historian James David Drake, "the reduction of Indian political power in New England did not make the orthodoxy of Puritans in Massachusetts more dominant; rather, the postwar Puritans eventually became like a minority ethnic group themselves. . . . The years after King Philip's War witnessed the Anglicization of the New England colonies, and their greater incorporation within London's imperial system."[1] With the demise of Indian power and sovereignty, the contest over land and authority among the colonies intensified around the Connecticut–New York border, around the southern parts of what would become the states of Maine and New Hampshire, and, of course, in the Narragansett country.

By the early eighteenth century, Puritanism as a distinct way of life was fading out, though the imprint of Puritan ideas of self-discipline, moral rectitude, and America as the "New Israel" continue to exert an enormous influence on the culture of New England and, indeed, that of the United States, right up to this day.

For the Indians, Metacom's War was an unmitigated catastrophe. The conflict, writes historian Jill Lepore, was the "defining moment, when any lingering, though slight possibility for [Indian] political and cultural autonomy was lost."[2] About four thousand Indians had died—more from starvation and exposure than in combat. At least that many fled southern New England entirely, seeking to retain some measure of their freedom and traditional lifestyle with other Native Americans in Canada, or among the Abenaki and other tribes in northern New England and New York. Some of these Indians would return as allies of the French to conduct a devastating series of raids on English settlements early in the eighteenth century.

Hundreds of Indians, perhaps as many as a thousand, were either sold into permanent slavery or long-term servitude in New England and the Caribbean. Even the children of those who'd surrendered based on promises of merciful treatment were sometimes sold into long-term servitude to New England households. According to contemporary reports, some native parents killed their own children or had them killed by others rather than see them suffer such a cruel fate.[3] Scores of Indians sold off into servitude undoubtedly had no connection at all to Philip's forces, as "most colonists accepted . . . that the vast majority of Indians were guilty by association."[4]

Many of the pro-rebellion sachems and war chiefs who were captured or surrendered were ultimately executed by either town or colony authorities. The Narragansett war chief Chuff was executed by firing squad in Providence soon after surrendering in August 1676. On August 23, a special court-martial was held in Newport in which four Indians were convicted of treason and later executed.

For those Indians who remained in southern New England, life was harsh and unforgiving. There would be no returning to traditional village life. The colonies placed all Indians, even those who had fought with the Puritan army, under close supervision, prohibiting them from assembling in large numbers, or from possessing firearms.

Hundreds of displaced Indians eked out a living as day laborers on English farms. An early-eighteenth-century missionary at Natick, the largest Christian Indian town, observed wistfully that the Indians throughout southern New England "are generally considered by white people, and placed, as if by common consent, in an inferior and degraded situation, and treated accordingly." The colonists "took every advantage [of the Indians] that they could . . . to dishearten and depress them."[5]

And what of the Narragansetts? In an October 25, 1676, letter to the colony of Connecticut, which laid claim to the entire Narragansett country by right of conquest, the government of Rhode Island stated explicitly that it had never made war on the Narragansetts, and that the tribe had remained at peace "till by the United Colonies they were forced to war, or such submission as it seems they could not submit to."[6] It was true—Rhode Island had raised no troops to fight the Narragansetts or any other hostile tribe. But that didn't mean its citizens were about to turn the other cheek after Canonchet and his warriors had laid waste to Rhode Island's settlements on the mainland and killed or wounded so many fellow colonists.

One of the more significant casualties of King Philip's War was the uniquely symbiotic relationship between the Narragansetts and the leaders of the colony of Rhode Island. Williams, Gorton, Randall Holden, John Easton, and many other Rhode Islanders had relied on the Narragansetts as neighbors, trading partners, and allies in their joint struggle against Puritan domination, just as the Indians had relied on them. But in the sorry aftermath of war, Rhode Island treated the Indians only marginally better than the Puritan colonies. Although slavery was formally banned by the Rhode Island General Assembly in March 1676, a number of Indians held by the Rhode Island authorities were taken to Plymouth or Massachusetts Bay and sold outright.

A committee in Providence arranged scores of indentured-servant contracts for Indians with English settlers in both New England and the West Indies.[7] Roger Williams was a member of that committee. Apparently the founder of Providence did not question the traditional seventeenth-century practice of victors retaining custody over war captives, though according to one of the leading scholars on this subject, Williams strongly favored servitude for a finite period over outright slavery.[8] Sadly, however, Indian slavery did become an accepted practice in Rhode Island in the early eighteenth century.[9]

We know for certain that some displaced Narragansetts found a new home close to their old one, among Ninigret's people. Although Ninigret died sometime in the fall of 1676, he and his people had maintained strict neutrality during the war, and were rewarded for doing so. The Rhode Island government made no attempt to confiscate Niantic lands in the immediate aftermath of the war. A large swath of land in southern Narragansett country "remained a place of sanctuary where remnant groups of Narragansetts could live in relative tranquility."[10]

By the early eighteenth century, this Niantic-Narragansett community included some Wampanoag, Pequot, Nipmuck, and probably some River Indians as well. Before long, this mixed community began to call itself "the Narragansetts," and the contemporary Narragansett Indians of South County, Rhode Island, today trace their ancestry directly back to this group.

The basic trajectory of Narragansett history from the early eighteenth until the mid-twentieth century is similar to that of many other "vanquished" tribes. Beset by prejudice, poverty, and high rates of alcoholism, a few hundred souls persevered from generation to generation under the "protection" of the Rhode Island legislature. The state proved unable, unwilling, or both to guard the Indians' interests against the predations of outsiders, or the excesses of a number of tribal leaders who either embezzled or gambled away limited tribal assets.

As tribal lands were sold off bit by bit to speculators or to the towns in South County to pay off debts, most of the people who identified as Narragansett assimilated into mainstream American culture. Many became stonemasons, fishermen, and carpenters—traditions that continue to this day with Narragansett people. Yet all the while, the Narragansetts retained their identity as descendants of a proud nation that had held on tenaciously to its autonomy and its traditional way of life for a long time, under great duress.

After transferring 135,000 acres of tribal land to the colony government in 1709 in exchange for protection of a sixty-four-square-mile reservation against rival claims of jurisdiction, tribal fortunes spun downward. From 41,000 acres of common land in the early eighteenth century, the reservation was reduced to a mere 922 acres by 1880. In that year the Narragansetts were formally detribalized by an act of the Rhode Island legislature, ostensibly to encourage economic self-reliance and full integration of the remaining members of the tribe into American society. The tribal council quitclaimed all 922 acres to the state for a mere $5,000. That sum was split equally among the 324 men and women deemed to be members of the tribe at that time.

Detribalization put an end to the tribe only in the eyes of the law. A loose form of tribal organization was maintained through the Narragansett Christian church, which had emerged in the Great Awakening of religion in America in the 1740s and remains a powerful force in Narragansett life today. Several hundred people throughout Rhode Island and in a number of other communities in New England kept in touch with one another, attended the annual August powwow in Charlestown, and passed down Narragansett stories and rituals to their children. For them, detribalization was but one more episode in a long and bitter history of dispossession.

Revitalization of the tribe began in the 1930s, when John Collier, commissioner of the US Bureau of Indian Affairs, and a cadre of Indian leaders from all over the country encouraged Native Americans once again to actively embrace their heritage. The Narragansetts retribalized as a nonprofit corporation in 1934, opening membership to all descendants of the 324 people on the tribal rolls as of 1880.

Narragansett people embraced the Indian rights movement that emerged in the late 1960s and 1970s, which called on both federal and state governments—indeed, the American people—to address the injustices and humiliations they had inflicted on the Indians over the centuries. The movement also encouraged Indians from all the nations to celebrate their history and culture among the wider community.

In 1975, the Narragansett tribe went to court against the State of Rhode Island, arguing that the 1880 detribalization act was a violation of a 1790 law requiring agents of the federal government to oversee the transfer of all tribal lands. In an out-of-court settlement, the tribe was awarded eighteen hundred acres of land within Charlestown. In return, the Narragansetts agreed that "the settlement lands shall be subject to the civil and criminal laws and jurisdiction of the State of Rhode Island."[11]

In 1983, the Department of the Interior granted the Narragansetts formal federal recognition, opening the door for the tribe to receive federal assistance for education, job training, and health care. Today, the tribe numbers about twenty-four hundred people, and plays an active, and at times combative, role in Rhode Island politics. The chief sachem, Matthew Thomas, and the elected tribal council continue to press for greater independence and economic opportunity for their people.

The colony of Rhode Island survived its battle against Puritan domination, thanks in large measure to the sustained and determined efforts of Williams, his allies in Rhode Island and London, and the Narragansett Indians. The State of Rhode Island and Providence Plantations is "the smallest state with the longest name" in the union. Celebrated as the birthplace of religious freedom in America, it is a popular tourist destination, known for its beautiful beaches, Newport mansions, and a long tradition of colorfully corrupt politics. Paradoxically an integral part of New England and a quirky enclave apart, in Rhode Island, people, as the expression goes, "think otherwise." Localism reigns supreme in Rhode Island culture and politics today, just as it did in Roger Williams's time. In a state only forty-eight miles long and twenty-three miles wide, there are more than thirty separate school systems and thirty-five city and town police departments.

Roger Williams remained an active participant in his community during the last years of his life, frequently providing testimony about the early history of the town of Providence and of the colony of Rhode Island to various interested parties. In May 1682, he wrote to Governor Simon Bradstreet of Massachusetts, asking for help in printing twenty-two sermons Williams had delivered over the years. It may not have been the last letter Roger Williams wrote, but it is the last to have survived. The sermons were never published, perhaps because their author was now "old and weak and bruised (with a rupture and colic) and lameness on both my feet."[12]

The founder of Providence died sometime between January 27 and March 15, 1683. We know nothing about his last days, and little about his funeral. Williams, who never found the time to pose for a portrait, would probably have wanted it that way. A contemporary witness reported that his funeral was marked by "a considerable parade." Guns were fired by the colony militia over his grave, located on the hill behind his house on Towne Street.[13]

Williams is still Rhode Island's most celebrated and historically significant individual. His extraordinary life and work continue to command the attention of both scholars and ordinary citizens who are curious about the origins of the dissenting tradition in America, and the meaning of political as well as religious liberty. Perry Miller, the Harvard historian, is surely correct when he writes that for Williams "the Christian predicament—which was also the glory of Christianity—was to hold what the believer conceives to be truth with fierce tenacity, yet never attempting to impose that truth upon the minds or souls of other men."[14] This early rebel against the established order in New England was ready to risk everything he had, and more, in pursuit of the mystery of human freedom.

Williams saw more clearly than any other first-generation English settler the dire implications for the Indians of the Puritans' inclination to mistake their own vision of truth and the good society for God's. For fifty years, he struggled to bring to light the yawning gap between Christ's teachings as he understood them, and the Gospel of the New England Way. He did so not only for the welfare of the Indians, but for the good of the colony that he helped to found, for in Williams's eyes the fate of the Narragansetts and the colony of Rhode Island went hand in hand. But above all, Roger Williams defended the Narragansetts and his fellow Rhode Island settlers against the predations of the Puritan establishment because he felt called to do so by the spirit of Christ. For Christ was Williams's anchor and inspiration in every facet of a long and varied career of public service.

As Puritan power became more entrenched and aggressive, and the Narragansetts' position more tenuous, Williams must have sensed that the day of reckoning was fast approaching. Yet he did not lose heart. He continued to lobby vigorously for peace and reconciliation up to the Puritans' preemptive strike against the Narragansetts in the Great Swamp. Even as the Indians razed Providence after nine months of horrific fighting, he put himself forward one last time as an instrument of peace.

"Concerning Indian affairs, reports are various," Williams had written to John Winthrop Jr. back in the spring of 1647. "Lies are frequent. Private interests, both with Indians and English are many; yet these things you may and must do. First, kiss the truth where you evidently, upon your soul, see it. 2. Advance justice, through a child's eyes. 3. Seek and make peace, if possible, with all men. 4. Secure your own life from a revengeful, malicious arrow or hatchet."[15] As a concise primer on the art of diplomacy—or the art of living a good life—it wasn't a bad start.

Williams has been justly celebrated as America's first advocate for religious liberty and separation of church and state, and for putting both those principles into practice in Rhode Island. But his role as peacemaker, as tireless servant of the public good—with *public* being expansively defined to include the Indians—hasn't been as widely appreciated as it should be. Williams's relationship with his Narragansett neighbors reveals early glimmerings of an alternative vision of Indian-white relations in America. He saw Rhode Island as an experiment in religious liberty and frontier democracy, where people of different races, faiths, and cultures could put aside their differences and live together in a spirit of cooperation and civility.

In the alliance between Williams and the Narragansett, and in Williams's quest to establish a tolerant and pluralistic haven in the heart of Puritan New England, we can glimpse at work ideas well ahead of their time. Those ideas would eventually rise up in powerful condemnation of the wanton and destructive treatment the Puritan oligarchy and its descendants inflicted on the people who were here long before Euro-American history began.

Acknowledgments

While researching and writing *God, War, and Providence*, I drew insight and inspiration from the work of scores of scholars who've toiled in the vineyard of Puritan-Indian relations in early New England far longer than a freelance writer ever could. Many of their names and works appear in the endnotes of this book, but a few deserve special mention here. The idea for this book emerged from my reading of Francis Jennings's *The Invasion of America*, a seminal work in the field if there ever was one, and a fascinating article in the *New England Quarterly* by Jack L. Davis, "Roger Williams among the Narragansett Indians."

William S. Simmons's fine work on the Narragansetts, and Glenn LaFantasie's meticulously edited *The Correspondence of Roger Williams*, proved absolutely indispensable in researching this story. Everyone seeking to understand American Puritanism and the novel ideas of Roger Williams owes a debt to the pioneering work of Perry Miller and Edmund S. Morgan. I'm no exception. It was Professor William G. McLoughlin who first piqued my interest in the Indian–Euro-American encounter when I was an undergraduate at Brown University in the late 1970s.

I am grateful indeed to several other Brown professors for their help and support on this project. Evelyn Hu-DeHart offered me a two-year post as a visiting scholar in the American Studies Department in 2012–14, during which time I conducted most of the research for the book. American Studies professor Patrick

Malone provided moral support in addition to many insightful comments on several early draft chapters. Linford D. Fisher, associate professor of history, read my initial proposal and sample copy and made some terrific suggestions.

Without the able and cheerful assistance of the librarians of Brown University, the University of Rhode Island, and the Rhode Island Historical Society, the book would never have seen print.

It's been my good fortune to publish this book under the wise and able direction of Colin Harrison, editor in chief of Scribner. Colin's superb editing improved my draft manuscript more than I can possibly say, and his enthusiasm for the story was infectious. Sarah Goldberg, assistant editor, responded to my many pleas for help and guidance with remarkable alacrity and good cheer. Copy editor Steve Boldt punched up the prose very nicely, and saved me from some embarrassing errors of chronology.

My agent, John F. Thornton, believed in the project from start to finish. He read many early drafts, and offered a wealth of sound editorial advice. Tom Verde, a fine writer himself with a keen interest in New England history, read the entire draft manuscript and urged me—strongly—to make the book less a study and more of a story. I have tried hard to follow his advice.

Thanks to Todd Mennillo, Mark Sutton, Amy Lipman, Ursula Brandl, Kate Robins, Dave Warren, Kay, Kat, Lucas, and John Ho, Peter Cornillon, Peter and Helen Flynn, and Vance and Ted Gatchel for their friendship and moral support.

Special thanks to my partner, Lynn Ho, for all kinds of support and encouragement . . . and for putting up with me when the going got tough, which it often did.

Notes

INTRODUCTION

1 Patrick M. Malone, "King Philip's War," in *The Oxford Companion to American Military History* (New York: Oxford University Press, 1999), 366.

2 Eliot quoted in Jean M. O'Brien, *Dispossession by Degrees: Indian Land and Identity in Natick, Massachusetts, 1650–1790* (Cambridge, UK: Cambridge University Press, 1997), 27.

3 Roger Williams, *The Correspondence of Roger Williams*, ed. Glenn LaFantasie (Hanover, NH: Brown University Press/University Press of New England, 1988), 605. Hereafter cited as *CRW.*

CHAPTER 1—1635: INDIANS AND PURITANS, SEPARATE AND TOGETHER

1 William Wood, *New England's Prospect*, ed. Alden T. Vaughan (1634; repr., Amherst: University of Massachusetts Press, 1993), 58–59. Hereafter Wood, *Prospect.*

2 Ronald Dale Karr, ed., *Indian New England, 1524–1674: A Compendium of Eyewitness Accounts of Native American Life* (Pepperell, MA: Branch Line Press, 1999), 19–23.

3 Patrick M. Malone, email correspondence with the author, September 19, 2017.

4 William Cronon, *Changes in the Land: Indians, Colonists, and the Ecology of New England* (New York: Hill & Wang, 1983), 34–37.

5 Roger Williams, *A Key into the Language of America* (1643; repr. of 5th ed., 1936, Bedford, MA: Applewood Books, n.d.), 135. Hereafter Williams, *A Key.*

6 Ibid, 124.

7 Ibid., 126.

8 Wood, *Prospect*, 88.

9 Paul A. Robinson, "Lost Opportunities: Miantonomi and the English in Seventeenth-Century Narragansett Country," in *Northeastern Indian Lives, 1632–1816*, ed. Robert S. Grumet (Amherst: University of Massachusetts Press, 1996), 19.

10 John Winthrop, *Winthrop's Journal: 1630–1649*, ed. James K. Hosmer, 2 vols. (New York: Charles Scribner's Sons, 1908), 1:65. Hereafter cited as Winthrop, *Journal*.

11 Wood, *Prospect*, 81.

12 John Winthrop, "A Model of Christian Charity," in *Pragmatism and Religion: Classical Sources and Original Essays*, ed. Stuart E. Rosenbaum (Urbana: University of Illinois Press), 22.

13 Edmund S. Morgan, *Roger Williams: The Church and the State* (New York: W. W. Norton, 2006), 11. Hereafter cited as Morgan, *Williams*.

14 Neal Salisbury, *Manitou and Providence: Indian, Europeans, and the Making of New England, 1500–1643*. (New York: Oxford University Press, 1982), 174. Hereafter cited as Salisbury, *Manitou*.

15 Alan Taylor, *American Colonies: The Settling of North America* (New York: Penguin Books, 2001), 159. Hereafter cited as Taylor, *American Colonies*.

16 Ibid., 5.

17 Francis J. Bremer, *The Puritan Experiment: New England Society from Bradford to Edwards* (New York: St. Martin's Press, 1976), 95.

18 John Winthrop, *Journal of John Winthrop*, eds. Richard Dunn et al. (Cambridge, MA: Belknap Press of Harvard University Press, 1996), 261.

19 William Bradford, *Of Plymouth Plantation: 1620–1647*, new ed. with an introduction by Samuel Eliot Morison (New York: Modern Library, 1952), 3. Hereafter cited as Bradford, *Plymouth*.

20 Edmund S. Morgan, *The Puritan Dilemma: The Story of John Winthrop*, 2nd ed. (New York: Longman, 1999), 8.

21 Ibid., 77.

22 Francis Jennings, *The Invasion of America: Indians, Colonialism, and the Cant of Conquest* (Chapel Hill: University of North Carolina Press, 1975), 182. Hereafter cited as Jennings, *Invasion*.

23 Wood, *Prospect*, 89.

24 Alden T. Vaughan, *The Puritan Tradition in America* (Hanover, NH: University Press of New England, 1972), 44.

25 William S. Simmons, "Cultural Bias in the New England Puritans' Perception of Indians," *William and Mary Quarterly* 38, no. 1 (January 1981): 56.

26 Salisbury, *Manitou*, 177.

27 Taylor, *American Colonies*, 192.

28 Unnamed Puritan source quoted in Salisbury, *Manitou*, 181.

CHAPTER 2—A GODLY MINISTER, BANISHED

1 Winthrop, *Journal*, 1:57
2 Roger Williams, *The Complete Writings*, 7 vols. (New York: Russell & Russell, 1963), 6:228. Hereafter Williams, *CW*.
3 Bradford, *Plymouth*, 257.
4 Winthrop, *Journal*, 1:63.
5 Taylor, *American Colonies*, 160.
6 Ola Elizabeth Winslow, *Master Roger Williams: A Biography* (New York: Macmillan, 1957), 104. Hereafter Winslow, *Williams*.
7 Williams to an Assembly of Commissioners, November 17, 1677, *CRW*, 2:750.
8 Williams, *A Key*, 143.
9 James T. Kloppenberg, *Toward Democracy: The Struggle for Self-Rule in European and American Thought* (New York: Oxford University Press, 2016), 65. Hereafter Kloppenberg, *Toward Democracy*.
10 *CRW*, 13, editorial note.
11 Ibid., 15, editorial note.
12 Quote from *The Bloody Tenet* in Kloppenberg, *Toward Democracy*, 65.
13 *CRW*, 16, editorial note.
14 Ibid., 18, editorial note.
15 Winthrop, *Journal*, 1:204.
16 Winslow, *Williams*, 119–20.
17 *CRW*, 22, editorial note.

CHAPTER 3—"FOR PERSONS DISTRESSED OF CONSCIENCE": PROVIDENCE

1 "Mr. Cotton's Letter Lately Printed," Williams, *CW*, 1:388.
2 *CRW*, 1:58, editorial note.
3 Williams to John Winthrop, before August 25, 1636, *CRW*, 1:54.
4 Williams to John Mason and Thomas Prence, June 22, 1670, *CRW*, 2:610.
5 Williams to an Assembly of Commissioners, November 17, 1677, *CRW*, 2:750–51.
6 Howard M. Chapin, ed., *Documentary History of Rhode Island and Providence Pla* (1916; repr., London: Forgotten Books, 2012), 27. Hereafter Chapin, *Documentary History*.
7 Irving B. Richman, *Rhode Island: Its Making and Its Meaning* (New York: G. P. Putnam's Sons, 1908), 84. Hereafter Richman, *Rhode Island*.
8 Samuel Greene Arnold, *History of the State of Rhode Island and Providence Plantations*, 2 vols. (Providence, RI: Preston & Rounds, 1899), 1:103. Hereafter Arnold, *Rhode Island*.

9 William G. McLoughlin, *Rhode Island: A History* (New York: W. W. Norton, 1978), 19. Hereafter McLoughlin, *Rhode Island.*
10 Barbara Ritter Daily, "Anne Hutchinson," in *The Reader's Companion to American History*, ed. Eric Foner and John Garraty (Boston: Houghton Mifflin, 1991), 530.
11 McLoughlin, *Rhode Island*, 16.
12 Morgan, *Williams*, 93–94.
13 Winthrop, *Journal*, 1:132.
14 Samuel H. Brockunier, *The Irrepressible Democrat: Roger Williams* (New York: Ronald Press), 126.
15 Winslow, *Williams*, 259.
16 Sydney V. James, *Colonial Rhode Island: A History* (New York: Charles Scribner's Sons, 1975), 76. Hereafter James, *Colonial Rhode Island.*
17 Jeffrey Glover, "Wunnaumwayean: Roger Williams, English Credibility, and the Colonial Land Market," *Early American Literature* 41, no. 3 (2006): 430.
18 Winslow, *Williams*, 131.
19 Williams to General Court of Commissioners of Providence Plantations, August 25, 1658, *CRW*, 2:485.
20 John Russell Bartlett, *Records of the Colony of Rhode Island and Providence Plantations, in New England*, 10 vols. (Providence, RI: A. C. Greene & Brothers, 1856), 1:26. Hereafter *RCRI.*

CHAPTER 4—TROUBLES ON THE FRONTIER: THE PEQUOT WAR

1 Winthrop, *Journal*, 1:139.
2 See, for example, Albert A. Cave, *The Pequot War* (Amherst: University of Massachusetts Press, 1996), in its entirety (hereafter Cave, *Pequot War*); Jennings, *Invasion*, 177–227; and Wilcomb E. Washburn and Robert M. Utley, *Indian Wars* (Boston: Houghton Mifflin, 2002), 36–44.
3 See Jennings, *Invasion*; Cave, *Pequot War*; and Salisbury, *Manitou*, by way of example.
4 Wilcomb Washburn, "Seventeenth-Century Indian Wars," in *Handbook of North American Indians: Northeast*, ed. Bruce Trigger (Washington, DC: Smithsonian Press, 1978), 15:89. Hereafter Washburn, "Seventeenth-Century Indian Wars."
5 Jennings, *Invasion*, 193.
6 Ibid., 186–207.
7 Winthrop, *Journal*, 1:139.
8 Ibid., 1:132.
9 Cave, *Pequot War*, 119.
10 Ibid., 132.
11 Williams to John Winthrop, October 24, 1636, *CRW*, 1:69.

12 Winthrop, *Journal*, 1:190.
13 Ibid., 1:118.
14 Williams to John Mason and Thomas Prence, June 22, 1670, *CRW*, 2:611.
15 Cave, *Pequot War*, 126.
16 Ibid., 126.
17 Winthrop, *Journal*, 1:193.
18 Ibid.
19 John Underhill, "News from America," in Charles Orr, *History of the Pequot War* (1897; repr., London: Forgotten Books, 2012), 80–81. Hereafter Orr, *Pequot War*.
20 Cave, *Pequot War*, 151.
21 Narragansett warriors quoted in Jenny Hale Pulsipher, *Subjects unto the Same King: Indians, English, and the Contest for Authority in Colonial New England* (Philadelphia: University of Pennsylvania Press, 2005), 25. Hereafter Pulsipher, *Subjects unto the Same King*.
22 Winthrop to Bradford, July 28,1637, in Bradford, *Plymouth*, 398.

CHAPTER 5—"DID EVER FRIENDS DEAL SO WITH FRIENDS?"

1 Salisbury, *Manitou*, 232–33.
2 John Winthrop et al., *Winthrop Papers* (Boston: Massachusetts Historical Society, 1863), 3:442. Hereafter *Winthrop Papers*.
3 Cave, *Pequot War*, 164.
4 Williams to John Winthrop, August 20, 1637, *CRW*, 1:112–17.
5 Michael Leroy Oberg, *Uncas: First of the Mohegans* (Ithaca, NY: Cornell University Press, 2003), 80. Hereafter Oberg, *Uncas*.
6 Williams to John Winthrop, July 15, 1637, *CRW*, 1:102.
7 Ibid., 1:101.
8 Williams to John Winthrop, after September 21, 1638, *CRW*, 1:182.
9 *CRW*, 1:187, editorial note.
10 Williams to John Winthrop, September 10, 1638, *CRW*, 1:180.
11 Oberg, *Uncas*, 85.
12 Williams to John Winthrop, May 9, 1639, *CRW*, 196–97.
13 John Mason, "A Brief History of the Pequot War," in Orr, *Pequot War*, 43.
14 Ibid.
15 Julie A. Fisher and David J. Silverman, *Ninigret, Sachem of the Niantics and Narragansetts: Diplomacy, War, and the Balance of Power in Seventeenth-Century New England and Indian Country* (Ithaca, NY: Cornell University Press, 2014), 43. Hereafter Fisher and Silverman, *Ninigret*.
16 Oberg, *Uncas*, 89–90.
17 Ibid., 90.
18 The relatively isolated settlements of colonial New England had an unquenchable thirst for news. Rumors and hard news alike traveled

extraordinarily quickly among the colonial towns, with correspondence transported by English messengers on horseback, or by Indian runners. The latter could traverse as much as eighty miles within twenty-four hours in good weather.

19 William Bradford to John Winthrop, June 1640, *Winthrop Papers*, 3:258–59.
20 Winthrop, *Journal*, 2:15.
21 Ibid., 2:74.
22 Recapitulation of Miantonomi's alleged speech in "Leift Lion Gardener his relation of the Pequot Warres." in Orr, *Pequot War*, 142.
23 Winthrop, *Journal*, 2:75–76.
24 Ibid., 2:77–78.
25 Unnamed Puritans quoted in Richman, *Rhode Island*, 188.
26 Winthrop, *Journal*, 2:81.
27 Ibid., 2:123.
28 Jennings, *Invasion*, 265.
29 Williams to the General Court of Massachusetts Bay, May 12, 1656, *CRW*, 2:451.
30 Daniel K. Richter, *Facing East from Indian Country: A Native History of Early America* (Cambridge, MA: Harvard University Press, 2001), 110.
31 Oberg, *Uncas*, 102.
32 Richman, *Rhode Island*, 166.
33 Winthrop, *Journal*, 2:132.
34 Ibid., 2:133.
35 Ibid., 2:135.
36 Ibid.
37 Ibid., 2:77.
38 Salisbury, *Manitou*, 232.
39 Karen Ordahl Kupperman, *Indians and English: Facing Off in Early America* (Ithaca, NY: Cornell University Press, 2000), 235.
40 Taylor, *American Colonies*, 197.
41 Williams to John Winthrop, *CRW*, August 20, 1637, 113.
42 Washburn, "Seventeenth-Century Indian Wars," 15:90.

CHAPTER 6—TO LONDON

1 Williams to Massachusetts General Court, October 5, 1654, *CRW*, 2:410.
2 Edwin S. Gaustad, *Liberty of Conscience: Roger Williams in America* (Grand Rapids, MI: W. B. Eerdmans, 1991), 64.
3 Winslow, *Williams*, 187.
4 Authors unknown, *New England's First Fruits* (London, 1643), 1–2.
5 James Axtell, *The European and the Indian* (New York: Oxford University Press, 1981), 135, 203.

6 "To the Reader," in Williams, *A Key*, n.p.
7 Jonathan Beecher Field, "A Key for the Gate: Roger Williams, Parliament, and Providence," *New England Quarterly* 80, no. 3 (September 2007): 372.
8 Williams, *A Key*, 9–10.
9 Ibid., 7.
10 Ibid., 70.
11 Ibid., 21.
12 Ibid., 142.
13 Ibid., 131.
14 Ibid., 123, 129.
15 Richman, *Rhode Island*, 207–8.
16 Chapin, *Documentary History*, 172–74.
17 Richman, *Rhode Island*, 210.
18 Winthrop, *Journal*, 2:140.
19 Arnold, *Rhode Island*, 184.
20 John Andrew Doyle, *The English Colonies in America*, 2 vols. (New York: Holt, 1889), 2:245.
21 Jennings, *Invasion*, 271.
22 *RCRI*, 1:134–35.
23 Ibid., 1:135.
24 See Winthrop, *Journal*, 2:157.
25 Ibid., 2:163.
26 Ibid., 2:169.
27 Williams, *CW*, 1:339.
28 Ibid., 1:326–27.
29 Ibid., 1:392.
30 Ibid., 2:268–69.
31 Chapin, *Documentary History*, 216.
32 Ibid., 215.
33 John M. Barry, *Roger Williams and the Creation of the American Soul: Church, State, and the Birth of Liberty* (New York: Viking, 2012), 305. Hereafter Barry, *Roger Williams*.
34 Ibid., 308.
35 Richman, *Rhode Island*, 176.
36 Williams, *CW*, vol. 3, preface, n.p.
37 Ibid., 3:127.
38 Morgan, *Williams*, 93–94.
39 Williams, *CW*, 3:206.
40 Timothy L. Hall, *Separating Church and State: Roger Williams and Religious Liberty* (Urbana: University of Illinois Press, 1998), 89.
41 Williams, *CW*, 3:358.
42 Ibid., 7:190.

43 Ibid., 3:249–50.
44 See Barry, *Roger Williams*, 339–40.
45 Winthrop, *Journal*, 2:198.
46 Richard Scott quoted in Chapin, *Documentary History*, 214.

CHAPTER 7—RUMORS OF WAR, UNITY AT LAST, 1644–57

1 Bradford instructions quoted in Edward Winslow, *Hypocrisie unmasked: a true relation of the proceedings of the governor and company of the Massachusetts against Samuel Gorton of Rhode Island* (1646; repr., Providence, RI: Club for Colonial Reprints, 1916), 83.
2 See Oberg, *Uncas*, 11.
3 Winthrop, *Journal*, 2:202–3.
4 Frances Manwaring Caulkins, *History of Norwich, Connecticut: From Its Possession by the Indians to the Year of 1866* (Chester, CT: self-published, 1866), 40–42.
5 Williams to John Winthrop, June 25, 1645, *CRW*, 225.
6 *Acts of the Commissioners of the United Colonies*, in *Records of the Colony of New Plymouth in New England*, ed. David Pulsifer, 2 vols. (Boston, 1859; repr., New York: AMS Press, 1968), 1:54. These words are attributed to Ninigret on page 88 of this volume. Hereafter *AOC*.
7 Ibid., 1:38–44.
8 Ibid., 1:55.
9 Paul A. Robinson, "The Struggle Within: The Indian Debate in Seventeenth-Century Narragansett Country" (PhD diss., State University of New York at Binghamton, 1990), 169–70.
10 From the General Court of Massachusetts Bay, August 27, 1645, *CRW*. See quotation from Roger Williams's reply in note 2, 226–27.
11 Winthrop, *Journal*, 2:261.
12 Ibid., 2:282–83.
13 Ibid., 2:292–93.
14 Ibid., 2:311.
15 Ibid., 2:310.
16 Ibid., 2:312.
17 Richman, *Rhode Island*, 241.
18 *RCRI*, 1:190.
19 Williams, *CW*, 3:331.
20 See Charles McLean Andrews, *The Colonial Period of American History*, 3 vols. (New Haven: Yale University Press, 1934), 2:25–29, for a detailed discussion of the statutes. Hereafter Andrews, *Colonial Period*.
21 *RCRI*, 1:156.
22 Ibid., 1:157.
23 Andrews, *Colonial Period*, 2:26.

24 Sydney V. James, *The Colonial Metamorphoses in Rhode Island: A Study of Institutions in Change* (Hanover, NH: University Press of New England, 2000), 40.
25 Bruce Colin Daniels, *Dissent and Conformity on Narragansett Bay: The Colonial Rhode Island Town* (Middletown, CT: Wesleyan University Press, 1984), 11.
26 *RCRI*, 1:285–86.
27 Ibid., 1:333.
28 Andrews, *Colonial Period*, 2:26.
29 Arnold, *Rhode Island*, 1:259.
30 *AOC*, 2:26.
31 Samuel Drake, *Biography and History of the Indians of North America* (New York: n.p., 1834), 72.
32 Ibid.
33 Williams to John Winthrop Jr., October 9, 1650, *CRW*, 323.
34 Williams to John Winthrop Jr., October 17, 1650. *CRW*, 3:326, see note.
35 See discussion of the Dutch-Narragansett alliance in Fisher and Silverman, *Ninigret*, 73–79.
36 *AOC*, 2:125.
37 Ibid., 2:151.

CHAPTER 8—A ROYAL CHARTER, AND NEW TROUBLES IN NARRAGANSETT COUNTRY, 1657–65

1 Carl Bridenbaugh, *Fat Mutton and Liberty of Conscience* (Providence, RI: Brown University Press, 1974), 12.
2 See James, *Colonial Rhode Island*, 87.
3 Williams to John Mason and Thomas Prence, June 22, 1670, *CRW*, 2:614.
4 *Winthrop Papers*, 4:44.
5 *AOC*, 2:247.
6 Ibid., 2:249.
7 Fisher and Silverman, *Ninigret*, 94.
8 Ibid.
9 *RCRI*, 1:465.
10 Williams to John Mason and Thomas Prence, June 22, 1670, *CRW*, 2:614.
11 Richard S. Dunn, "John Winthrop, Jr., and the Narragansett Country," *William and Mary Quarterly* 13, no. 1 (January 1956): 68, 77.
12 Ibid., 78.
13 James, *Colonial Rhode Island*, 69.
14 Williams to the Town of Providence, January 15, 1682, *CRW*, 2:775.
15 Nathaniel B. Shurtleff, *Records of the Governor and Company of the Massachusetts Bay in New England: Printed by Order of the Legislature* (Boston: W. White, 1853), vol. 4, pt. 2, 161–62.

16 Pulsipher, *Subjects unto the Same King*, 49.
17 Ibid., 55.
18 Ibid., 56.
19 Ibid., 81.
20 *RCRI*, 2:60.
21 Pulsipher, *Subjects unto the Same King*, 57.
22 Ibid., 61.

CHAPTER 9—"IN A STRANGE WAY": KING PHILIP'S WAR

1 Williams to John Winthrop Jr., June 25, 1675, *CRW*, 2:694.
2 Williams to John Winthrop Jr., June 27, 1675, *CRW*, 2:698.
3 Benjamin Church, *Diary of King Philip's War* (1716; repr., Little Compton, RI: Lockwood, 1975). Hereafter Church, *Diary*.
4 John Easton, "A Relacion of the Indyan Warre," in Mary Rowlandson, *The Sovereignty and Goodness of God: With Related Documents*, ed. Neal Salisbury (1682; repr., New York: Bedford Books, 1997), 116–17. Hereafter Rowlandson, *Sovereignty and Goodness*.
5 Nathaniel Philbrick, *Mayflower: A Story of Courage, Community, and War* (New York: Viking, 2006), 206. Hereafter Philbrick, *Mayflower*.
6 Pulsipher, *Subjects unto the Same King*, 94.
7 Douglas Edward Leach, *Flintlock and Tomahawk: New England in King Philip's War* (1958; repr., Woodstock, VT: Countryman Press, 2009), 28. Hereafter Leach, *Flintlock*.
8 Pulsipher, *Subjects unto the Same King*, 99.
9 William Hubbard, *The History of the Indian Wars in New England* (1677; repr., Baltimore: Genealogical, 2002), 87.
10 Taylor, *American Colonies*, 200.
11 Leach, *Flintlock*, 93.
12 Patrick M. Malone, *The Skulking Way of War: Technology and Tactics among the New England Indians* (Lanham, MD: Madison Books, 1991), 105–6.

CHAPTER 10—THE NARRAGANSETT WAR

1 Smith, quoted in Pulsipher, *Subjects unto the Same King*, 122.
2 Ibid., 126.
3 *Winthrop Papers*, reel 11, Massachusetts Historical Society.
4 *AOC*, 2:357.
5 Church, *Diary*, 98-99.
6 Unnamed Puritan quoted in Philbrick, *Mayflower*, 302.
7 Rowlandson, *Sovereignty and Goodness*, 105.
8 Ibid., 106.
9 Ibid., 78–79.

10 Ibid., 100.
11 Leach, *Flintlock*, 160.
12 Williams to Robert Williams, April 1, 1676, *CRW*, 2:722.
13 Ibid., 2:723.
14 William Hubbard, *A Narrative of the Indian Wars in New England* (1677; repr., Brattleboro, VT: William Fessenden, 1814), 162.
15 Church, *Diary*, 126.
16 Edmund S. Morgan, *American Slavery, American Freedom: The Ordeal of Colonial Virginia* (New York: W. W. Norton, 1975), 269.
17 Connecticut War Council directive quoted in Jennings, *Invasion*, 319.

CHAPTER 11—AFTERMATH

1 James David Drake, *King Philip's War: Civil War in New England, 1675–1676* (Amherst: University of Massachusetts Press, 1999), 170.
2 Jill Lepore, *The Name of War: King Philip's War and the Origins of American Identity* (New York: Knopf, 1998), 3.
3 Linford D. Fisher, "'Why shall wee have peace to bee made slaves': Indian Surrenderers during and after King Philip's War," *Ethnohistory* 64 (January 2017): 99.
4 Ibid., 103.
5 Taylor, *American Colonies*, 203.
6 *RCRI*, 2:556.
7 John A. Sainsbury, "Indian Labor in Early Rhode Island," *New England Quarterly* 48, no 3 (September 1975): 383. Hereafter Sainsbury, "Indian Labor."
8 Margaret Ellen Newell, "The Changing Nature of Indian Slavery in New England, 1670–1720," in *Reinterpreting New England Indians and the Colonial Experience*, ed. Colin G. Calloway and Neal Salisbury (Boston: Colonial Society of Massachusetts, 2003), 106–8.
9 Sainsbury, "Indian Labor," 385.
10 Paul R. Campbell and Glenn LaFantasie, "Scattered to the Winds of Heaven: Narragansett Indians, 1676–1880," *Rhode Island History* 37, no. 3 (1978): 70.
11 Robert A. Geake, *A History of the Narragansett Tribe of Rhode Island: Keepers of the Bay* (Charleston, SC: History Press, 2011), 133.
12 Williams to Simon Bradstreet, May 6, 1682, *CRW*, 2:777.
13 Winslow, *Williams*, 288.
14 Perry Miller, "Roger Williams: An Essay in Interpretation," in Williams, *CW*, 7:5.
15 Williams to John Winthrop Jr., May 28, 1647, *CRW*, 1:234.

Selected Bibliography

Andrews, Charles McLean. *The Colonial Period of American History.* Vol. 1, *The Settlements.* New Haven, CT: Yale University Press, 1934.

Arnold, Samuel Greene. *History of the State of Rhode Island and Providence Plantations.* 4th ed. Providence, RI: Preston & Rounds, 1899.

Axtell, James. *Beyond 1492: Encounters in Colonial North America.* New York: Oxford University Press, 1992.

———. *The Invasion Within: The Contest of Cultures in Colonial North America.* New York: Oxford University Press, 1985.

Barry, John M. *Roger Williams and the Creation of the American Soul: Church, State, and the Birth of Liberty.* New York: Viking, 2012.

Bartlett, John Russell. *Records of the Colony of Rhode Island and Providence Plantations, in New England.* Providence, RI: A. C. Greene & Brothers, 1856.

Berkovitch, Sacvan. *The Puritan Origins of the American Self.* New Haven, CT: Yale University Press, 1975.

Bodge, George M. *Soldiers in King Philip's War: Being a Critical Account of That War, with a Concise History of the Indian Wars of New England from 1620–1677.* Leominster, MA: Printed for the author, 1896.

Bonomi, Patricia U. *Under the Cape of Heaven: Religion, Society, and Politics in Colonial America.* Updated ed. New York: Oxford University Press, 2003.

Bradford, William. *Of Plymouth Plantation, 1620–1647.* New ed. New York: Knopf, 1952.

Bragdon, Kathleen. *The Columbia Guide to American Indians of the Northeast.* New York: Columbia University Press, 2001.

———. *Native People of Southern New England.* Norman: University of Oklahoma Press, 1996.

Breen, Timothy. *The Character of a Good Ruler: A Study of Puritan Political Ideas.* New Haven, CT: Yale University Press, 1970.

Bremer, Francis J. *First Founders: American Puritans and Puritanism in an Atlantic World.* Durham: University of New Hampshire Press, 2012.

Brockunier, Samuel Hugh. *The Irrepressible Democrat: Roger Williams.* New York: Ronald Press, 1940.

Campbell, Paul R., and Glenn LaFantasie. "Scattered to the Winds of Heaven: Narragansett Indians, 1676–1880." *Rhode Island History* 37, no. 3 (August 1978).

Cave, Alfred. *The Pequot War*. Amherst: University of Massachusetts Press, 1996.

Chapin, Howard M. *Documentary History of Rhode Island*. London: Forgotten Books, 2012. First published in 1916.

———. *The Trading Post of Roger Williams: With Those of John Wilcox and Richard Smith*. Providence, RI: E. L. Freeman, 1933.

Cronon, William. *Changes in the Land: Indians, Colonists, and the Ecology of New England*. New York: Hill & Wang, 1983.

Daniels, Bruce Colin. *Dissent and Conformity on Narragansett Bay: The Colonial Rhode Island Town*. Middletown, CT: Wesleyan University Press, 1984.

Davis, Jack L. "Roger Williams among the Narragansett Indians." *New England Quarterly* 43, no. 4 (1970).

Drake, James David. *King Philip's War: Civil War in New England, 1675–1676*. Amherst: University of Massachusetts Press, 1999.

Dunn, Richard S. "John Winthrop, Jr., and the Narragansett Country." *William and Mary Quarterly* 13, no. 1 (January 1956).

———. *Puritans and Yankees: The Winthrop Dynasty of New England, 1630–1717*. New York: W. W. Norton, 1971.

Field, Jonathan Beecher. "A Key for the Gate: Roger Williams, Parliament, and Providence." *New England Quarterly* 80, no. 3 (2007).

Fisher, Julie A., and David J. Silverman. *Ninigret, Sachem of the Niantics and Narragansetts: Diplomacy, War, and the Balance of Power in Seventeenth-Century New England and Indian Country*. Ithaca, NY: Cornell University Press, 2014.

Fisher, Linford D. "'Why shall wee have peace to bee made slaves': Indian Surrenderers during and after King Philip's War." *Ethnohistory* 64 (January 2017).

Forbes, Allyn B., ed. *Winthrop Papers*. 5 vols. Boston: Massachusetts Historical Society, 1929–45.

Gaustad, Edwin S. *Liberty of Conscience: Roger Williams in America*. Grand Rapids, MI: W. B. Eerdmans, 1991.

Geake, Robert A. *A History of the Narragansett Tribe of Rhode Island: Keepers of the Bay*. Charlestown, SC: History Press, 2011.

Gibson, Susan G. *Burr's Hill, a 17th Century Wampanoag Burial Ground in Warren, Rhode Island*. Providence, RI: Haffenreffer Museum of Anthropology, Brown University, 1980.

Glover, Jeffrey. "Wunnaumwayean: Roger Williams, English Credibility, and the Colonial Land Market." *Early American Literature* 41, no. 3 (2006).

Grumet, Robert Steven, ed. *Northeastern Indian Lives, 1632–1816*. Amherst: University of Massachusetts Press, 1996.

Gura, Philip. *A Glimpse of Sion's Glory: Puritan Radicalism in New England, 1620–1660*. Middletown, CT: Wesleyan University Press, 1984.

———. "Samuel Gorton and Religious Radicalism in England: 1644–1648." *William and Mary Quarterly* 40, no. 1 (January 1983).

Hall, David D. *The Faithful Shepherd: A History of the New England Ministry in the Seventeenth Century*. New York: W. W. Norton, 1974.

———. *Worlds of Wonder, Days of Judgment: Popular Religious Belief in Early New England*. New York: Knopf, 1989.

Hall, Timothy L. *Separating Church and State: Roger Williams and Religious Liberty*. Urbana: University of Illinois Press, 1998.

Hirsch, Adam J. "The Collision of Military Cultures in Seventeenth-Century New England." *Journal of American History* 74, no. 4 (1988).

History of the Pequot War: The Contemporary Accounts of Mason, Underhill, Vincent and Gardener. Introduction by Charles Orr. Cleveland, OH: Helman-Taylor, 1897.

Hubbard, William. *A Narrative of the Indian Wars in New-England: From the First Planting Thereof in the Year 1607, to the Year 1677*. Brattleboro, VT: William Fessenden, 1814.

Kupperman, Karen Ordahl. *Indians and English: Facing Off in Early America*. Ithaca, NY: Cornell University Press, 2000.

LaFantasie, Glenn. "Roger Williams and John Winthrop: The Rise and Fall of an Extraordinary Friendship." *Rhode Island History* 47, no. 3 (August 1989).

Leach, Douglas Edward. *Flintlock and Tomahawk: New England in King Philip's War*. Woodstock, VT: Countrymen Press, 1958, reprinted in 2009.

Lepore, Jill. *The Name of War: King Philip's War and the Origins of American Identity*. New York: Knopf, 1998.

Main, Gloria L. *Peoples of a Spacious Land: Families and Cultures in Colonial New England*. Cambridge, MA: Harvard University Press, 2001.

Malone, Patrick M. *The Skulking Way of War: Technology and Tactics among the New England Indians*. Lanham, MD: Madison Books, 1991.

March, Kathleen. "Uncommon Civility: The Narragansetts and Roger Williams." PhD diss., University of Iowa, 1985.

Miller, Perry. *Errand into the Wilderness*. New York: Harper & Row, 1964.

———. *The New England Mind: The Seventeenth Century*. Cambridge, MA: Harvard University Press, 1954.

———. *Roger Williams: His Contribution to the American Tradition*. Indianapolis, IN: Bobbs-Merrill, 1953.

Morgan, Edmund S. *The Puritan Dilemma: The Story of John Winthrop*. 2nd ed. New York: Longman, 1999.

———. *Roger Williams: The Church and the State*. New York: Harcourt, Brace & World, 1967.

Oberg, Michael Leroy. *Uncas: First of the Mohegans*. Ithaca, NY: Cornell University Press, 2003.

———. "'We Are All the Sachems from East to West': A New Look at Miantonomi's Campaign of Resistance." *New England Quarterly* 77, no. 3 (2004).

Philbrick, Nathaniel. *Mayflower: A Story of Courage, Community, and War.* New York: Viking, 2006.

Potter, Elisha R. *The Early History of Narragansett.* N.p.: S. S. Rider, 1886.

Pulsipher, Jenny Hale. *Subjects unto the Same King: Indians, English, and the Contest for Authority in Colonial New England.* Philadelphia: University of Pennsylvania Press, 2005.

Richman, Irving Berdine. *Rhode Island: Its Making and Its Meaning: A Survey of the Annals of the Commonwealth from Its Settlement to the Death of Roger Williams, 1636–1683.* New York: G. P. Putnam's Sons, 1908.

Robinson, Paul A. "The Struggle Within: The Indian Debate in Seventeenth Century Narragansett Country." PhD diss., State University of New York at Binghamton, 1990.

Rubertone, Patricia E. *Grave Undertakings: An Archaeology of Roger Williams and the Narragansett Indians.* Washington, DC: Smithsonian Institution Press, 2001.

Sainsbury, John A. "Miantonomo's Death and New England Politics, 1630–1645." *Rhode Island History* 30, no. 4 (1971).

Salisbury, Neal. *Manitou and Providence: Indians, Europeans, and the Making of New England, 1500–1643.* New York: Oxford University Press, 1982.

Sehr, Timothy J. "Ninigret's Tactics of Accommodation—Indian Diplomacy in New England, 1637–1675." *Rhode Island History* 36, no. 2 (1977).

Shurtleff, Nathaniel B., and David Pulsifer. *Acts of the Commissioners of the United Colonies of New England, 1643–1679*, in *Records of the Colony of New Plymouth, in New England.* Boston: Press of W. White, 1855.

Simmons, William S. *Cautantowwit's House: An Indian Burial Ground on the Island of Conanicut in Narragansett Bay.* Providence, RI: Brown University Press, 1970.

———. "Cultural Bias in the New England Puritans' Perception of Indians." *William and Mary Quarterly* 38, no. 1 (1981).

———. "The Narragansett." In *Handbook of North American Indians: Northeast*, edited by Bruce Trigger. Washington, DC: Smithsonian Institution, 1978.

———. *Spirit of the New England Tribes: Indian History and Folklore, 1620–1984.* Hanover, NH: University Press of New England, 1986.

Simpson, Alan. "How Democratic Was Roger Williams?" *William and Mary Quarterly*, 3rd ser., 13, no. 1 (February 1956).

Slotkin, Richard, and James King Folsom. *So Dreadfull a Judgment: Puritan Responses to King Philip's War, 1676–1677.* Middletown, CT: Wesleyan University Press, 1978.

Taylor, Alan. *American Colonies: The Settling of North America.* New York: Viking, 2001.

Vaughan, Alden T. *New England Frontier: Puritans and Indians, 1620–1675.* 3rd ed. Norman: University of Oklahoma Press, 1995.

Williams, Roger. *The Complete Writings.* New York: Russell & Russell, 1963.

———. *The Correspondence of Roger Williams*. Edited by Glenn W. LaFantasie. Hanover, NH: Brown University Press/University Press of New England, 1988.

Winslow, Ola Elizabeth. *Master Roger Williams: A Biography*. New York: Macmillan, 1957.

Winthrop, John. *Winthrop's Journal, "History of New England," 1630–1649*. Edited by James K. Hosmer. New York: Charles Scribner's Sons, 1908.

Wood, William. *New England's Prospect*. Edited by Alden T. Vaughan. Amherst: University of Massachusetts Press, 1993.

Yale Indian Papers Project. Yale Library. Available at http://www.library.yale.edu/yipp.

Image Credits

iv Courtesy of the Rhode Island Historical Society

1 Courtesy of the Art and Picture Collection, the New York Public Library

9 Courtesy of the Archives Division, Office of the Secretary, Commonwealth of Massachusetts.

12 From *The Invasion of America: Indians, Colonialism, and the Cant of Conquest* by Francis P. Jennings. Published by the Omohundro Institute of Early American History and Culture. Copyright © 1975 by the University of North Carolina Press. Used by permission of the publisher.

39 Courtesy of the Rhode Island Historical Society

57 Photograph by Erik Gould, courtesy of the Rhode Island School of Design Museum of Art, Providence

64–65 Drawing by Ray Houlihan, from *Becoming a City* by Margaret Uroff. Copyright © 1968, renewed in 1996 by Houghton Mifflin Harcourt Publishing Company. Reprinted by permission of Houghton Mifflin Harcourt Publishing Company. All rights reserved.

77 Courtesy of the Brown University Library

83 Courtesy of the Rhode Island Historical Society

95 Courtesy of the Rhode Island Historical Society

123 Courtesy of the Rhode Island Historical Society

153 Courtesy of the Art and Picture Collection, the New York Public Library

156 Courtesy of the State of Rhode Island

187 Courtesy of the Brown University Library

205 Courtesy of the Rhode Island Historical Society

218–19 Map © Jeffrey C. Ward

225 Photograph courtesy of Keith R. Wahl, Made from RI, LLC

245 Courtesy of the Rhode Island Historical Society

IMAGE CREDITS

INSERT

1 Courtesy of the Brown University Library
2 Courtesy of the Rhode Island Historical Society
3 Courtesy of the New York Public Library
4 Courtesy of the Rhode Island Historical Society
5 Courtesy of the Massachusetts Historical Society
6 Photograph by Erik Gould, courtesy of the Rhode Island School of Design Museum of Art, Providence
7 Courtesy of the Rhode Island Historical Society
8 © President and Fellows of Harvard College, Peabody Museum of Archaeology and Ethnology, PM# 17-16-10/87069
9 Gift of the American Antiquarian Society, 1890 © President and Fellows of Harvard College, Peabody Museum of Archaeology and Ethnology, PM# 90-17-10/49333
10 © President and Fellows of Harvard College, Peabody Museum of Archaeology and Ethnology, PM# 04-21-10/63432
11 Courtesy of the Haffenreffer Museum of Anthropology, Brown University
12 Courtesy of the Haffenreffer Museum of Anthropology, Brown University
13 Courtesy of the Brown University Library
14 Courtesy of the New York Public Library
15 Courtesy of the New York Public Library
16 Courtesy of the Brown University Library
17 Courtesy of the New York Public Library
18 Courtesy of the Rhode Island Historical Society
19 Courtesy of Roger Williams University

Index

Numbers in italics refer to pages with images.

About the Author

JAMES A. WARREN is a writer and a former visiting scholar in the American Studies Department at Brown University. Currently a regular contributor to *The Daily Beast*, Warren is the author of *Giap: The General Who Defeated America in Vietnam* and *American Spartans: The U.S. Marines: A Combat History from Iwo Jima to Iraq*, among other books. His articles have appeared in *MHQ: The Quarterly Journal of Military History*, *Vietnam* magazine, *Society*, and the *Providence Journal*. For many years Warren was an acquisitions editor in the fields of history, religion, and ethnic studies at Columbia University Press. Educated at Brown, he lives in Saunderstown, Rhode Island.